AWARENESS

D1284162

AWARENESS

exploring
experimenting
experiencing

John O. Stevens

Eden Grove Editions

ISBN 1 870845 02 1

Original U.S. Publication by Real People Press
in Moab, Utah, U.S.A. 1971

This edition published in Great Britain, 1989 by
Eden Grove Editions
26 Eden Grove
London N7 8EF

Printed in Great Britain by BPCC Wheatons Ltd., Exeter

to
Fritz Perls

Dear Fritz:

I remember mostly your love, your warmth, and your gentleness whenever someone was open and honest—whether honestly saint or honestly bastard. I also remember how brutal you were in the face of dishonesty, refusing to tolerate deception of any kind. I know that you disliked being brutal—you much preferred to live and flow with people in awareness. Your brutality was actually the greatest kindness, bringing many of us to life by confronting us with our manipulations and games.

You touched many people with your life; I wish you could see how many you are reaching through your legacy of books, tapes and films. There are tears of love in my eyes as I write this, and I can hear your deep rich voice saying "There's some beautiful melting going on." Thank you, Fritz, for leading me and frustrating me to the edge of discovery, and for showing me the tools for my continuing journey.

Steve

Contents

New Preface

It is hard to recall what a wasteland the field of psychology was when I was a college student in the late 1950's. Essentially there was Freud or Behaviorism, and both were pretty pessimistic. Although they disagreed in many areas, they both agreed that if you loved someone it was only because she reminded you of your mother! Abraham Maslow's *Motivation and Personality* (1954) was a fresh cool breeze of hope and possibility blowing across the desolate desert of mechanism and fatalism.

As I went to graduate school at Brandies to study with Maslow (abandoning a career in chemistry), I began to hear others singing faintly in remote corners of this wilderness: Carl Rogers, Viktor Frankl, Virginia Satir, Erich Fromm and others dissatisfied with current dogma and groping for new understandings. When I went on to teach psychology in junior college I did some groping of my own.

When I first saw Fritz Perls in 1967, I saw some of these understandings made manifest. Fritz insisted that talking be transformed into the lived experience of action and feeling, and he was always willing to demonstrate what he did. People became transparent in Fritz's presence, and they often used that awareness to become more alive and real.

This book AWARENESS was born out of my involvement with Gestalt Therapy and my need to adapt Fritz's methods to my junior college classes. It is now nearly twenty years since I wrote this book, with a lot of living, loving, and learning under the bridge since then. Periodically someone warms me by telling me how useful the book has been to them, either personally or in their work with groups. It has often been excerpted, and it has been translated into German, Japanese, Spanish and Portuguese.

Now I look back at this book from over ten years' involvement with Neuro-Linguistic Programming (NLP), a method derived from the work of Fritz Perls, Virginia Satir, and Milton Erickson. NLP has taught me many ways to bring about change more quickly, including ways to facilitate useful communication between conflicting parts. Other than that, there is very little in AWARENESS that I would change.

As I wrote in the Afterword "I hope you will take this book simply as a report of some of my tools and explorations as of this moment. I feel like an explorer who has paused to make crude maps and notes describing my travels." My journey of discovery goes on, and I wish you well in your use of this book for yours. The methods outlined in this book still work as well as they did twenty years ago, and awareness is still badly needed to discover what it means to become a loving human being in a society that often does not support this ongoing search and discovery.

Steve Andreas
(formerly John O. Stevens)
November 1988

Introduction

This book is about awareness, and how you can explore, expand and deepen your awareness. Most of the book consists of experiments which ask you to focus your awareness in certain directions to see what you can discover. It's incredible how much you can realize about your existence by simply paying close attention to it and becoming more deeply aware of your own experiencing. What the sages have said for centuries is really true: the world is right here—all we have to do is empty our "minds" and open ourselves to receive it.

The experiments in this book have grown out of my Gestalt Therapy work with groups of adults, and the application of these methods to my college teaching of psychology. These experiments provide opportunities for you to discover more about yourself, either working alone or with other people in pairs or groups. Whether you make use of these opportunities or not depends on how much you are willing to invest yourself in them.

As I began writing this book I often wondered how useful it would be to individuals using it alone, without a leader or guide. One day when Jackie was typing part of the manuscript, she turned to me with tears streaming down her cheeks and told me what was going on

in her. Even though her attention was divided between the typing
and the fantasy journey she was typing, she became involved in the
fantasy and discovered something within her. Now I know that the
book can be useful to you, even when you work with it alone. She
later took several of her friends on the same fantasy, and they also
learned quite a bit about themselves. One of these friends then went
on to do it with some other friends of hers, with good results. So I
know now that quite a lot can be done even when someone unskilled
uses these methods. It is even better, of course, if a leader has
explored his own awareness considerably, become familiar with this
approach, and feels comfortable with it. This book is an outgrowth
of Gestalt Therapy, and I wholeheartedly recommend Fritz Perls'
book *Gestalt Therapy Verbatim* to anyone who wants to get deeply
involved and fully understand this approach.

The experiments in this book are tools. Like any tools, they can
be used skillfully or clumsily; they can be unused or misused. I
would not write this book if I were not convinced that there are a
great many people who can make good use of it. I hope that you will
use it as you would any new tool—tentatively, with care and respect,
and with awareness of your degree of understanding. I discuss a
number of the ways this approach can be misused in the section *To
the Group Leader or Teacher*. If you misuse this book while working
with yourself, that's your responsibility, but if you work with others,
please read this section carefully and keep it in mind.

There are a lot of self-improvement books that tell you how to
change yourself. When you try to change, you manipulate and
torture yourself, and mostly you just become divided between a part
of you that tries to change and a part of you that resists change.
Even when you do accomplish change in this way, the price is
conflict, confusion and uncertainty. Usually, the more you try to
change, the worse your situation becomes.

*This book is based on the discovery that it is much more useful
to simply become deeply aware of yourself as you are now.* Rather
than try to change, stop, or avoid something that you don't like in
yourself, it is much more effective to stay with it and become more
deeply aware of it. You can't improve on your own functioning; you

can only interfere with it, distort it, and disguise it. When you really get in touch with your own experiencing, you will find that change takes place by itself, without your effort or planning. With full awareness you can let happen whatever wants to happen, with confidence that it will work out well. You can learn to let go and live and flow with your experiencing and happening instead of frustrating yourself with demands to be different. All the energy that is locked up in the battle between trying to change and resisting change can become available for participation in the happening of your life that is both passive and active. This approach will not provide you with answers to the problems of your life. It does provide you with tools that you can use to explore your life, simplify and clarify your problems and confusions, and help you discover *your* answers—what *you* want to do.

This book will definitely not "adjust you to society." It can help you to adjust to *yourself*—help you to discover your own reality, your own existence, your own humanness, and be more comfortable with it. Often this will be in opposition to what your society or your spouse or your friends say you "should" be. If enough of us get really in touch with our own human reality, perhaps we can build a society that is appropriate to what we *are*, instead of what we "should" be. But most important, the exploration of awareness leads to a continuing ongoing enrichment and involvement with your life that has to be experienced to be known.

A few years ago, on my way to an evening meeting, I met a young woman who had just been killed in an accident. I did not know that she was dead, so I did what I could for her until I realized that there were no signs of life and I saw that the moisture on her open eyes was drying. The memory of that young woman stayed with me vividly all that evening, and she is with me now. Later that evening I watched the blood pulsing in another woman's throat as she slapped and scolded her child, and I screamed silently *"Wake up! Be glad you're alive!"* All of us have been given a precious gift of life—and how little we usually appreciate it. Thank you, dead woman of my memory, for waking me up and reminding me to life.

Awareness

My experience can be divided into three kinds of awareness, or zones of awareness:

1) *Awareness of the outside world. This is actual sensory contact with objects and events in the present:* what I now actually see, hear, smell, taste, or touch. Right now I see my pen sliding over the paper, forming words, and I hear a humming noise. I smell smoke from the fire, I feel the texture of the paper under my hands, and I taste the sweet fruity taste of strawberries in my mouth.

2) *Awareness of the inside world. This is actual sensory contact with inner events in the present:* what I now actually feel from inside my skin—itches, muscular tensions and movements, physical manifestations of feelings and emotions, discomfort, well-being, etc. Right now I feel pressure in the tip of my left index finger as it holds the paper down. I feel an unpleasant tightness in the right side of my neck, and as I move my head it feels somewhat better, etc.

These first two kinds of awareness encompass all that I can know about present reality as I experience it. This is the solid ground of my experience; these are the facts of my existence here, in the moment that they occur. No matter how I or others think or feel *about* this awareness, it *exists,* and no amount of arguing, theorizing or complaining can make it non-existent. The third kind of awareness is quite different, namely, my awareness of *images* of things and events that do *not* exist in present ongoing reality:

3) *Awareness of fantasy activity. This includes all mental activity beyond present awareness of ongoing experience: All explaining, imagining, interpreting, guessing, thinking, comparing, planning, remembering the past, anticipating the future, etc.* Right now I am wondering how long it will take me to write this book. I have an image of what it will look like when it is finished, and I wonder how you, the reader, will respond to it—will you find this book useful, and will you like me for writing it? All this is unreality. The book is not done; I cannot see it, and you cannot see it or respond to it. It is all my fantasy, my imagination.

And yet within this fantasy there is some reality hidden. I can discover more about this reality if I invest myself in my fantasy and become aware of my physical feelings, perceptions and activities as I do this. As I think of how long the book will take, I become aware of the tiredness in my body and I realize that the wish for the book to be done arises out of this tiredness now. As I imagine your response to the book, I am aware that I want you to like me and I want to be of use to you. As I write this, the warm feelings in my body and the tears in my eyes confirm its truth. Now I stay with these feelings for awhile, and something else begins to develop—something more basic than your liking me or my being of use to you. Whether you like me or not, I love to be with you honestly, with reality firmly beneath our feet, and I know that this book can help us toward that. As I write this, my body feels solid and confident, saying "yes."

It is really difficult to bring home the realization that everything exists in the momentary now. The past exists only as parts of present reality—things and memories that I *think about* as being "from the past." The idea of the past is sometimes useful, but at the same time it is an idea, a *fantasy* that I hold *now.* Consider the following problem: "Prove to me that the world was not created two seconds ago, complete with artifacts and memories."

Our idea of the future is also an unreal, though sometimes

useful fiction. Our idea of the future, like our conception of the past, is based on our understanding of the present. Past and future are our guesses about what preceded the present moment and our guesses about what will follow. And all this guessing occurs *now*.

Now

It is only this,
no draft nor final manuscript
survives with which to speculate,
for I have burned them.
No edition has a date,
I distinguish no printings,
number and sign no copies
so what you hold, collector,
will not appreciate.
Do not put this on your shelf, critic,
for the special paper dissolves in air.
Read, that is all;
now is the only time
to take the wafer of our sacrament
before it vanishes
This is all there is.

—Peter Goblen

In the instructions that follow, I ask you to explore your own awareness and to notice some basic properties of your awareness. Three periods (. . .) indicate a pause. Stop reading when you come to these pauses and take some time to explore your own awareness as directed. Unless you take time to discover your own experience, these directions will be useless to you—like a map of a place you have never seen. To fully discover what a place is like, you have to spend some time really looking around while you are there, and you will discover much more if you return at different times and different seasons. A peaceful stream may become a raging torrent in rainy weather, or a barren stony ditch in drought. The same is true of what you discover about your own existence through these experiments. At one time you will become aware of certain things, while at a later time what you discover may be quite different. Each of these different experiences is a valid part of your reality at that time.

I know that many of you will read quickly through this book without actually doing most of the experiments. If you do all the experiments, it will take you quite a while to work through the book. Sometimes you may get bored when a number of somewhat similar experiments are grouped together. At the same time, many of these experiments have little twists and reversals that can be much more useful if they are unexpected. If you have already read them through casually, you will know what's coming and you may cheat yourself out of some important discoveries.

In all of these experiments, I ask you to pay attention to one, or a few, aspects of your awareness. Although I present these experiments as individual units, the reality that they point to is a whole. All these ways of increasing your awareness and maintaining your contact with your existence can become an integral part of your everyday life. As you move through these experiments, you can discover more in the later ones through applying what you have learned from earlier ones. Likewise, you can then return to the earlier experiments, and gain more from them by applying what you have discovered in the later ones. Some experience with the basic experiments in these first three sections is necessary to fully understand and make use of the rest of the book. You will be cheating yourself if you don't invest yourself fully in these three sections before going on.

Be sure to try some of the basic awareness experiments that immediately follow, and return to them at least one or two times to give yourself an opportunity to discover their usefulness. What you discover in these first experiments may not seem very important, but they are the root and foundation of this approach.

Zones of Awareness

Take some time to pay attention to your own awareness now. Just be an observer of your awareness, and notice where it goes. Say to yourself "Now I'm aware of—" and finish this sentence with what you are aware of at the moment, and then notice whether this is something *outside*, something *inside*, or a *fantasy*. ... Where does your awareness go? ... Are you mostly aware of things outside your body, or sensations inside your skin? ... Now direct your attention to whichever area you are least aware of, inside or outside, and become more aware of this. ... To what extent are you occupied with fantasies, thoughts and images? ... Notice that while you are occupied with a thought or an image, your awareness of inside and outside reality decreases or disappears. ... If you can just solidly learn the distinction between a fantasy and the reality of your actual experience you can take a big step toward simplifying your life.

Focusing

Continue experimenting with your awareness, and realize that your awareness is like a searchlight. Whatever you focus your attention on is pretty clear, but other things and events tend to fade out of awareness. If I ask you to become aware of what you hear, you can probably hear quite a few different sounds and noises. ... And while you are doing this, you are mostly unaware of the sensations in your hands. ... As I mention your hands, your attention probably moves there, and you become aware of the sensations in your hands. ... As your attention moves there, your awareness of sounds fades away. ... Your awareness can shift from one thing to another quite rapidly, but you can only be fully aware of whatever is in the focus of your awareness at the moment. Take some time now to become more aware of how you focus your awareness, and what comes into the focus of your awareness. ...

Generalizing

Notice when you begin generalizing, such as "Now I'm aware of the whole room," or "I hear all the sounds." Generalization is a fantasy activity of the "mind" as it stores up individual images and then boils them down into generalizations. Awareness is much sharper and much more localized. Again pay attention to your awareness. If you notice that you are generalizing, return your attention to the focus of your awareness in the present moment, and see what you can actually contact clearly. ...

Selection

Now notice what *kinds* of things and events you become aware of. Of all the millions of experiences possible to you at any moment, only a few actually emerge into your awareness. There is a selective process that directs your attention toward certain kinds of things that are somehow relevant to you, and tends to ignore others. For instance, you may mostly notice colors, shapes, textures, imperfections, coverings, sounds, movements, tensions, or physical sensations, etc. Again take some time to just be an observer as you let your awareness wander. Notice what kinds of things and events emerge spontaneously into your awareness, and see if you can discover something about what your selective process is like. . . .

Now try saying "I'm selecting (or choosing) to be aware of—" and finish the sentence with whatever you are aware of in that moment. Do this for a few minutes. . . .

Avoiding

Now realize that this selective focusing on certain kinds of experience is also a way of *not* focusing on something else—a way of avoiding and excluding certain experiences. Pay attention to your awareness again and after you become aware of something, follow this by saying "—and I left out—" and finish the sentence with something that you skipped over just before. Do this for a few minutes, and become aware of what you are skipping. . . . What kinds of things do you skip? . . .

There are always other things and events that are nowhere near your focus of awareness. You can discover what these are by noticing what you are not aware of. Right now, what are you *not* aware of? . . . Try directing your attention toward those things or events that are not in the focus of your awareness at the moment, and take some time to actually contact them and be more aware of them. . . .

Now say to yourself "Right now I'm not aware of—" and complete the sentence with something you are not aware of at the moment. As you do this, you will become aware of something here and now that you were not aware of a moment before. Stay with this experience for a little while and see what more you can discover about it. Then repeat this process, and again discover what you are not aware of at that moment. Do this for several minutes now, and notice what kinds of experiences you discover as you do this. . . .

Now try something very similar, but a bit more specific. Say to yourself "Right now I'm *avoiding—*" and complete the sentence with whatever you discover you are avoiding at that moment. As you do this, you will become aware of something that you were previously excluding from your awareness. Stay with this awareness for awhile and see what more you can discover about it. Then repeat this process, and discover something else that you are avoiding. Do this for several minutes now, and notice what kinds of experiences you are avoiding and how you feel as you do become aware of them. . . .

Duration and Flow

Now again become an observer of your awareness as you let it wander, and become aware of how long you stay with an awareness. . . . Notice whether your awareness jumps quickly from one thing to another, or whether it moves more slowly—giving you plenty of time to really explore and contact whatever you are aware of. . . . Now experiment with speeding up the flow of your awareness from one thing to another. . . . Now slow down your flow of awareness and experience this. . . . What do you notice about your awareness when it moves rapidly or slowly? . . . Now let your awareness wander freely again, and simply be an observer. . . . Be aware of the difference in the time you spend with different things and events—you probably stay longer with some experiences, and stay only a short time with others. . . . Notice which experiences you dwell on for awhile, and which you pass over quickly. . . . Now continue doing this and adjust your timing to even the flow of your awareness. When you become aware of staying with one experience for some time, move on; when you become aware of moving quickly, slow down or return to what you passed over quickly and stay with it for awhile. . . . Now become more aware of the flow of your awareness, as it moves from one thing to another. . . . Do you notice any pattern or direction in this flow? . . . Do you find your awareness returning repeatedly to one thing, or one kind of thing or event, or alternating between one kind of thing and another? . . .

Connection and Interruption

Continue to pay attention to this flow of awareness, and notice what connection there is between the successive things you become aware of. . . . As your awareness moves from one thing to another, how are these things related to each other? . . . Follow this flow and learn more about its direction and what it is like. . . . Notice when your flow of awareness is interrupted. When it stops or suddenly changes its character or direction, return to what you were aware of just before this interruption and focus your attention there for awhile. . . . See if you can discover more about this. . . . How do you feel as you stay with this awareness? . . .

Pleasant-Unpleasant

Again, take a few minutes to become aware of the flow of your awareness, and as you become aware of something, notice whether this awareness is pleasant or unpleasant to you. . . . What differences do you notice between your awareness of something pleasant and something unpleasant? . . . Does your awareness stay longer with one or the other? . . . Are you less aware of detail with one or the other? . . . Is there some pattern or similarity in what you experience as pleasant and unpleasant? . . . Continue this for awhile and learn more about how your awareness of pleasant and unpleasant experience differs. . . .

An interruption in the flow of awareness is sometimes a response to a sudden change in our surroundings. But more often it is a response to an awareness of something unpleasant. We usually avoid something unpleasant, and interrupting our awareness is a way of keeping unpleasant experiences at a distance. This is one of the major ways that we reduce and limit our awareness. If you become aware that you are avoiding and alienating an experience, it is possible to reverse this process. If you notice an interruption of your awareness, you can focus your attention on the experience that immediately preceded the interruption and seek to learn more about what it is that you are avoiding. Try this again now. . . .

Shuttling

Now try shuttling back and forth between awareness of something outside and something inside for a few minutes. First become aware of something in your surroundings. . . . and then become aware of some physical feeling inside your body. . . . Continue to move between awareness of inside and outside events. . . . As you do this, also be aware of the flow of your awareness, the interruptions in this flow, and the connections between the successive events of your awareness. Continue this for awhile, and learn more about how your awareness of inside events is related to your experience of your outside surroundings. . . .

Now continue this shuttling, and try considering your awareness of inside events to be a response to your awareness of something outside. Be aware of something outside, and then say "—and my response to this is—" and finish this sentence with whatever you become aware of as you shuttle back to your awareness of something inside. For instance, "I'm aware of the thick soft rug, and my response to this is a relaxed feeling in my thighs." Continue this for a few minutes. . . .

Intending

Continue to pay attention to your continuum of awareness and be aware of any intention in this. Is your awareness actually flowing by itself with you as an observer? Or are you doing something specific, imposing some intentional activity? For instance, you might be straining or trying hard to do a "good job." You might be shutting out some kind of awareness or "just going through the motions" of what these instructions ask you to do. Take some time now to notice when some intention guides your awareness instead of letting it flow by itself. . . .

Process

Our language tends to structure our world as a bunch of things that occasionally change, interact with each other, etc. Viewing the world as a set of ever-changing processes and happenings is more difficult, and also often much more valid and useful. Continue to pay attention to your continuum of awareness and state your awareness in terms of processes and happenings, rather than things. For instance, instead of saying "I feel a tension," say "I feel tensing." Instead of "I hear birds," say "I am listening to twittering and chirping." Instead of

"I feel a breeze" say "I am feeling the air moving gently over my arm." Take some time to get in touch with the flow and process of your experiencing of the world around you.

Physical Activities

Now focus your awareness on your body and your physical sensations. Wherever you notice some movement, tension, or discomfort, express this as an ongoing activity such as pushing, tensing, or holding. . . . Now exaggerate this activity slightly, and become more aware of it. If you are tensing your shoulder, tense it more, and be aware of which muscles you use and how you feel as you do this. . . . Now take responsibility for this muscular activity and its consequences. For instance, say to yourself "I am tensing my neck, and hurting myself," or "I am holding my right arm tightly, and stiffening myself," All of your muscular tension is self-produced, and much of your physical discomfort is a result of this. Take some time now to become more aware of your physical activities, and take responsibility for what you are doing to yourself. . . .

Releasing Your Body

We interfere with our functioning by preventing expression of much of what happens in ourselves. You can learn to let your body take over and release itself from this interference. Begin by lying down on a rug or a firm bed in a position that is really comfortable for you. A good position is lying on your back with your knees drawn up until your feet rest flat on the floor and your knees rest lightly against each other. Close your eyes, and get in touch with your body. . . . Are you really comfortable? See if you can get even more comfortable by changing your position slightly. . . . Now become aware of your breathing. . . . Notice all the details of how you are breathing. . . . Feel how the air moves into your nose or mouth, . . . and down your throat, and into your lungs. . . . Notice all the details of how your chest and belly move as the air flows in and out of your lungs. . . .

Now notice whenever thoughts or images come into your mind. . . . Notice how these words and images interfere with your awareness of the physical sensations of your breathing. . . . Pay attention to these thoughts and images now, and be aware of what happens if you try to stop them. ... What do you experience as you try to stop your thoughts? ... What do you feel in your body now? ...

Now try something different. Instead of trying to stop your thoughts, just focus your attention on your breathing. ... Whenever you realize that your attention has wandered to thoughts or images, just refocus your attention on the physical sensations of your breathing. ... Don't struggle or battle—just notice when you become preoccupied with words and images, and then return your attention to your breathing. ...

Now focus your attention on your body, and notice which parts of your body come into your awareness spontaneously. ... Which parts of your body emerge into your awareness? ... And which parts are you less aware of? ... Now scan your body and notice which parts of your body you can easily become aware of and feel clear, distinct sensation from. ... And which parts of your body feel unclear and indistinct even when you focus your attention on them. ... Do you notice any difference between the left side and the right side of your body? ...

Now be aware of any physical discomfort you feel, and focus your attention on it. ... Get more in touch with it, and become deeply aware of it in detail. ... As you become more aware of this experience, you may find that it slowly develops or changes. A movement, a feeling, or an image may develop out of what you are focusing on. Allow this change and development to take place without interference, and continue to focus your attention on whatever emerges. Let your body do whatever it wants to do, and let happen whatever wants to happen. Continue this for five or ten minutes and see what develops out of this focusing of your attention on whatever emerges into your awareness. ...

Contact-Withdrawal

Look around you and get in touch with your surroundings. What do you experience here? ... Now close your eyes. ... Withdraw from the situation here, and go away from here in your imagination. Go anywhere you like, and experience what it is like to be there. ...

What is it like there?... And how do you feel there?...

Now open your eyes and be aware of the situation here. What is it like to be here? ... And how do you feel now? ... Compare your situation here with the situation there. ...

Go away again wherever you like, either the same place or somewhere else, ... and again experience this situation fully. ...

Open your eyes now, and again contact the situation here. ... Compare it to the there situation. ...

Continue to shuttle back and forth between here and there, and be aware of what you experience. Notice any changes in your experience as you continue this shuttling for a few minutes. ...

Now come back here, and open your eyes, ... and quietly absorb your experience of this shuttling. ...

This contact-withdrawal shuttling can be useful to you in sever al ways. By withdrawing briefly from a situation—either into your physical experience or into your fantasy or both—you can usually get some rest and support, and then return with more energy to the present situation you have to cope with. Also, if you examine the there situation carefully, you can usually discover *there* what is missing in the *here* situation. If you are having difficulty with people in the here situation, you will most likely withdraw to a fantasy situation where you are alone, or with people that you don't have difficulties with—a place you can rest and be more comfortable.

Another thing you can discover in the there situation is unfinished situations that need to be completed in some way—an unresolved disagreement with someone, a lawn to be mowed, etc. When you withdraw in fantasy, you often get reminders of these unfinished situations that won't let you rest. If you hang on grimly to what you are doing, you may be avoiding dealing with these unpleasant unfinished situations, and these unfinished situations will prevent your full involvement in the present. Here's a simple but useful example. If you are doggedly studying a book, you are probably reading it without understanding. Your eyes may run down the page, but a minute later you can remember nothing, because too many other situations are crying for your attention. If you withdraw temporarily to something else—a stretch, a cookie, a fantasy, etc., then you can return to the book with renewed energy. If you don't withdraw from a situation like this, all you do is exhaust yourself without benefit.

If you totally avoid a difficult situation, it often gets worse and seldom goes away; if you hang onto it grimly, you exhaust yourself. If you alternately tackle the problem, and then withdraw temporarily to gather strength, you can be most effective. Most people realize that over-extended withdrawal is bad. Fewer people realize that over-extended contact is just as bad. As you read this book, occasionally stop and be aware of whether you are really in contact with it, or whether most of your attention is somewhere else. If it is somewhere else, leave this book for awhile, and return when your attention is less divided.

The brief excerpts that follow are transcripts of tape recordings of people beginning to explore their continuum of awareness in a group. They illustrate some of the aspects of awareness that the previous experiments ask you to focus on. The leader's comments are enclosed in slashes, like this: /L: What do you experience from moment to moment?/

Don't read further until you have tried the previous experiments on your own.

I'm aware of the silence. I wish I were somewhere else. /L: O.K., close your eyes, and go somewhere else in fantasy./ I know where I was going already—to the Spaghetti Factory (a restaurant)—I already pictured things. /L: Do it. Close your eyes. I want you to really invest yourself in this, and really pay attention to your process. What is it like there?/ Umm. There's big, big salad bowls—they're gigantic and they're dark brown, wooden, and there's a bunch of spaghetti in them. And there's a lot of sauce on the spaghetti, (laughing) and I feel like having some. /L: You're laughing. Can you tell us what's funny to you?/ Well, because I thought salad should be in the bowls, not spaghetti, 'cause it looks more like a salad bowl. It's dark, there's candles, there's a low long counter—I don't have to close my eyes. Um—yes I do. There's a lot of people. /L: How do you feel there?/ Comfortable, and hungry. /L: Come back here now, and contrast the two experiences./ A little nervous, a little uptight. And it's light here, and I wish it were dark. /L: Do you see the contrast? Here you're uncomfortable and it's light; there you're comfortable and it's dark. Go there again and discover some more./ People seem real relaxed. I'm relaxed there. People are smiling—people in separate booths, down long aisles. It's crowded and people seem relaxed and happy, and they're eating a lot. /L: Now come back here. How do you experience being here?/ Everything seems so, so—not dead, just light. I don't know what it is. It's really dark there, and you kind of hide away, and kind of get lost. /L: You can't hide here./ No. /L: How do you feel here, now?/ A litte more relaxed than I was, 'cause I've been there for awhile. /L: Exactly. This is something you can use on your own. In any situation that you're uptight, go away for a little while, and then come back./ Isn't that escaping? /L: Only if you do it permanently. If you do it temporarily it's called resting./

I'm aware that I feel sticky—when I sat down, sort of sweaty. /L: You went briefly into the past with "when I sat down."/ I feel a nervousness in my stomach. I can feel my heart beating faster, and I'm aware of the color of the room—there's so much of it. And I'm aware of those two girls who look a lot alike, and I was wondering if they were sisters. /L: Wondering is fantasy./ Yeah. I'm aware that I'm hot, and my feet don't touch the floor. And I'm aware that people right there were moving, squirming. /L: You said "were" which puts it in the past, and "those people" is generalization. Specifically who did you see, and what did they do?/ Her and her. (pointing) She was moving her foot, and she was moving her hands. I'm aware of increasing nervousness, in myself. /L: How do you feel that? What, exactly, do you feel that you call nervousness?/ I guess you'd say butterflies, I guess because I'm aware of so many eyes, and I see people, in a semi-circle, almost engulfing me. (pause) /L: Are you aware that you're looking at me?/ Umhmn. (pause) I'm aware of other things, but—I think I'll leave it there. /L: You'd like to stop./ Umhmn. /L: O.K. Thank you. Do you notice *where* you stopped?/ *Yeah.* When I started talking about the people engulfing me, and all those *eyes!* I didn't realize that until you asked me. /L: Would you like to explore this a little more?/ O.K. /L: Look around at the people here, and tell us what you see. What are you aware of?/ I'm aware of a lot of eyes. (laughs) Also colors. I notice hair colors, clothes, skin tones, um— /L: Could you be specific—exactly what do you see, moment-to-moment? Rather than generalizing and lumping them together as colors or skin tones, say which colors you see and whose skin tones you notice./ I notice her red pants, and I notice her tan, and her hair is very dark. There are a lot more girls than there are boys—I notice that one boy who is frowning. /L: Do you feel engulfed now?/ Not really, no. I don't feel the same feeling that I felt a minute ago. I don't feel that they're all people together; I can pinpoint individuals more, rather than a collective group—a massive group. When I began looking at individuals rather than grouping, then I began to feel more comfortable. /L: You begin to *see* them instead of *imagining* them. They were engulfing you in your imagination; they were actually just sitting there in reality. As you get more in touch with your awareness of these individuals, the fantasy of a group engulfing you then fades away./

I'm aware that my stomach is tight. And I'm holding my breath. And I'm breathing, and my heart's pounding faster. I'm thinking of what to say—and tapping my fingers. I feel like I'm looking for something. /L: You're mostly aware of your activities—holding, breathing, thinking, tapping. You're also intending somehow, searching, trying to think what to say./ Yeah. I'm aware that I have my feet crossed. And I'm aware of her shoes. And she has long fingernails. /L: Are you aware that you started with your own body—your feelings in your chest—and then gradually worked out to your fingers and feet, and then to her feet and fingers? As if gradually moving out to the other people./ (laughing) Just before you said that I started to come back inside and feel tightness. /L: Try shuttling back and forth between inside and outside awareness./ I feel like the inside of my body is sealed from the outside—like everything is inside and it's tight. /L: Say "I'm tightening myself."/ I'm tightening myself inside. I see her face. I still feel the tightness. I notice her purse underneath the chair, and his feet—he's wiggling his toes, and his hands are tight. /L: You are aware of tightness outside, now./ (pause) I'm searching. All I feel is tight inside, and I'm trying to think of something else inside that I feel, that's different from being tight. /L: Your awareness keeps returning to the tightness, and you intentionally *try* to be aware of something else, rather than stay with your actual awareness of your tightness./

I'm aware that I'm too short to sit down in this chair. I'm aware of the wind in the trees, and—you know, it—they move kind of slowly, but if you watch them for awhile, it kind of relaxes you, because— /L: Could you say "I"? You're talking about your own experience. "As I watch the trees, I relax."/ I'm aware that it happened there (pointing to where she had been sitting) but it isn't happening now, because I'm too nervous. /L: So this is not awareness, you're actually remembering the past./ Yeah. /L: So what's happening now?/ I'm really nervous. I'm aware that my feet are moving. I'm aware that other people are kind of bored. /L: That's a fantasy. You don't know that they're bored./ No. I'm aware of him, especially: He's kind of smirking, and I'm—I guess I'm trying to figure him out. /L: That's fantasy again. Now try saying "I'm avoiding—" and finish the sentence with something that you're avoiding at that moment and become more aware of it./ I'm avoiding looking at people I don't know. I'm avoiding thinking about how I look—I'm avoiding that. And I'm avoiding saying a lot of things I'd like to say—about feelings inside me. You know, especially feelings— I'm avoiding feelings that are—you know, you know, those kind of feelings. (laughs) I'm avoiding—you know, I'm avoiding, um, telling people that they're—they're handsome, or that, you know—that kind of—I'm avoiding that. And I'm avoiding looking at—at Ruth, and I don't know why. /L: Try looking at Ruth. Try contacting some of these things that you're avoiding./ (pause) When I look at Ruth, I see her just kind of sitting there, and she's holding her hands, and—and in—in my mind—I guess I'm not aware, I think that she's not very happy with me or something. I don't know why. /L: This is fantasy again; you imagine disapproval./ Yeah—of me. /L: You contact your awareness briefly, and then you jump into fantasy—thinking, remembering, wondering, imagining./

I'm shaking all over, and my heart's beating very fast, and my hands are sweaty. And I'm aware of him looking at me, and my voice is shaking. (laugh) /L: After each awareness you report, say whether it is pleasant or unpleasant. "My voice is shaking--"/ That's unpleasant. Being nervous is unpleasant. He's looking at me--kind of through me. That's (laughs) unpleasant. I'm aware of the noises outside-- that's pleasant. This chair is very hard, and that's pleasant--it's firm and smooth. And the floor under my feet feels good. I'm very aware of what's inside, what's happening--/L: Tell us about this./ Well, first of all, my thoughts are spinning around and around--that's kind of unpleasant. And I have this--a pain. (laughs) It's a nervous type of pain in my stomach. (laughs) Um. Mostly I'm aware of everybody looking at me. I don't like that. I'm very aware of outside--the trees moving. /L: I notice that you went from people looking at you to the trees outside, and I recall earlier when you saw a fellow looking at you, you next became aware of the noises outside./ Yes. /L: You're aware of people looking at you. Could you look back at them and tell us what you see?/ I'm stuck on him, uh, just a face, I don't know, kind of looking out. I'm not really sure what's there. /L: Can you see his face?/ Yes. /L: What do you see?/ Um. (laughs) Um, I see his eyes and his face. I see his moustache. He's got very clear eyes, very penetrating. /L: Do you see how you are stuck with the eyes?/ Yeah. I'm aware of Ann, sitting there--she's pleasant. /L: How are you aware of her? What do you see?/ (laughs) I see--well, why she's pleasant is because I've talked to her, but that--she's pleasant from other things that I know about her. /L: So this is the past--memories, rather than awareness. Look at Ann now: what do you see?/ It's hard to see. /L: Right now the other people have eyes, but you have no eyes./ Yeah. /L: All you can see is their eyes. Let's follow this up a bit. What do you imagine they see as they look at you?/ Oh. (laughs) Uh. Sort of a nervous, shaky, sweaty (laughs) person. (laughs) /L: What would you say to a nervous, shaky, sweaty person?/ Cool it. Be calm. Quiet down. /Are you by any chance saying this to yourself?/ Sort of--yeah, I am. /L: How are your symptoms? Do you still feel nervousness?/ Yeah. I'm moving around, trembling. There's a pain in my stomach. /L: Try exaggerating this nervousness and trembling. So far you've been fighting these symptons. You experience them as unpleasant and you try to reduce them. Reverse this, and try to increase these symptoms./ O.K. I'm moving my feet more, I'm trembling, I feel the pain and tightness in my stomach. /L: Can you focus on that tightness, and make it tighter?/ Yeah. I feel like it's getting into a ball. /L: Say this, "I'm tightening myself."/ I'm tightening myself. (pause) Now it's not happening—it's, it's fading away. I think I'm getting less upset. It feels like an ice-cream cone would feel if it melted. /L: You feel O.K. now? This always happens if you really get in touch with yourself and become fully aware of what is actually happening in you./ Yeah. /L: Now look out again./ All right. I see people. /L: Do you see them? How do you see them?/ Well, I see *her* now, she's smiling. And she looks very relaxed. She—I don't know—she's moving her arm, maybe she's nervous because I saw her—I'm thinking that because I would be nervous, if she saw me. /L: Notice that now you look at her, and you make her nervous. Before, they made you nervous by looking at you./ (laughter).

Wherever you are, whatever you are doing, you can do this kind of observing and experimenting. Just pay attention to the process of your awareness. You can make good use of time that you would otherwise waste in boredom, waiting, fidgeting, etc. As you become aware of your own process, you can discover how you avoid, block, disrupt and distort your own functioning. As you discover how you interfere with your functioning, you can learn to let go of this interference. You can bring more and more awareness into your daily activities, and your life can become more flowing and alive.

Daily Task

Choose some everyday task that you have to do, such as washing dishes, brushing your teeth, taking out the garbage, etc. Do this task, and pay close attention to how your body feels as you do it. . . . Try doing it at half-speed for a few minutes, to give you more time to be aware of what goes on in you as you do this. . . . Notice if you are holding or moving your body in an awkward or uncomfortable way. Then exaggerate this tension or awkwardness and get more in touch with it—really experience it. . . . Now let go and explore other ways of doing the same task that might be more comfortable or pleasing for you. . . . Try letting your movements flow. .... Let these movements slowly become a dance, and enjoy this dancing. Play with your awareness of doing this task, and explore it as if it were a foreign country—for most of us, it really is a foreign country.

Listening to Your Surroundings

Look around now at whatever is in your environment and become more aware of what is there. Really contact your surroundings, and let each thing speak to you about itself and its relationship to you. For instance, my desk says "I am messy and full of work you have to do. Until you tidy me up, I'll irritate you and keep you from concentrating." A wood sculpture says "See how I can flow even though I am still. Slow down and discover your beauty." Take about five minutes to let the things in your enviroment speak to you. Listen carefully to these messages that you are getting from all around you. ....

If you can learn to really listen to your surroundings, you can realize what effect they are having upon you without your being aware of it. As you become more aware of these influences, you can change your surroundings to make them more comfortable and less distracting, irritating, etc. I have used this experiement in the classroom to point out the oppressive effect of its structure. The blackboard says "Look this way, everything important will happen here. " The hard chairs say "Don't go to sleep, don't have fun, be orderly, and look this way." The clock says "Be prompt, and don't waste time," etc. After becoming aware of the deadening influence of the orderly classroom, we do what we can to make it a more comfortable place for human beings to live in. We get a rug, get rid of most of the chairs and rearrange the rest, put up something colorful, etc.

Next I want you to try some experiments that involve you with another person. These experiments will be most effective if you do them with someone whom you don't know well, but if no one else is available, do them with a friend or spouse.

Contacting

Sit down facing this person and don't talk. Just look at your partner's face for a couple of minutes and try to really see this other person. . . . I don't want you to make this into a staring contest, and I don't want you to spend your time imagining what your partner is like. I want you to look at your partner and simply be aware of all the details of his face. Become aware of the actual characteristics of his features—the colors, shapes and textures, how his face moves or doesn't move, etc. I want you to really become aware of this other person. Try to really see him. . . .

Is there anything going on in you now that makes it difficult for you to focus your attention on your partner? . . . If something else is competing for your attention, take a little time to become more aware of this. . . .

Rehearsing

Continue to look at each other, and at the same time imagine what you think will happen and what you will do in the next few minutes. You are probably doing some of this rehearsing anyway, so take some time to focus your attention on your fantasies and expectations. . . . Become aware of them in detail. . . . What do you think is about to happen? . . .

Now become aware of what is going on in your body. . . . Notice any sensations of tension, excitement, nervousness, etc. . . . To what extent are these symptons a response to your fantasies and expectations about the future, rather than a response to what is actually happening at this moment? . . .

Withdrawing

Now get more in touch with your actual experience of the moment. Close your eyes and withdraw into your physical existence for a few minutes. . . . Become aware of your body and your physical sensations. . . . Notice any tension, nervousness, or excitement, etc., and get in touch with this. . . . Focus your awareness on any discomfort you find, and notice how it changes as you stay in touch with it. . . .

Now open your eyes and look at this other person again. . . . Is it any easier to see him now? . . . Try to discover even more about this person. . . . What can you see now that you didn't notice before? . . . To what extent can you really *see* this person, and to what extent are you still occupied with fantasies—guessing, imagining, or assuming what he is like, wondering what he sees as he looks at you, wondering how long this will last, etc.? . . . Whenever you find yourself doing this, just refocus your awareness on your partner's . face and expressions. . . .

Continue to look at your partner, but focus your attention on your physical existence. . . . What is going on in your body now? . . . Notice any tension, nervousness, discomfort, ease, or excitement that you feel, and get more in touch with it. . . . Become aware of exactly where you feel these sensations, and what these sensations are like. . . .

In a moment I want you to tell each other all the details of how you feel physically—where you feel tension, nervousness, ease or excitement, etc., and exactly what it feels like to you. Don't explain or justify your experience, just describe what you feel in detail, and be aware of how your experience of your body changes as you tell your partner about it. Take a few minutes for this. . . .

Memory Image
Again close your eyes and withdraw into your body. . . . Again get in touch with what is going on inside your skin, and notice what happens as you focus your attention on these sensations in your body. . . . Really get in touch with your physical existence. . . . Now keep your eyes closed and visualize your partner's face that you were looking at only a few moments ago. How completely can you do this? Which features are clear in your imagination, and which features are dim or absent? . . . Can you recall the shape of his nose, the color of his eyes, the texture of his skin, etc.? Be aware of where your image is distinct, and where it is incomplete or fuzzy. Which parts are difficult or impossible for you to visualize? . . . Realize that quite a lot of what escaped your memory must have also escaped your full awareness. . . .

Now open your eyes and compare your image with the reality of your partner's face. . . . Which details of your image were incorrect? . . . Now look at the parts of his face that were absent or fuzzy in your image, and discover what these parts are like. . . . Discover even more about this person's face. . . .

In a minute I'm going to ask you to tell each other what you see—not what you imagine or guess, but what you are actually aware of now as you look at your partner's face. Don't fall back on your memory of what you saw before, and don't explain why you noticed this or apologize for seeing it, etc. Just say what you are aware of now, from moment to moment, and give all the details of your awareness. Don't just say "Now I see your eyes," say "Now I see your wide-set dark brown eyes; they are shining and I like to look at them, " or whatever your experience is. Take about five minutes for this. . . .

Censoring

Now stop talking and silently look at your partner and be aware of what you have been censoring—the things that you have noticed about your partner but haven't told him for some reason. . . . Realize that you imagine some unpleasant comsequence—he would become sad, displeased, angry, rejecting, etc. Also realize that this fantasy of yours inhibits or prevents the full expression of your awareness, and that this holding back is also a kind of dishonesty: you refuse to fully reveal your awareness to your partner. . . .Again focus your attention on the things you are censoring, . . . and now close your eyes and imagine that you tell your partner about these things. . . . What happens now? Let your imagination go, and discover in detail what it is that you fear would happen if you told your partner about these things. . . . What are your expectations of catastrophe, and how do you feel now as you imagine this catastrophe? . . .

Now open your eyes. In a moment I want you to tell your partner what would happen if you told him the things you are censoring. Say, "If I tell you what I'm censoring—" and finish this sentence with what you think would happen. After you have each done this, respond to your partner's catastrophic expectations and discuss whether these expectations are likely, and whether they are really disasters or only inconveniences. Then if you are willing, tell each other at least a few of the things that you are censoring, and compare your expectations with what actually happens when you do this. Go ahead. . . .

Sit quietly for a little while now, and absorb your experiences and what you have learned from these experiments. . . . Now take five or ten minutes to tell each other what you have learned and experienced. . . .

As you have been talking during the last few minutes, to what degree have you been really contacting each other and really communicating? . . . Have you been looking at each other as you talk, or have you been avoiding contact by looking away or staring at your hands or the wall? . . . Have you been talking directly to this person, or have you been broadcasting your words, or scattering generalities on the floor? . . . Take a few more minutes to discuss this. . . .

I hope you had some experience of how difficult it is to do even a simple thing like seeing someone's face, as long as you are preoccupied with threatening fantasies about the future and with your physical symptoms of nervousness and excitement in response to these fantasies. This nervousness and excitement is often called anxiety. Anxiety is what you experience when your body prepares for a challenge that is not here in reality. If the challenge actually exists, your excitement and energy can flow into the activity of coping with the challenge. Since the challenge only exists in fantasy, there is nothing you can actually do, and all your energy and excitement gushes out in trembling and other symptoms of anxiety. This also happens if the challenge is present in reality, but you don't dare attempt it yet and are still preoccupied with rehearsing and catastrophic expectations.

If you can even realize that you are preoccupied with fantasies and expectations and that these fantasies are not real, this alone can help you get more in touch with what is actually happening. Even more useful is the temporary withdrawal into your body. When you close your eyes, you temporarily break contact with the threat, and by focusing your attention on your body sensations you regain contact with your physical reality. As you do this, you are also withdrawing your attention from the fantasies and you become less involved with them.

Whenever I become involved with fantasies I lose awareness of ongoing reality, and at the same time I interfere with my own functioning. All the things my body does on its own require awareness, so any loss of awareness causes my functioning to be less adequate. In addition, I begin to physically respond to the fantasies instead of reality. If I am actually threatened in reality, a fast heartbeat and a tense stomach may be useful to me. When I am not threatened, the same symptoms are a useless waste of energy, and they may also disturb other tasks that I do need to do in reality. In addition to these difficulties, these fantasies require that I use a lot of energy to inhibit and censor the expression of many aspects of my awareness and activities. For instance, if I am talking to you and I begin to imagine that I will make mistakes and that you will judge and criticize me, I will experience what is called "self-consciousness." My fear of this fantasied disaster urges me to run, and my energy will begin to flow into excitement and movement. But my fear of your criticism also requires that I conceal these symptoms from you, so I have to use additional energy to subdue my excitement and stop my urge to run. So much energy may go into this conflict between excitement and inhibition that there isn't enough left for the simple task of talking to you. Also, both the symptoms and my attempts to oppose them often interfere with my talking to you—my voice may become quavery or stuttering and I may be so aware of this that I lose awareness of what I want to tell you.

These disturbances of my functioning leave me more and more scatttered and confused. My awareness is divided between fantasies and reality. I am responding partly to what is real and partly to what is unreal, and my responses to my fantasies further interfere with my activities in reality. My energy is divided between the tasks that are required by reality and the tasks that my fantasies require. My energy is also divided between expressing myself and inhibiting that expression. I have become dis-integrated: I no longer function as an integrated whole, but instead scatter my awareness, my responses, my activities and my energy. I become confused, frustrated and ineffective—and all of us suffer from this to some degree.

If you can explore your awareness in detail and learn more about it, you can work toward becoming less scattered and less confused, and more whole and integrated. Mostly this is a matter of letting go, learning how to not interfere with your own functioning, and learning how to get out of your own way.

Contacting

Again I want you to pair up with someone you don't know well and sit facing this person without talking. Look at your partner's face for a couple of minutes and try to see this other person. . . . Become aware of all the details of this person's face—the shape, size, color, and texture of all the different features, etc. . . . Let your eyes move around as you continue to discover more about this person's features and expressions. . . .

Accepting Symptoms

Continue to look at your partner, and at the same time focus your attention on what you feel physically. . . . What is going on in your body that tends to interfere with your seeing your partner? . . . Probably you feel some excitement and nervousness—your heart pounding, some tension, or butterflies in your stomach, etc. Probably you are also rejecting these sensations, judging them as "bad" and uncomfortable, and that you must not reveal your "weakness" to your partner. Try reversing this judgment, even if this reversal seems to be a phony game. Instead of calling these symptoms "nervousness," call them "excitement" and see if you can *enjoy* them. . . . Notice how your symptoms change as you accept them more and become more aware of them. . . .

Exaggerating Symptoms

Now experiment with trying to increase or exaggerate any symptoms you feel, instead of trying to decrease or minimize them. If you feel some trembling, let this trembling become more intense. If you feel some tension, increase the tension in those muscles for awhile. Be aware of what happens as you encourage your symptoms instead of fighting them. . . .

Now try expressing your symptoms even more. Continue to stay in touch with your symptoms and exaggerate them, and let them flow into some kind of noise. Make some kind of noise that expresses what is going on in you now. . . . Now increase this noise until it is much louder. . . . Now silently absorb what you have just experienced. . . .

Now take a few minutes to tell each other what you experienced during these experiments. . . .

Now again sit quietly and look at your partner's face to see what you can discover about it in this moment as you look at it. . . . Continue to look at your partner, and at the same time become aware of your own body. . . . Become aware of any tension, nervousness or other discomfort that you feel. . . . Particularly notice any tension or discomfort in your face. . . . What does this express? . . . Do you have any objection to being looked at by your partner in this way? Is there something you don't want him to see? . . .

Reality Testing

Now deliberately imagine what your partner sees as he looks at you. You are probably doing some of this anyway, so pay attention to these imaginings and become more aware of them. . . . What exactly do you imagine he sees, and what do you imagine his response is to what he sees? . . . Notice how these fantasies get between you and your experiencing. . . . One way to get rid of these disturbing fantasies is to express them and check them out in reality. Now take several minutes to tell your partner what you imagine he sees as he looks at you and find out if he was aware of these things before you mentioned them. . . .

Shuttling

Now I want you to continue to look at each other and silently become aware of some aspect of your own physical existence. . . . Then become aware of something in your partner. . . . And continue to shuttle back and forth between awareness of your own physical sensations and awareness of your partner. . . . As you do this shuttling, be aware of how your own private experience of yourself is connecting with your awareness of your partner—something outside yourself. . . . Now silently talk as you do this: "Now I'm aware of your bushy eyebrows; now I'm aware of stiffness in my left knee; now I'm aware of your full, soft lips; now I'm aware of a pleasant warm feeling in my stomach," or whatever your experience of this shuttling is. ... Now continue this for a couple of minutes, but whisper it out loud so that your partner can hear you. ... Now take turns with this shuttling for a few minutes. Listen for awhile as your partner shuttles, and then you shuttle as he listens to you. ...

Now take some time to share your experiences in these experiments and tell each other what you have discovered about yourself and your partner. ...

If you really invested yourself in these experiments, you have had some more experience of how your fantasies keep you from expressing yourself, and also some more awareness of what those fantasies are. If you can become really aware of these fantasies, you can explore what they express about you and then check them out in reality. And if you can really become aware of what you hold back and how you hold yourself back, then you have a chance to let go and reverse the process, and discover how well you can function without interference.

The aim of this book is to show you how you can increase your contact with inner and outer ongoing reality, and decrease your preoccupation with the fantasy activity which prevents your contact with experiencing. Fantasy *can* be useful, but *only* if you invest yourself in it fully, with awareness, and integrate the fantasy with your experiencing of reality in the present. I gave one example of this previously, when I related my fantasies about this book to my physical experience at the time.

Another example: A student spent a lot of time for several months imagining asking a particular girl in his class for a date. This fruitless preoccupation with his fantasy wasted a sizable chunk of his life. If he had really used this fantasy, he could have realized that although useless as a fantasy, asking her for a date could be very useful in reality. If he actually asks her for a date, either she says yes and they can develop their relationship further, or she says no and he can turn his attention toward some other girl who might be more receptive. In either case his life begins to move and flow again, instead of remaining stuck in an unactualized fantasy. Who knows how many other friendly girls may have been available, or may have even approached him while he was preoccupied with this fantasy?

Of course, if he asks her for a date, he runs the risk of rejection if she says no, or the challenge of a close personal relationship if she says yes. He avoids confronting the situation and so it remains unfinished. This is the typical conflict situation. His urge in one direction is opposed by an urge in the opposite direction: his wish to be close to her is opposed by fears of closeness or rejection. However, there is an important difference between these two urges. His desire to be close to her is at least partly his response to her presence now, and he can probably feel this response clearly in his body. His fears are in response to his fantasy about the future—what he imagines may occur if he tells her of his liking her and asks her for a date. His fantasy of the future kills the expression of himself in the present.

The remedy for this kind of situation is first for him to fully realize that his fears are *fantasies,* and next for him to fully realize that these are *his* fantasies—that they express much more about him than they do about the girl, and that they are his responsibility. For instance, if his fantasy is mostly of rejection, he must realize that it is he who rejects himself, not the girl. He doesn't give the girl a chance to reject him! He does it himself, but without realizing it. He alienates his own rejection and imagines that the girl will reject him. If he can really become deeply aware of this part of himself that rejects, and identify with it, he can become free of his catastrophic fantasies and free to express himself. With awareness, his fantasies can support his life instead of paralyzing it.

The usefulness of fantasies and imagination—planning, thinking, etc.—is apparent to most people. A certain amount of reflecting on the "past" and guessing about the "future" can save us some difficulty and make our lives fuller and more satisfying. But this is true only if we make use of this guessing in reality and realize that a fantasy is only a guess *about* reality. For instance, all scientific "knowledge" is entirely fantasy: There is no real difference between a scientist talking about electrons and radiation, and a witch doctor talking about spirits and demons. Each is expressing his images and his thinking about imaginary processes that he can't see, in order to try to understand the events that he can see—atomic bombs and sick patients. The *only* difference between the two is their attitude toward their fantasies. The witch doctor confuses his fixed fantasies with reality, and invents endless explanations when reality doesn't fit his preconceptions. The scientist knows that his fantasies are guesses, and he insists that they be continually tested, changed and adapted to fit the reality that he observes. A scientist does not demand that his guesses and theories are proved to be "true." He is content if they fit what he observes and are useful in further exploration and interaction with reality.

> Not truth, nor certainty. These I foreswore
> In my novitiate, as young men called
> To holy orders must abjure the world.
> "If . . ., then . . .," this only I assert;
> And my successes are but pretty chains
> Linking twin doubts, for it is vain to ask
> If what I postulate be justified,
> Or what I prove possess the stamp of fact.
>
> Yet bridges stand, and men no longer crawl
> In two dimensions. And such triumphs stem
> In no small measure from the power this game,
> Played with the thrice-attenuated shades
> Of things, has over their originals.
> How frail the wand, but how profound the spell!

> —Clarence R. Wylie Jr.,
> Mathematician*

Creative imagination is useless in itself, but when it flows into awareness and interaction with existing reality, something new grows in the world. A creative person is aware of the qualities and characteristics of his surroundings, and responds to these surroundings with awareness of his own individual process—his own feelings, needs and

*From "The Imperfections of Science" by Warren Weaver. *Proceedings of the American Philosophical Society*, Vol. 104, No. 5, October, 1960.

wishes. A creative response is one that integrates awareness of self and world in a form that is appropriate to both. A creative product satisfies something in the creator, and it also has to satisfy the demands of the materials of which it is made.

Although imagination can be useful, realize that whatever time you spend in thoughts and fantasies is time that you spend out of awareness and contact with your life. Most of us spend a lot of our lives hoping and planning for things that will never come, and worrying about things that will never happen. Our fantasies can be valuable as long as they are integrated with our life, support our living, and leave room for awareness and experiencing. But when imagination is split off from the rest of life, it becomes a dead end—an escape from life and an avoidance of living. A great deal of fantasy activity is intended to do just that—avoid the challenges, the risks, and the unpleasant experiences that are a necessary part of living. With every avoidance we become deader and deader, less in contact with ourselves and less in contact with our surroundings. When you lose contact with an unpleasant area of your life, you also lose contact with pleasantness and other valuable potential. Earlier I gave an example of the student who spent a lot of time imagining asking a girl for a date. His dead-end fantasies are the means by which he avoids the risk of the unpleasantness of possible rejection. But as he does this he also avoids any possibility of gain—enjoying her company, her appreciation or love, etc. The walls that keep out arrows and spears also keep out kisses and roses.

Full awareness is identification with my experience and my process now: acknowledging that this is my experience, whether I like it or not, and that this liking or not liking is also part of my experience. The avoidance of unpleasantness and risk is both a reduction of my awareness and an alienation of my experience. This alienation is the process of saying "that's *not* me, that's something alien, something different."

The remedy for alienation of awareness is simple, namely identification, saying "That *is* me, I *am* like that." I can rediscover myself by noticing whatever I am aware of, and identifying with it. I look up now and become aware of the fire in front of me. What happens if I identify with it? "I am burning, making small contented fluttery noises. I am giving off heat; I warm you and make you comfortable. I feel good and steady. I consume old wood, producing gases that will nourish leaves, and ashes that will nourish roots." This is me, as fire, now. At some other time I may discover something different when I become fire, or I may choose something quite different to identify with. Whenever I do this, I will discover more about what my experience is like at that moment. This identification is a beautiful vehicle for expressing feelings, and is far more accurate and expressive than psychologists' tests. Read the following poem, which uses this identification process, and be aware of the degree to which you can identify with this poet's expression of his existence.

Crabs

If you were to leave a burlap bag,
bunching and clicking, full of live crabs,
on the beach, tied at the top, stuffed
with shifting shells inside its sag,
each sticky stalk-eye blind and tender,

claws pinching claws—or nothing—clacking,
hard, hollow bodies scraping as
legs worked them through the bodies, backing,
you would know how full of things I lie,
dry, out of reach of the folding sea,

inert and shapeless, were it not
for rattling crabs inside of me
that hear, perhaps, the long waves crushing,
the flute of the wind through grass and sand,
remember the water, the cool salt hushing,

struggle to slit the burlap and
scatter in sideways, backwards courses,
like beetles, devils, flat as clocks—
these snapping wants, these shelled remorses—
to drag themselves beneath the rocks.

—Judson Jerome*

*From *Light in the West* by Judson Jerome. Golden Quill Press, Francestown, N. H., 1962, p. 19.

Object Identification

Now try this identification experiment yourself. Wherever you are, let your awareness wander, and notice something that stands out in your awareness, or something that you return to and notice repeatedly. . . .

Now focus your awareness on whatever emerges and become more aware of it. What is it like? . . . What are its characteristics? . . . What does it do? . . . Take a little time to discover still more details about it. . . .

Now *identify* with this thing and *become* it. Imagine that you *are* this thing. As this thing what are you like? . . . What are your qualities? . . . Describe yourself: Say to yourself silently, "I am—" . . . What do you do, and what is your existence like as this thing? . . . See what else you can discover about your experience of being this thing. . . .

Now take some time to quietly *absorb* this experience. If you begin to analyze it or think about it, just return to the experience itself. Explaining only takes you away from your experience. If you want to really understand your life, simply learn to stay in contact with your awareness. . . .

Now I want you to ask yourself to what extent you became really involved in this experience, and how much you discovered about yourself. To what extent can you accept your experience as really being an accurate statement about some aspects of your existence? Do you feel "Yes, this is me" or do you feel some doubt or distance, as if the experience were "out there?" Did you become aware of any strong physical feelings, or did you feel untouched and remote from the experience? People differ in their willingness to give up their idea of what they are like and discover themselves as they are. Try the same experiment again with something different, and see if you can get even more into the experience of identifying with it and really becoming this thing. . . .

This method of identification is the basis of the Buddhist idea that full concentration and meditation on anything can lead to full knowing of our inner nature. This begins as a somewhat artificial identification with something outside and different from you, and can grow into a direct personal experience of deepened awareness. When you identify with something in your surroundings, you are somewhat limited by the characteristics of what is actually present there. When you identify with your own internal processes and events you are much closer to yourself and much less limited by your environment. When you find yourself spontaneously thinking of a proverb, remembering a phrase or a snatch of conversation, or humming a tune, take some time to become more aware of it and really invest yourself in it and identify with it. Last week as I was driving I found myself humming a theme from the movie *High Noon.* I began to sing it and identify with it. Tears welled up as I sang:

"And I must face a man who hates me—
or lie a coward,
a craven coward,
or lie a coward in my grave."

As I continued to sing I had more tears for awhile, and then gradually fewer tears and a feeling of strength and conviction. I know that I must face a "man who hates me"—a part of myself that criticizes, judges and condemns. And I also know that another part of me is cowardly and would rather die than confront the judge. As I write this, some of these same feelings return to me, and I know I haven't fully confronted that judge yet. I use words to tell you about my experience, but I want to be sure that you understand that what is important is the *experience* itself, not the words. The world, and most of our experience, is *drowning* in words. Get in touch with your own experiencing.

Humming
Sit alone quietly and take a little time to get in touch with your own experience of your body right now. . . . When you feel ready, begin to hum very softly and without intending to do anything but follow your humming, identify with it, and let it lead you somewhere. Focus your awareness on your humming and let it begin to change by itself. . . . Just be aware of what it is like and what it does as it changes in tone and volume. Don't try to change it; just be aware of the qualities and feelings in your humming and see where it

leads you. Your humming may drift into a tune that you recognize, and perhaps some words will come to you. Identify with whatever comes to you and become the feelings in the tune and the meanings of the words, to see what you can discover. . . .

You can do the same kind of investment and identification with a waking fantasy in your mind. In fantasy anything is possible, and even if you start with a particular imagined thing or situation, you create it and its characteristics out of yourself. The dream is the best kind of fantasy to use in this way because it is almost completely spontaneous and free of our intentional control, and originates completely from within ourselves.* A waking fantasy can be manipulated and controlled somewhat, but if you are willing to let your fantasy develop spontaneously, you can learn a great deal about your existence. The next experiment can give you an experience of discovering yourself through fantasy identification. If you can, do it with a group of 5-7 people so that you can share your experiences with others and learn from their experiences as well.

Rosebush Identification

Find a comfortable position, lying on your back if possible. Close your eyes and become aware of your body. . . . Turn your attention away from outside events and notice what is going on inside you. . . . Notice any discomfort, and see if you can find a more comfortable position. . . . Notice what parts of your body emerge into your awareness, . . . and which parts of your body seem vague and indistinct. . . . If you become aware of a tense area of your body, see if you can let go of the tensing. . . . If not, try deliberately tensing that part, to see which muscles you are tensing, . . . and then let go again. . . . Now focus your attention on your breathing. . . . Become aware of all the details of your breathing. . . . Feel the air move in through your nose or mouth. . . . Feel it move down your throat, . . . and feel your chest and belly move as you breathe. . . . Now imagine that your breathing is like gentle waves on the shore, and that each wave slowly washes some tension out of your body, . . . and releases you even more. . . .

Now become aware of any thoughts or images that come into

*Examples of this productive use of dreams can be found in *Gestalt Therapy Verbatim* by Frederick S. Perls.

your mind. . . . Just notice them. . . . What are they about, and what are they like? . . . Now imagine that you put all these thoughts and images into a glass jar and watch them. . . . Examine them. . . . What are these thoughts and images like, and what do they do as you watch them? . . . As more thoughts or images come into your mind, put them into the jar too, and see what you can learn about them. . . . Now take this jar and pour out the thoughts and images. Watch as they pour out and disappear, and the jar becomes empty. . . .

Now I'd like you to imagine that you are a rosebush. Become a rosebush, and discover what it is like to be this rosebush. . . . Just let your fantasy develop on its own and see what you can discover about being a rosebush. . . . What kind of rosebush are you? . . . Where are you growing? . . . What are your roots like, . . . and what kind of ground are you rooted in? . . . See if you can feel your roots going down into the ground. . . . What are your stems and branches like? . . . Discover all the details of being this rosebush. . . . How do you feel as this rosebush? . . . What are your surroundings like? . . . What is your life like as this rosebush? . . . What do you experience, and what happens to you as the seasons change? . . . Continue to discover even more details about your existence as this rosebush, how you feel about your life, and what happens to you. Let your fantasy continue for awhile. . . .

In a little while I'm going to ask you to open your eyes and return to the group and express your experience of being a rosebush. I want you to tell it in *first-person present tense, as if it were happening now.* For instance, "I am a wild rose, growing on a steep hillside, on very rocky soil. I feel very strong and good in the sunshine, and little birds make their nests in my thick vines—" or whatever *your* experience of being a rosebush is. Also try to express this *to* someone. Speak to anyone you like, or to different people at different times, but communicate *to* someone—don't just broadcast your words to the ceiling or scatter them on the floor. Now open your eyes when you feel ready and express your experience of being a rosebush. . . .

Sample Responses

The examples below were transcribed from a tape recording of a group's responses to the rosebush identification fantasy. They can give you some idea of the tremendous variety of experience possible with this kind of fantasy. These examples can serve as background and comparison to what you experience, and they may help you discover aspects or possibilites in this kind of fantasy journey that you can explore further. However, these are *others'* experiences. Although you can learn from them, you can only learn about yourself from *your own* experiences.

Don't read further until you have tried this fantasy identification yourself.

1(F)* I am against the side of a house. I have lots of blossoms on me. I'm partly in the shade of the house—sometimes I'm in the sun. I have other bushes alongside of me, there's grass in front of me, and every once in awhile I change—I look different, I look like a different kind of bush, and then I come back to the way I was before. Finally I grow into one big flower—I'm not a bush at all, I'm just one huge flower—rose flower. . . . /Leader: Do you have any feelings about being this rosebush, or any experience as the seasons change?/ I can feel myself growing and changing—it's nice.

2(M) I'm a rosebush, and I live in a greenhouse. I'm sheltered—young roots, um. I live in a greenhouse, sheltered from the elements, and since I'm in a greenhouse, people come and look at me, but they don't pick my blossoms. There was a lady that took care of me, but I can still feel small animals eating at my limbs. There are lots of different flowers with me, but they're not my type of flower and they're not as beautiful. I feel secure in my greenhouse—feel that I can't be hurt and the lady won't—the only thing that can get to me are these animals, small animals that crawl across my limbs. My thorns are protection, but they can't keep out small animals. They keep out the big ones.

3(F) I am in a back yard, by a fence, and it's my back yard and I can see over the fence, and I keep climbing it, I keep growing, so that I can see more of what is going on around me. I can feel the soil under me and it's moist soil, but it's cold and my roots go down deep into it, and I don't like being rooted, I don't like not being able to see. And there are other bushes around me, but they're not flower

*(F) indicates female; (M) indicates male.

bushes. And they're not—I just look at them—there's no communication with—between myself and the other bushes. And I really—I have very few other buds, I'm more or less one—kind of single flower, really—with a large blossom at the top, and smaller buds around me, and I notice—I can feel the seasons change. I don't like the winter. I don't like it when it's cold and rainy. And I'm vulnerable, because I have no protection, and I lose all my flowers. And I like it in the springtime, and I'm in blossom again, and people—people come and pick all the flowers. But it doesn't make me sad because I like—I like it when people pick the flowers because they think the blossoms are beautiful.

4(F) I'm next to a big white house, and I have a camellia bush next to me, and I have flowers growing beneath me. I like the feel of my roots in the ground, I like the cold earth, and it—it's a good feeling. I don't feel that my flowers are really me, I just felt like they were something I produced, something nice to look at. I was sad when they left, but, um, they weren't really a part of me, they were just something I produced. /L: Present tense./ And I can get inside my veins and I feel the water from my roots going through my veins. And I like to look at the people walking around me. I look at people around me, and I've lived by this house for a long time and I've seen a lot happen here. /L: How do you feel being this rosebush—you just shook your head./ Ah, it was just amazing. I've never done this before. It's nice.

5(M) I'm a rosebush, and I'm sitting in a clearing and there's trees around me and there's green grass and there's yellow grass. I think it—it is spring when I first start this. And I can feel buds on me, there's three, and as I go along—before the seasons change there's three buds, and one is my head, and one is my heart, and I can't—I don't know what the other one is. And there's a beautiful woman who finds this clearing; she comes over to me and sees my buds and finally my blossoms are open, and at the end of summer she picks the one that's my heart. . . . And it isn't a bad feeling—it's a good feeling. And she takes the flower and she leaves, and it's a kind of a feeling of waiting from then on. And then it's sadness; /L: Instead of "It's sadness," say *"I'm sad, I'm waiting."*/ I'm sad, I'm waiting, and it's feelings of autumn and winter and cold—and then after the snows are melting, I'm feeling warm again, and still waiting. I end up waiting.

6(M) I'm a rosebush with a very intricate root system that goes deep into the ground, and I have main roots, but I don't feel those, I'm not aware of those as much as I'm aware of this system of string-like roots that go into the ground everywhere, like fingers and toes all over the earth. And they're going in all directions as though they're reaching for every source of nourishment and liquid source that they can find. And I can go back up my root system and feel, as I'm going through, some thicker roots that lead to my body, but there's not as much awareness about that. But as soon as I become—I come through the earth, I look at myself as the stems and as the body of the plant, I have very *sturdy*, green, *thorny*—but I don't feel as though they're thorny, I feel as though it's part of me, and as if someone else might look at it as a scar, but I look at it as part of myself—neither beauty nor ugliness. I have many leaves and many stems going off in many directions. Most of them are straight, going in different directions, but there are shoots off these main stems. Quite a few leaves, I have leaves throughout most of the—myself. And when the seasons are changing, I'm especially aware of the cold, and at this point I had a feeling of receding, of recession—and not something that one might look at and see, but this feeling within myself of combining my resources so that they're within one area, so that I can use them to my benefit the best I can against the cold or the wind or the rain or whatever. Some of my leaves fall; most of them stay during the cold weather. I didn't have people cutting my stems, but I reflected on how I felt about people cutting my stems. And the feeling was one of—I was thinking these people were the ones who helped me to become—planted, put me here, cultivated— and these people would come at times and cut my limbs. And I felt somewhat sorry for them, that they weren't aware of my needs, rather than what they *thought* my needs were. They would cut limbs that would look dead, or would look like they needed to be cut—*to them*—but they were actually stems or leaves that need not be cut. And I didn't mind so much the people cutting them; I was more sorry for the reason that they were cutting them—that they were very closed. Here I was growing, doing what I knew best to do—was to grow. They had planted me here, and uh, I was neither pleasing them nor—well, I was pleasing myself. But I wasn't pleasing myself and then pleasing them, necessarily, but that happened. They were pleased with me—but not totally, or they wouldn't have cut the leaves and the stems that I still needed.

7(M) I'm a rose trying—trying to grow but there's grass all around me. I have to get close to this fence, because I feel the heat from the fence, and it's coming from the other side. And I have to grow higher than this fence in order to get this heat. Every time that I just get up to the fence, just getting over it, the heat's already gone, and it's winter and all my leaves are beginning to fall. I feel like I'm shedding, and I'm just—falling back down, below the fence again, and disappearing into the ground. I want someone to come and take me away, take me inside so that I won't be cold, and take me back out when it's summer again so that I can grow and perhaps get over the fence.

8(M) I'm two rosebushes. One is, uh, big white roses, and the other one is a bush with tea roses—yellow, pink, and orange. And I keep going back and forth between these two colors. The predominant color is the white—a large bush that sits in the backyard next to a fence /L: Say "I—"/ that gets pruned /L: "I get pruned."/ with patience. /L: Say "I get pruned."/ I get pruned with patience—that is to say I *sustain* the pruning with patience, because it's for my growth. I've been there a long time: I'm a very old bush. I've seen many, many, of the inhabitants of the houses around me come and go, change. When winter comes, I recede into myself, and again there's a waiting. I look forward to the spring, and when spring comes, I feel myself growing. I sort of hibernate in the winter. When the summer comes, I feel like I'm just bathed in energy, and I *tingle* all over, I feel very warm, and I feel heat all through me. Everything flows easier, kind of like melted honey. I'm very glad that the very fact that I breathe is very pleasant to the people around me. I watch the seasons come and go and watch the people come and go. I get mad every once in a while when bugs come and chew me up, and then I understand that it's O.K. because lots and lots of things are

gonna happen to me but I'm not really gonna die. I watch my leaves
and petals fall in the fall, and I know that I'm going to take them
into myself again and grow bigger when the heat comes. With the
very things that are falling this year, I will sustain myself and grow
even more. I have thorns, but I don't know why I have them. They
have no meaning to me—it's almost like I have something that used
to have meaning to me but no longer has meaning to me. I feel
well-rooted in the ground, and I feel the two parts of me—the part
above the ground and the part below the ground—each one is
contributing to the other.

9(F) I'm a huge rosebush, a lot of stems, thick tall stems— a lot
of them, coming from the same roots. I'm about five feet behind a
big house—the house that I live in now—at the bottom of a small hill.
I have a lot of thorns, about three or four yellow roses, and to the
left of me are some bars—jungle gym bars that kids play on a lot, and
I watch them. And to the right of me were—/L: Present tense./ To
the right of me are rosebushes, more rosebushes. I'm not too aware
of those, I don't know what color flowers they have. And there's also
some corn growing right next to the house. My roots are small and
deep and white. It's raining out, and the rain feels refreshing. It feels
real good—it feels like I've just gotten out of the shower, or just
washed my face. And the wind is blowing me back and forth and
that feels good—it's like being rocked. And I felt very comfortable—I
feel very comfortable. I was in this season—I'm in this season,
springtime, and I'm anticipating summer because it sounds peaceful.
Winter sounds noisy to me. Someone picked me and took me into
the house and put me in a vase on a table, and I don't like that—I like
being outside, all connected to the bush where I'm supposed to be.
That's where I stopped.

10(F) I feel really ugly; I don't feel pretty at *all*. And all that I
can see are just three long stems out of the right of me. I'm in the
middle of a huge open field. It's fresh damp soil, but there's nothing
around. And there's just two buds on me that haven't opened. I'm so
covered—I'm just those three stems with *thorns* that—I *hate* it. I feel
very lonely, but I don't feel fear because there's nothing there. And I
don't know what the rest of me looks like, and I can't feel my roots

and I feel really strong and healthy, but I don't feel any food coming. And every once in a while there's this big hand coming out at me and it goes to the part where I can't see, and a big, red, beautiful flower is picked. I see the hand with the flower in it—I can see the hand having one finger plucked out of it, off the hand, but not really feeling pain. The hand—it's ugly and it's—I don't like it. I just keep looking at the thorns, and the buds on the—next to the thorns, never blossom. But I always see a red flower passing by me in a hand. The blossom comes out of me but it comes out of a part that has nothing to do with what I can see. /L: You say part of you, you can see and part of you, you can't. As you're sitting now, what part of you can you see, and what part of you can't you see?/ I see just three—just wicked stems out of the right of me. I feel tall, I know there is a part of me beneath that and around in back of me, but I can't see it. I don't see a person in front of me, I just see the hand. There's no seasons, the weather never changes, it's just always the same.

11(M) I'm a—pink rose in my grandmother's garden, right next to the well—it's an old well, a flowing well. I am this pink rose, and it's just—just *bliss*—I don't know how to say it. I'm *so* content, so happy. I'm like—my grandmother, she's always taking care of me. She's—I'm always neat and clean, plenty to eat, lots of water, and all those beautiful flowers around me. Beautiful flowers—they're not roses, I'm the only one. I'm just sitting next to the well, growing, and just happy.

12(M) I'm a young rose growing in dirt in a green garden. And I'm really afraid of the first winter, where it's beginning to feel really cold. And I seem to shrink, and finally relax—the cold goes over me, and then I seem to be constantly awakening from that, and spreading in spring. I don't seem to know anything but spring and summer, and then nothing, and then I'm spreading again and I'm smaller than I was the last time. I have a lot of stems and a few flowers. The flowers and the thorns seem to be my reason for existing. When my flowers are picked, I feel very pleased—that's my reason for being there, for living, for growing. The thorns are—are green also, they're not gnarly and thorny, they're green and I like them, too, so I nourish them as much as I do the flowers. There don't seem to be very many leaves. I'm sinking my roots deep into cool, dark earth, and finally I sink a root into an underground fountain.

13(F) My roots are in the ground down very far. The dirt is really warm. It's not real wet, it's just damp. It's very soft and very rich and dark. My roots are white, and they have a lot of hair on them, and there's a lot of nourishment coming up through the soil. It feels good and tastes good, and it travels up the stems and up into the flowers. The flowers aren't open yet. The sun is coming in, and as the sun comes in and meets the nourishment that is coming up the stem, the flowers seem to—/L: "*My* flowers."/ My flowers are blossoming. First they are coming up very small, and as the sun comes in and gets warmer and warmer, they get larger and larger, soaking up the sun. There's a white house behind me that's very, very old, and I know that I've been here a long time, and yet I feel very young. There's grass in front of me, miles and miles and acres of grass, and it's green—a beautiful green color and it's thick and deep, and very tall. And I can see forever, and at the same time I feel all this nourishment coming up through the ground, coming up to the sun. The bees are coming in to my flowers and the bees are taking honey and nourishment from my flowers, and then they're flying away and I want to fly with them. I want to fly over the hills and over the grass. As summer ends and fall is coming, my flowers fall off, but it's not as if they've died. They fall into the soil and nourish the soil and go back up in nourishment again. And I'm starting to get dry and the earth is starting to dry up, and I'm feeling sort of waiting for winter to come. And winter comes and it comes very strong. There's a lot of frost, a lot of dark clouds, and the wind is strong. It feels so good to blow in the wind. It's not soft, it's a very strong wind. And the rain comes down and the rain feels so good on my face—my stems. And it goes into the ground and I feel the enrichment, the nourishment and water coming up through my stems. I can feel my whole body expand with the water that is coming up inside of me, being so dry. And then it keeps raining and keeps raining, and then finally I know it's time for spring to come. Spring comes, and I feel the sun on my face. It's very warm, but not real hot, and there's a very gentle breeze. And the grass is coming back again, the grass is very green. It had turned a beautiful golden color, and then the fields had been plowed, and now the grass is coming up again. And the soil is damp again; the sun is heating it and it's getting warm. And the water comes up and the sun comes in and the flowers bloom again. They come out and are just beautiful. It's—it's the freedom that I feel that when the bee comes and takes the honey and flies away, this is *my* freedom to burst out into flowers. But I still feel a—a containment. I want to fly somewhere and I want to go on. And yet I know that my roots and my stems are important to the flower and blooming, and being what I am, and that now I have to understand who I am as a bush. And people pick my flowers, and I—I like that. It's not as if they're cutting things off of me and taking something away. It's a sharing that I like to give. I think that's all. And my flowers die and—anything that falls back in the soil or anything that comes into me or goes away—that is a part of me, flying away with the bee. I am all the things. It's like I am a bee, too, picking up nourishment and flying away. I feel like a base, and I also feel like the things that come to that base and leave from that base.

14(F) I'm just a stem, just—and I'm in a little green plastic pot. And it's square, about four inches by four inches, and I'm just one straight green stem and it's got thorns on it and—/L: "I—"/ I'm growing up, and I get just somehow where I can't see me any more, and I look down and I see me coming up again, out of the pot; I grow up again. And I just keep growing higher, and then drop back down again, and see that I start all over again. I come up, and I go down, and come back up again. And then I look to see my roots, and I am a bush, and I'm just—I have no flowers, just the one stem, a lot of thorns. And I don't like having thorns, and I don't want to tell anybody that I have thorns. And, um, my roots are—half of them nice—well, um, I'm in the dirt, part in the dirt and the other part are a whitish yellowish color, and they're crawling, they're moving back and forth, and hanging out of the dirt. And I don't have any seasons. /L: You say some of your roots are hanging out of the dirt?/ Out of the dirt. It's like the dirt's broken away from me, half of it is broken away. /L: You're gesturing on your right side./ Ah, yeah, on the right

side, and the other side is good dirt. And the roots that are out—I
don't see the roots that are in the dirt—I only see the ones that are
out, and they're crawling and moving back and forth. /L: Do you
have any feeling about that—these exposed roots?/ I just—I—they're
moving around in the air. When I see them, I see them as—as
grasping, but I don't feel that way, just moving. And, um, it's just
black all around me except for the little piece of dirt that the roots
grow in. I'm—I don't have any surroundings but that piece of dirt.
It's awful hard to be the rosebush; I'm tired of trying to stay there
and be the rosebush; I want to smile and be happier, so I make
it—make me disappear, and then I'm just lying there.

15(M) I'm a pretty good-sized bush—pretty good-sized. I've
been here for quite a while. I can see over everything. I can see out in
front some; I can see in the back because that's where everything's
at. A lot of little kids in the neighborhood, they play ball—little kids
play ball, and the ball goes in my stickers— I *stick* 'em. Yeah. I stick
'em. A lot of kids got tired of me sticking them, they got a rope and
tied it around my vines and then they pulled me out. But they didn't
get all of me. They left part of me, and I'm growing back.

16(F) I'm a very tough old gnarled rosebush, growing alone in
the desert. The soil is very rocky and sandy, and my roots are very
strong and tough, plunging into the rock for moisture—*nothing* is
going to pull me out. Above the ground I'm mostly short, very thick,
gnarled stems. Right after a rain I come out with a few small leaves
for a little while, before the animals come and nibble them off again.
My tough gnarled stems are safe; they're too woody to eat.

17(M) I'm a rosebush in a garden, and I'm trained up against a
trellis beside a house. I feel very strained—all my stems are tied to
this framework, and I feel tied down and straining. When my shoots
are young, someone ties them down to this trellis, and then I have to
grow unnaturally. And off to my right in the middle of the lawn is a
tree rose that isn't tied down like I am. It's covered with blossoms,
and I'm very *envious* of this other rose's freedom to grow. I'm just
burning with envy and straining to get loose.

Within this small sample of seventeen responses there is a wide
range of experience. The instructions ask you to become a rosebush

in fantasy, and to explore your existence as this rosebush. The variety of responses to the same instructions should convince even the skeptic that what a person experiences in this fantasy is not completely determined by the instructions. On the contrary, what a person experiences has *much* more to do with who he is and how he experiences his existence.

Even when different people have similar events in their fantasy, their responses to this event may be quite different. Several people had their roses picked in the fantasy, but how they felt about this "same" event was very different. Some are very pleased and enjoy being able to share their roses with others, two feel sadness or dislike, and one person feels a horror at a rose being picked by a mutilated hand. How does a person experience his thorns? One enjoys sticking kids with them, another needs them for protection, two feel little about their thorns, one dislikes them, another feels disgust for the ugly thorns, and others either don't have thorns or are not aware of having them. There can be no standard "symbolic meaning" for any person's experience. Attaching symbolic meanings with a symbol dictionary is at best a fruitless intellectual game.

But if you tell me in detail *what* you experience, and also *how* you experience this, then I can share your experience and begin to understand your life as you experience it. You don't need an "expert's" guidance to understand another human being; all you need is sensitivity and openness to his experience.

Soon I am going to point out aspects of some of these responses and compare different responses. As I contemplate doing this, I am afraid that you, the reader, will immediately begin deliberately changing any "bad" experiences you have to "good" ones, manipulating your fantasies as you manipulate your life. If you have unpleasant experiences, any attempt to avoid them and cover them up will only add to the unpleasantness. Jim Simkin has an excellent image that illustrates this. Garlic, when it is well-distributed throughout an Italian lasagna, adds a pleasant flavor to the food. If you keep the garlic separate and only eat it in the last bite, it is very unpleasant and disgusting. The longer you avoid the garlic in your life, the more unpleasant the later bite will be. For instance, many people avoid experiencing and expressing their anger, because anger is disruptive and sometimes destructive. So their anger accumulates until something triggers an explosion of violence and destruction. Anger is not necessarily violent and destructive; it can be supportive of life. Anger can be a reasonable expression of my response to actually being injured or mistreated, or it can be an unreasonable response to imaginary injuries. Whatever its source, it exists and will be an obstacle to your life until you are willing to express it, explore it, and become deeply aware of it and assimilate it into your experience. Whatever you experience in a fantasy is a fact—a fact that must be respected and explored further if you are to make use of it. In order to respect something, you have to be willing to allow it to exist as it is, and you also have to be fully aware of it—the original meaning of respect is "to look at a thing." I hope that my comparing responses and pointing out aspects will help you to become more aware of them in detail. Then you can become more sensitive to your own and others' experiences, and particularly become more aware of avoidances—where there is unawareness and no respect.

I want to begin with two responses which are very different. Reread responses 10 and 13 and compare them. Response 10 is a nightmare, with quite a lot of ugliness, disgust, hate and mutilation. There are also large areas of unawareness. She is only aware of three thorny stems on her right, and the rest of her existence is a void—an absence of awareness. She can't see the rest of herself, she can't feel her roots or any food, and even the mutilated hand feels no pain. The only interaction with her surroundings is with this hand. With these strong feelings of ugliness and hate, there is also a strong sense of repetition and stagnation. The disembodied, mutilated hand repeatedly picks the flower, the buds never blossom, and she says, "There's no seasons, the weather never changes, it's just always the same."

Response 13 is almost the exact opposite: Instead of ugliness, hate, unawareness and stagnation, there is beauty, warmth, full awareness, growth, and change. She can both see *and* feel her roots, and she can feel *and* taste the nourishment that flows up through the soil into her roots and up the stems to her flowers. Not only are her surroundings nourishing, but she also nourishes others, sharing and giving freely to the bee that takes honey, and the people who pick her flowers. Even the coming of a very strong winter, with frost, rain, and very strong wind is enjoyable and nourishing—not a dangerous threat. There is some feeling of containment in not being able to move and travel as the bee does, but she even feels a participation in this traveling too. All of this woman's energy is available for growth, living, interacting, and coping with her surroundings. Response 10 shows a person whose energies are mostly locked in stagnant conflict and avoidance. When she can really get in touch with her conflicting energies, the stagnation will change into movement and her buds will begin to blossom.

Aspects of Experience

There are a great many aspects of experience. An encyclopedia of them would be enormous and also enormously dull. I do want to mention a few important aspects, and give some examples of them, to give you some ideas about what to look for and how to further develop your own sensitivity.

Avoidances, lack of awareness. The lack of awareness in response 10 is obvious. Not so obvious is 1, which is pleasant, but expresses no physical sensations or emotional feelings. It is essentially a visual experience, and is much shallower than response 13, which also includes sensations of touch, warmth, taste, movement, etc.

Change vs. stagnation. The change and growth in 13, and the repetition and stagnation in 10 have already been mentioned. In 7 there is a degree of repetition as the rose repeatedly strains to get above the fence and falls down again as winter comes.

Self-support vs. environmental support. A good example of self-support is 13. There is no suggestion of any outside assistance. She supports herself and even contributes support to the bees and the people who pick her flowers. In contrast, 11 is completely taken care of by the grandmother "She's always taking care of me." In 2, environmental support is provided by the greenhouse and the lady who takes care. His thorns provide self-support against large animals but not against small ones.

Self-environment relationship. In 13, there is a healthy, growing, joyful and creative interaction. Response 16 shows a person who is also providing her own self-support, but has to work tremendously hard to do it. All her energy goes into a battle with her environment—hanging on, getting moisture and growing tough woody stems that the animals can't eat. No energy is left over for foliage or joyous blooms. Response 6 is midway between 13 and 16 in this respect.

Barriers and frustrations. In two responses, fences are barriers that prevent the bush from getting the full heat of the sun. Animals, bugs, winter cold, storms, people who pick and prune, etc. are also frustrations to be suffered or resisted in other responses.

Overall emotional mood. In 17 there is straining and envy, in 15 there is defiance, in 5 there is sadness and waiting, in 11 there is bliss, and in 7 there is mostly frustration and inadequacy.

Degree of involvement in the fantasy. The extent to which a person is willing to become involved in the fantasy experience, and then to own it by expressing this experience in first-person present tense is very important. It is a measure of the person's willingness to contact his existence and experience himself. In 10, despite the ugliness and disgust she feels, she is willing to experience it and report it as herself and her existence. In contrast, although response 1 is relatively pleasant and unthreatening, there is also relatively little emotional involvement.

In response 9, there is good involvement as long as the experience is pleasant, but when she is picked and brought into the house, she doesn't like that and "That's where I stopped." In 14, she struggles to identify with the unpleasantness and frustration, but it remains essentially a visual experience, and then she wants to "smile and be happier," so she makes the rosebush disappear. Many people put distance between themselves and their experience by relating it in the past tense and not identifying with their experience by saying "I." When I say "it was—" I am speaking about something "out there" at a distance from me in both space and time.

This kind of fantasy is very useful in evoking alienated feelings and experiences, and quite a few people quickly get in touch with very deep feelings. Although some people rediscover things of great beauty and power in a fantasy, more often what is avoided and alienated is unpleasant or frightening. In order for a fantasy to be useful to you, you have to be willing to get fully involved in it, and let it develop on its own, without manipulation. It is possible to stay removed from the fantasy and have merely a shallow visual experience which you can easily change to something else when it gets unpleasant. If you do this, realize that you are unwilling to really experience your existence, and that you would rather hang onto your image of yourself than let go and discover what your life is like. Often you will start out on a fantasy with a good deal of control and direction, and then the fantasy gradually deepens and takes on a life of its own, independent of your efforts to guide and change it.

For many people, a fantasy will start out pleasantly and only as it deepens will unpleasant aspects appear. If you fail in your attempts to change something unpleasant into something more pleasant, this is a good sign that you are letting go enough for the fantasy to develop on its own, free of your efforts to control and manipulate it. Quite a few people discover experiences of great strength and beauty in their fantasies; most people, if they are honest, will also discover something that is unpleasant or threatening. If this unpleasantness is fully experienced, it will also blossom into a kind of strength and beauty. But when something unpleasant does develop, most people will avoid it by reducing their involvement with that experience.

It is this avoidance of unpleasantness that keeps parts of my experience separate from me, and reduces my awareness. In order to regain awareness and understanding, I have to be willing to contact these unpleasant areas of my experience and rediscover them. It would be very convenient if I could remove unpleasantness from my life simply by avoiding it, but this seldom—perhaps never—works. All I do is reduce my awareness of these unpleasant experiences and add confusion to my difficulties. If I avoid a scary situation, I am left with nagging doubts, vague feelings of unease, a sense of weakness, etc., that continue to bother me until I deal with the situation. Like an unattended toothache, fears and discomforts tend to worsen if they are not recognized and dealt with. The only way to really get through unpleasantness is to fully experience it, understand it, and act upon this understanding. When I am willing to fully suffer this unpleasantness, there are several rewards. One is fuller awareness and understanding. Another is a sense of freedom and greater power as I confront and work through the unpleasantness that I had previously been unwilling to face. In addition, my avoidance of unpleasantness requires a certain amount of energy which now becomes available for more useful tasks.

So if you discover an area of unpleasantness in fantasy or in your life, realize that this is an untapped resource, a source of power and freedom, *if* you are willing to suffer the discomfort of facing it and accepting it fully. As long as you avoid something unpleasant, it will continue to affect your life and have power over you. If you are willing to face and accept this unpleasantness now, something can grow and develop out of this experience, and you can become more whole, more fully alive.

A student in a class I was visiting told me vehemently that she disliked the brown shirt that I was wearing. Her voice expressed strong feelings, and I asked her to say something more about my shirt and what she disliked about it. "It's grim and depressing; it reminds me of my father's funeral." Clearly she still had strong feelings about her father and his death that she was not yet willing to fully accept and express. These alienated feelings continue to struggle for expression and appear in her surroundings. She sees my *shirt* as grim and depressing, but doesn't yet realize how grim and depressed *she* is. This kind of alienation is called *projection*—what we "see" around us is often part of our own alienated experience, rather than the world itself. When this girl accepts and works through her feelings, she will be able to see my shirt as it is, and not as a convenient location for her unexpressed feelings.

What I have asked you to do in these identification experiments is to encourage and amplify this process of alienation and projection, and then to reverse it by asking you to identify with your own projections. If you can become aware of how you alienate your experience, it is a relatively simple matter to recover your awareness by reversing this process through re-identification. If you are willing to make this kind of self-correction in your everyday life, you can

live more in the real world of awareness, and less in the confusion of
your fantasies. If you imagine that someone is angry with you, try
the reverse, "I'm angry with him," and really identify with this. See
if you can discover how you are angry with him, what you dislike
about him, etc. If you find yourself wanting to help someone else,
try reversing this to "I want you to help me," and then explore how
you might want him to help you. Try the following reversal experiments. If you can, do them with a group of 5-7 people so that you
can share your experiences with others and learn from their experiences as well.

Reversal Identification

Lie down and find a comfortable position. . . . Close your eyes
and let go. . . . Notice any tension. . . . See if you can release this
tension or adjust your body so that you are more comfortable. . . .
Focus your attention on your breathing and continue to let go as I
talk to you. . . . We all tend to build up an image of how things
"really are," and an image of who and what we are. This image of
ourselves might be somewhat true, but it is a fantasy. There are
always aspects of ourselves that don't fit this image. If we hang onto
this image tightly, we restrict and deaden ourselves, and we prevent
ourselves from discovering the parts of our experience that are
unknown and alienated. If you can let go, even a little, of your *idea*
of who you think you are, you have a chance to discover more of
what you actually experience at this moment. What I want to do
next is to give you some experience in reversing the way you
experience parts of your world and how you experience yourself. It's
a simple way of loosening some of your binding prejudices about
reality. It can even be a way of finding new ways of functioning, and
discovering things about yourself that you usually are not aware of.
If nothing else, it's an interesting way to pass time when you are
bored.

Breathing

Now focus your attention on your breathing. . . . Become aware
of all the details of your breathing. . . . Feel the air moving in

through your nose or your mouth, . . . feel it move down your throat and into your lungs, . . . and notice how your chest and belly expand and contract gently as you breathe. Be aware of whatever else you experience in your body as you breathe. . . . Now imagine that instead of you breathing air, that *air* is breathing *you.* Imagine that the air is gently moving into your lungs, . . . and then slowly withdrawing. . . . You don't have to do anything at all, because the air is doing your breathing for you. . . . Just experience this for awhile, . . . and now switch back. . . .

Sex

Now I'd like you to imagine that your sex is reversed. If you are a male, you are now a female; if you are a female, you are now a male. . . . How is your body different now? . . . Become really aware of this new body, particularly the parts that have changed. . . . If you don't want to do this, that's O.K. But don't say to yourself "I *can't* do this." Say "I *won't* do this," and then add whatever words come to you next. By doing this you may get some idea of what it is that you are avoiding by refusing to do this reversal. . . . How do you feel in this new body? . . . And how will your life be different now? . . . What will you do differently, now that your sex has changed? . . . And how do you feel about all these changes? . . . Continue to explore your experience of being the opposite sex for awhile. . . .

Now change back again and get in touch with your real body and your real sex. . . . Silently compare the experience of being yourself with being the other sex. . . . What did you experience as the other sex that you don't experience now? . . . Were these experiences pleasant or unpleasant? . . . Continue to explore your experience for a little while. . . .

Race

Now imagine that your skin color is reversed: If you are black or dark-skinned, you are now white. If you are white-skinned, you are now black or dark-skinned. . . . Become really aware of your new body. . . . How is your body different now? . . . And how do you feel in this body? . . . How will your life be different, now that your skin color has changed? . . . And how do you feel about these changes? . . . Continue to explore your new existence for awhile. . . .

Now change back to your own skin color and your own body. . . . Silently compare the experience of being yourself with the experience of having a different skin color. . . . What differences do you notice between the two, and how did you feel in each? . . .

Self-Chosen

Now I'd like you to try a reversal of some typical event in your life. Choose anything you like—washing the dishes or shopping, for instance—and first explore the actual sequence of events as you experience them. . . . Now reverse this usual sequence. Stay with this reversal for awhile and see what you can discover from it. . . .

In a minute, I want you each to open your eyes and tell the others in the group about your experiences in these reversal experiments *in first-person present tense as if it were happening now:* "When I reverse my sex, I feel soft and loving as a girl—" or whatever your experience is. Take about ten minutes for this sharing. . . .

Reversing our usual way of thinking is a way of saying "Maybe some things and events in the world could actually be the reverse of how I see them." It is one way of temporarily discarding our preconceptions and prejudices, and seeing if another way of looking at the world could be more accurate. Any image or preconception limits our experiencing because it tells us ahead of time what our experience will and will not be. This is particularly true if the image is about myself. For example, if my image of myself is that I am strong and tough, and that only women are tender and loving, then I must deny any weakness, or warmth and tender feelings that I have. If I am willing to temporarily give up my image, when I reverse roles and become a woman in fantasy I become *my image* of what a woman is like. Since *my image* of a woman permits weakness and tender feelings, as a woman I can experience my own real feelings of weakness and tenderness that I did not previously permit myself to experience because they did not fit my image. Since different people have different images, they will have somewhat different reversals, and often quite different feelings while experiencing a reversal. Every person, almost every day, experiences some degree of every feeling and emotion that a human being can feel. Reversals are one way of uncovering whatever feelings you have right now but which your images do not permit you to experience—another way of regaining contact with your actual ongoing experience and releasing your potential as a person.

Communication Within

In contrast to the approach of this book, many psychologists talk about how it is healthy to develop a strong ego, a good self-concept, a strong character, etc. Any such image of myself is a fantasy, an idea. To the extent that I am preoccupied with this fixed idea of myself, I lose touch with the flow of my actual present experiencing. At best a strong self-image will cause me to become a rigidly predictable, socially useful automaton—a person who identifies with an *idea* of myself instead of with the *reality* of my actual feelings, experiences, and actions. My living becomes split between image and reality, between what I think I am and what I am.

I also become fragmented in another way: As soon as I try to achieve a goal, I become prey to fears of failure. If I want to impress you with what a nice guy I am, I begin to fear that you'll think me a louse. The more I fear your bad opinion, the more I will try to convince you that I am a good guy. Hopes and fears feed and grow upon each other, and each of these two opposing fantasies takes me farther from the reality of my experiencing at the moment.

It is possible to re-establish communication between these fragments of myself and gradually work toward recognizing and relin-

s, and toward regaining contact with my actual
y real responses. When I am in solid contact with
ng in a flexible flowing with events as they really
for a "self-concept" or a "strong ego" to tell me
or what I "should" do. This is the Zen teaching of
"no-mind." If my "mind" is empty of images, ideas, intentions,
prejudices, and demands, then—and only then—can I be in touch
with my actual experiencing of the world, balanced and centered in
the present moment of my sensing and responding.

Full awareness of my experience requires complete acceptance
of that experience as it is. Any demands—by myself or others—to be
different than I am, reduces my contact with what I actually experience. This begins the falsification of my life through acting differently than I feel and playing roles. I might try to be nicer or tougher
than I feel to impress others, or "society" might demand that I act
tougher or more tender than I feel, less or more sexual than I feel,
etc. The next experiment gives you an opportunity to become aware
of some of the demands that you place on yourself, and how you are
split between what you are and what you demand of yourself. If
possible, do this in a small group and ask someone to read the
instructions to you; if not, read through the instructions and then try
the experiment alone by yourself.

Demand and Response (topdog-underdog)

Sit comfortably and close your eyes. . . . Now imagine that you
are looking at yourself, sitting in front of you. . . . Form some kind
of visual image of yourself, sitting there in front of you, perhaps as if
reflected in a mirror. . . . How is this image sitting? . . . What is this
image of yourself wearing? . . . What kind of facial expression do you
see? . . .

Now silently criticize this image of yourself as if you were
talking to another person. (If you are doing this experiment alone,
talk out loud.) Tell yourself what you should and shouldn't do.
Begin each sentence with the words, "You should—" "You
shouldn't—" or their equivalent. . . . Make a long list of criticisms.
. . . Listen to your voice as you do this. How does your voice sound?
. . . How do you feel, physically, as you do this? . . .

Now imagine that you change places with this image. Become this image of yourself and silently answer these criticisms. . . . What do you say in response to these critical comments? . . . And what does your tone of voice express? . . . How do you feel as you respond to these criticisms? . . .

Now switch roles, and become the critic again. As you continue this internal dialogue, be aware of what you say, and also how you say it—your words, your tone of voice, and so on. . . . Pause occasionally to just listen to your own words in your mind and experience them. . . .

Switch roles whenever you want to, but keep the dialogue going. Notice all the details of what is going on in you as you do this. . . . Notice how you feel, physically, in each role. . . . How do these two speakers differ? . . . Do you really talk *to* each other, or do you avoid real contact or confrontation? . . . Are you listening to each other as well as talking, or are you only broadcasting and not receiving? . . . How do you feel about this other speaker as you talk? . . . Tell this to the other speaker, and see what he or she responds. . . . Do you recognize anyone you know in the voice that criticizes you and says "You should—"? . . . What else are you aware of in this interaction? . . . Bring this awareness into the conversation between you. . . . Continue this silent dialogue for a few minutes longer. . . . Do you notice any changes as you continue the dialogue? . . .

Now just sit quietly and review this dialogue. . . . As you look back, is there anything else about this conversation that you notice? . . .

In a minute I'm going to ask you to open your eyes and come back to the group. I want each person, in turn, to share your experiences with the group in as much detail as possible. I want you each to express what happened in your dialogue in *first-person present tense, as if it were happening now:* "As the critical person, I feel strong and I say 'You shouldn't goof off so much. You ought to work harder,' " or whatever your experience is. Open your eyes now and do this. . . .

Probably you experienced some kind of split or conflict, some division between a powerful, critical, authoritative part of you that demands that you change, and another less powerful part of you that apologizes, evades, and makes excuses. It is as though you are divided into a parent and a child: the parent, or "topdog," always trying to get control to change you into something "better" and the child, or "underdog," continually evading these attempts to change. As you listened to the voice that criticized and made demands on you, you may have recognized that it sounded a lot like one of your parents. Or it might have sounded like someone else in your life who makes demands on you—your husband or wife, a boss, or some other authority who controls you. If you do recognize someone specific in this dialogue, it is valuable to continue the dialogue as if you are speaking directly to this person.

At the same time, I want you to realize that everything that you experience in this dialogue happens in your own head. Whether your dialogue is with another specific person or with "society," it occurs in your own world of fantasy. When the other speaks in this dialogue, it is not "society" or an actual person who speaks, but your *image* of this other. Whatever occurs in your fantasy dialogue goes on between different parts of *yourself*. If there is a conflict in your dialogue, this conflict is between two parts of yourself, even if you alienate and disown one part and call it "society," "mother," "father," etc. We usually assume that our problems and conflicts are with *other* people, so we struggle to be free of their demands, and don't realize how much of the conflict is actually *within* us. Kahlil Gibran expresses this beautifully in *The Prophet:**

> And an orator said, Speak to us of Freedom.
> And he answered:
> At the city gate and by your fireside I have seen you prostrate yourself and worship your own freedom,
> Even as slaves humble themselves before a tyrant and praise him though he slays them.
> Ay, in the grove of the temple and in the shadow of the citadel I have seen the freest among you wear their freedom as a yoke and a handcuff.
> And my heart bled within me; for you can only be

free when even the desire of seeking freedom becomes a harness to you, and when you cease to speak of freedom as a goal and a fulfillment.

You shall be free indeed when your days are not without a care nor your nights without a want and a grief,

But rather when these things girdle your life and yet you rise above them naked and unbound.

And how shall you rise beyond your days and nights unless you break the chains which you at the dawn of your understanding have fastened around your noon hour?

In truth that which you call freedom is the strongest of these chains, though its links glitter in the sun and dazzle your eyes.

And what is it but fragments of your own self you would discard that you may become free?

If it is an unjust law you would abolish, that law was written with your own hand upon your own forehead.

You cannot erase it by burning your law books nor by washing the foreheads of your judges, though you pour the sea upon them.

And if it is a despot you would dethrone, see first that his throne erected within you is destroyed.

For how can a tyrant rule the free and the proud, but for a tyranny in their own freedom and a shame in their own pride?

And if it is a care you would cast off, that care has been chosen by you rather than imposed upon you.

And if it is a fear you would dispel, the seat of that fear is in your heart and not in the hand of the feared.

Verily all things move within your being in constant half embrace, the desired and the dreaded, the repugnant and the cherished, the pursued and that which you would escape.

These things move within you as lights and shadows in pairs that cling.

> And when the shadow fades and is no more, the light
> that lingers becomes a shadow to another light.
> And thus your freedom when it loses its fetters be-
> comes itself the fetter of a greater freedom.

There are real problems in the world, and I can really deal with these problems only when I am clear in myself about how I feel and what I want to do. When I am in conflict, I identify partly with my own feelings and wants and partly with fantasies that conflict with this awareness—ideas about what I should be, catastrophic expectations, fears of what others will do, etc. Much of my communication and activities are directed toward myself instead of toward the world. To the extent that I do this, I become ingrown, autistic, and isolated from others. My energy becomes divided and in opposition, so that very little energy is available for my struggles with the real world. When I participate in outside conflicts before I have cleared up the conflicts within me, I just create more conflict both inside and outside.

As long as I believe that my conflict is only with someone or something outside myself, I can do very little except complain about it, or try to change or destroy it. When I realize that much of the conflict is within me, then I can do something much more productive. I can take responsibility for my own difficulties, and stop blaming the world for problems that are my own. I can seek to discover more about these different and conflicting parts of myself, identify with them, and learn from them. The first step in this process is to become aware of the autistic activity that goes on in my "mind" or fantasy life. The next step is to direct it outward, so that the autistic self-to-self activity becomes relational self-to-other activity. As I direct this activity outward toward the world, it becomes more explicit and more detailed. Often I can discover who these messages are really intended for, or where they come from.

Listening to Yourself

Everyone says, "I tell myself," nobody says, "I listen to myself." So try listening to yourself for a change. Begin by paying attention to the thoughts going on in your head, and simply observe them. ... Now begin to say these thoughts, but like very soft whispering, so the words barely get past your lips. ... Now say them a bit louder, ... and keep increasing the volume until you reach your normal speaking level. ... Imagine that you are actually talking to someone. ... Continue to say your thoughts, and pay attention to what is communicated by the sound of your voice. ... What is your voice like? ... Is it strong or weak, clear or unclear, harsh or mellow, etc.? ... Is it judging, complaining, angry, pleading? ... Does this voice sound like anyone that you know? ... Who might these words be directed to? ... Choose some person to say these words to. Imagine that you actually do this, and see whether they fit. ... How do you feel as you talk to this person? ... Does this person reply to what you say? ... Now quietly absorb your experience for a little while. ...

The value of this is that although you are actually still talking to yourself, you do it *as if* you were talking to someone else. As you do this, your autistic activity becomes more relational, and you begin to regain contact with the world and your own experience. When you develop this into a dialogue, each side of a conflict contrasts with the other and clarifies it.

You can really do a lot for yourself through having these dialogues. You do have to be willing to suffer the unpleasantness of experiencing and expressing both parts of the conflict, and the two parts have to be willing to confront, encounter, and communicate honestly with each other. It is best if you can find a time or place where you can talk out loud, and bring your physical postures and movements into the dialogue. Often the tone of voice, a pointing finger, a frown, a fist, slumped shoulders, etc. express much more about what is going on in the dialogue than the words. Try to be aware of your total experience as you do this. As long as the dialogue is not just empty words but expresses your real feelings and experience, then as you become more and more deeply aware of these feelings and experiences, some change and development will take place.*

*See *Gestalt Therapy Verbatim*, by Frederick S. Perls, and *Don't Push the River* by Barry Stevens, for examples of such dialogues.

Any time you are aware of a conflict of opposites in yourself, or between yourself and someone else or something else, you can use this kind of fantasy dialogue to get communication started between the conflicting parts. In a previous experiment, the conflict is between what you are and what you "should be." For most people this is like an argument or struggle between a parent and a child. As long as this conflict continues to be a battle for control—with the "parent" preaching and threatening, and the "child" apologizing and evading—nothing will change. If you can really identify with both sides of this conflict, you can gradually begin to understand more about the conflict between them. As your understanding of both sides grows, the interaction between them will gradually change from fighting and avoiding each other, into more contact and communication. As the two sides start to listen to each other and learn from each other, the conflict will decrease and can even come to resolution.

Usually we are unbalanced because we identify mostly with one side of a conflict and don't realize our part in the opposing side. As both sides become clear and as we identify with both sides, we become more balanced and centered. We can act more from this balanced center, instead of from one of the conflicting sides. Resolution of conflict releases the energy that has been locked up in the struggle between the opposing sides, and this energy then becomes available in increased vitality and a sense of clarity, strength, and power. *This process is not something that can be forced or manipulated.* It is what happens *by itself,* when you deepen your identification with, and your awareness of, both sides of a conflict.

Letting Go of the "Past"

All of us carry around parts of our "past" with us in the form of memories. Our memories, even if they are exact images of previous things and events, are *images* and not the events themselves. Often these images and fantasies that we call memories are quite different from the things and events that actually happened. Some people are so burdened with the past, and so involved in their memories, that they have very little involvement with the present. If you want to reduce your involvement with your memories, you can invest yourself in them in the same way as any other fantasy; you can discover what awareness is hidden in these fantasies through identification and dialogue. Your involvement in the memory does something for you, and before you can let go of this memory you will have to find out what it does for you—what need is served by hanging onto it.

You might be escaping from a present that is unsatisfactory in some way to a memory of a time that was more fulfilling. If so, you can discover what it is that you are missing in your life now. If you can realize that the satisfactions of memory are a pale substitute for the satisfactions of reality, then you can face the challenge of working toward making the present more satisfactory for you, instead of retreating into memory.

If the memory is unpleasant, there is probably an unfinished situation in which you held back and have not expressed yourself fully. By investing yourself in this unfinished situation you can rediscover these unexpressed feelings and actions and let them complete themselves. The next experiment can give you an experience of working with this kind of unfinished situation.

Yes-No Situation

Lie down on your back and find a comfortable position. . . . Close your eyes, and keep them closed until I ask you to open them. . . . Let go, and get in touch with your body. . . . Notice any discomfort you feel, . . . and see if you can change your position so that you are more comfortable. . . .

Now focus your attention on your breathing. . . . As you become aware of your breathing, does it change? . . . Without interfering with your breathing, just observe it and be aware of it in detail. . . .

Now imagine that your whole body is like a balloon that slowly fills as you breathe in, and becomes very taut and stiff when you have a full breath, . . . and then slowly releases as you breathe out, so that you are completely released when your lungs are empty. . . Do this three or four times. . . .

Now just be aware of your natural breathing. . . . and imagine that each breath washes some of any remaining tension out of your body, . . . so that you become even more released with each breath. . . .

Now remember a specific situation in which you said "Yes" but you really wanted to say "No." Try to visualize this situation as if it were happening now. . . . Where are you? . . . What are your surroundings like, and how do you feel there? . . . Who is there with you and what has just been said? . . . Really invest yourself: Get in touch with being in the situation, and relive it as if it were occurring now. . . .

Now focus on the moment when you say "Yes." What tone of voice do you use as you say "Yes," and how do you feel as you do this? . . . What does it do *for* you to say "Yes"? . . . What do you gain by saying "Yes"? . . . And what do you *avoid* by saying "Yes"? . . . How do you feel about saying "Yes" in this situation? . . .

Now go back to the moment just before you said "Yes." Now say "No," and say anything else that you didn't express previously. . . . What tone of voice do you use as you say "No," and how do you feel as you do this? . . . How does the other person respond to you after you say "No"? . . . How do you feel now, and what do you reply to this person? . . .

Now change places and become the person to whom you said "No." What are you like as this person? . . . And how do you feel? . . . As this person, what do you say, and what tone of voice do you use? . . .

Now become yourself again and continue the dialogue. . . . How do you feel as yourself now, and how is this different from how you feel as the other person? . . . Do you feel more powerful as yourself, or as the other person? . . . Speak directly to this person, and tell him about how you are different from him. . . .

Become the other person again, and continue this dialogue and interaction. . . . Try to really get into the full experience of being this other person. . . . Continue this dialogue and switch places on your own each time the other person begins to reply, so that you always identify with the one who is speaking. . . . How are the two of you interacting now—are you fighting and arguing, or do you begin to communicate with each other? ... What are you aware of that you are *not* expressing—what are you holding back? ... Now express how you feel toward each other. ... If this is too difficult for you, at least say to the other "I am still holding back," and then say something about this holding back. ... Continue this dialogue for a few more minutes. Get even more into the experience of being these two people and exploring how you interact. ...

Take a little while to quietly absorb your experience. ... In a minute I'm going to ask you to open your eyes and relate your experience to the others in the group in first-person present tense, as if it were happening to you now. For example: "I'm reading in the living room; I'm very tired and my wife comes in and asks me to go to the store," etc. Be sure to include how you feel saying both "yes" and "no" in this situation, what it did *for* you to say yes or no, and what you learned from the dialogue after you said "no." Open your eyes now and share your experiences with the group. ...

When I ask you to remember this kind of situation, whatever emerges is an event that is still alive in your memory because there is energy still invested in it. By re-experiencing it in the present through identification and dialogue, you can discover what is unfinished and unexpressed, and assimilate both the experience and the energy that is bound up in it. There is a real parallel between taking in an experience and eating food. If you only gobble without chewing thoroughly, it sits inside you and continues to give you trouble until you vomit it up or digest it. Until you digest and absorb any food, the energy in it is not available to you, and the same is true of any experience you have. Probably you were not able to fully digest this experience of saying "yes" when you really wanted to say "no" but I hope you got some experience of chewing and digesting. You can return to this or any other experience repeatedly, until you really chew it up, experience it, and absorb it.

In this particular experiment you can also get quite a lot of understanding of your compliance behavior—what actually goes on when you comply with another person's wishes although you would really prefer not to. Try to realize what complying does *for* you, as well as what it does *to* you. Realize that when you comply, you do it *for yourself*—to get love and approval, to avoid a quarrel, or so that you can think of yourself as "nice" or "capable," etc. There are some people who spend most of their lives complying, others who spend most of their lives *not* complying, and some who give the appearance of complying, but actually don't. Very few people take time to fully realize what goes on in them as they comply. If you are really aware of what goes on in you when you comply, then you can work through the opposing forces within you and realize whether you *really* want to comply in a particular situation or not. In this way you can become more flexible, and free to act according to the actual situation and how you really feel. The extremes of compliance are the conformist who *always* complies and the rebel who *never* complies. Both are equally trapped in a rigid response to the outside demands of parents, society, etc. The conformist believes that he always has to do the approved thing, while the rebel believes he always has to *not* do the approved thing so that he can be "free." Full awareness of how you trap yourself can bring real freedom as you re-identify with this power you have given away to others—the power to respond honestly and directly without the need of outside support, approval or permission.

> when serpents bargain for the right to squirm
> and the sun strikes to gain a living wage—
> when thorns regard their roses with alarm
> and rainbows are insured against old age
>
> when every thrush may sing no new moon in
> if all screech-owls have not okayed his voice
> —and any wave signs on the dotted line
> or else an ocean is compelled to close
>
> when the oak begs permission of the birch
> to make an acorn—valleys accuse their
> mountains of having altitude—and march
> denounces april as a saboteur
>
> then we'll believe in that incredible
> unanimal mankind(and not until)

e. e. cummings*

Most of us still hang onto our parents and other significant people in our lives in this way, continuing to ask for their approval and support long after we are capable of making our own decisions— and often long after they are dead. Almost all of us have a great many unfinished situations with our parents and many unexpressed feelings toward them. These situations and feelings are more bits and pieces of history that clutter our lives. These unfinished situations interfere with your present relationships with parents, because to the extent that you hang onto previous situations, you lose contact with what is happening now. You are partly in contact with your memory fantasies of your parents and yourself, and only partly in touch with the reality of you and your parents *now*. Even in less intense relationships with friends and acquaintances, you are more likely to meet your memories of them than to meet them as they are now. Until you can deal with these unfinished situations and accept and express the feelings that you have held back, you will continue to be stuck with these burdens, and also stuck in your static relationship with your parents. I have seen seventy-year-olds still tied up in a bitter struggle with their memories of long-dead parents. It is hard work to deal with these unfinished situations, but until you do, you will continue to think of yourself as a child who needs support from a parent or someone else. Maturing is discovering that you are capable of your own support and that you are no longer a child who needs support and approval from parents. The next experiment can get you started on clearing up some of the unfinished situations that you have with your parents.

Parent Dialogue

Sit comfortably and close your eyes. . . . Visualize one of your parents, sitting facing you. Take some time to really see your parent sitting there in front of you, and make contact with him or her. How is he sitting? . . . What is he wearing? . . . What kind of facial expression does he have? . . . Notice all the details of your parent in front of you. . . . How do you feel as you look at your parent? . . . Now begin by being completely honest with your parent. Express all the things that you never told him and say these directly *to* him as if you were actually talking to him now. Express everything that comes to your mind—resentments you held back, anger you were afraid to show, love that you didn't express, questions that you never asked, etc. Be aware of how you feel as you do this, and notice if you begin to tense your body somewhere, etc. Be sure you stay in contact with your parent as you do this. Take about five minutes to do this. . . .

Now become your parent, and respond to what you have just said. As your parent, how do you reply to what your child just said? . . . Be aware of how you feel as you do this. . . . How do you feel toward your child? . . . Now tell him how you feel toward him, and tell him what you think of him. . . . What kind of relationship do you have with him? . . .

Switch places again and become yourself. How do you respond to what your parent just said? . . . What do you say now, and how do you feel as you say it? . . . Tell him how you feel toward him now, and tell him what you think of him. . . . How do you experience this relationship? . . . Now tell him what you need and want from him. Take some time to tell him exactly and specifically what you want him to do for you, and be aware of how you feel as you do this. . . .

Now become your parent again. As parent, what do you reply to this expression of needs and wants from your child? . . . How do you feel as you do this? . . . What understanding do you have of what he is asking for? . . . Have you experienced anything similar in your life? . . . Now tell your child what you need and want from him. . . .

Switch places and become yourself again. How do you respond to what your parent just said? . . . Do you have any better understanding of him now? . . . Now tell him what it does for you to hang onto him in fantasy like this. . . . What do you gain by holding onto all these unfinished feelings toward your parent? . . .

Now become your parent again and respond to this. . . . What do you say in reply? . . . What is your relationship like now? . . . Is any understanding developing, or is it still mostly fighting and conflict? . . .

Switch places and become yourself again. How do you respond to what your parent just said? . . . How do you experience your relationship, and what understanding do you have of your parent's situation? . . . Tell him whatever understanding you have of him now. . . .

Now I want you to tell your parent what you appreciate in him. No matter how difficult your relationship is, there must be something about him that you appreciate. Tell him about these things now, and be specific and detailed. . . .

Now become your parent again. How do you respond to these appreciations? . . . Can you really accept them, or do you minimize or reject them? . . . Now express your appreciations of your child. Tell him in detail what you appreciate in him. . . .

Now become yourself again. How do you respond to the appreciations you just got from your parent? . . . How do you feel toward each other now? . . . Continue this dialogue on your own for some time, and switch back and forth between being yourself and your parent whenever you want to. Pay attention to what is going on in this interaction and make this explicit. For instance, if you realize that the parent is scolding and blaming, point this out and demand that he express himself more directly. Notice when you are tense and holding back, and express yourself more fully. See how much you can express and clarify about this relationship. . . .

It takes time to clarify a relationship, and often you will arrive at a place where both sides are stuck in an unyielding deadlock. As you become more aware of the details of this deadlock, it will gradually become more flexible; when you become fully aware of the conflict, it will disappear. This may take many sessions of struggling, but each time there can be some clarification and deepening of awareness. Eventually you can arrive at letting go of parents, giving up your demands that they be different, and forgiving them for their faults, and what they did or didn't do for or to you. You can recognize that they couldn't be other than they were, and that even "forgiving" is irrelevant. Perhaps hardest of all is to let go of a lost relationship. When an important person in your life has died or left you, he continues to exist in your fantasies as if he were still alive. In a kind of self-hypnosis, you continue to be involved with a dead relationship. When you can complete this dead relationship and say goodbye, you can wake up from your hypnosis and become involved with the living people around you.

One of the ways we give away our power to be ourselves is by hypnotizing ourselves with the words that we use to describe our own actions. We put ourselves to sleep and become less aware of our own feelings and wishes. Whenever I say "I should—" I am hypnotizing myself with this demand. I tend to assume that this demand is reasonable, legitimate, and not open to question; I lose the realization that I can choose whether to accept the demand or not. I also lose awareness of my own response to this demand—my resentment, resistance, dislike, etc. My resistance and resentment still exist—even though I have lost awareness of it—and will continue to frustrate my attempts to change myself into what I "should" be. An earlier experiment focuses on this conflict. The next experiments focus on other ways that we hypnotize ourselves.

I Have to—I Choose to—

Pair up with someone else, and sit facing this person. Throughout the experiment, maintain eye contact and talk directly to this person. Take turns saying sentences to each other that begin with the words "I have to—" Make a long list of things that you have to do. (If you do this experiment alone, say these sentences out loud and imagine that you are saying them to some person you know.) . . . Take about five minutes to do this. . . .

Now go back to all the sentences you just said and replace "I have to—" with "I *choose* to—" and take turns saying these sentences to your partner. Say exactly what you said before except for this change. I would like you to realize that you do have the power of making a choice, even if that choice is between two undesirable alternatives. Take time to be aware of how you experience saying each sentence that begins with "I choose to—" Then repeat this sentence and immediately add any sentence that comes to you next. For example, "I choose to stay with my job. I feel safe and secure." Again take about five minutes to do this. . . .

Now take a few minutes to tell each other what you experienced as you did this. Do you have any actual experience of taking responsibility for your choices—any feeling of waking up a little from your self-hypnosis, any discovery of more power and possibilities? . . .

I Can't—I Won't—

Now take turns saying sentences to your partner that begin with the words "I can't—" Take about five minutes to make a long list of things that you can't do. . . .

Now go back to all these sentences you just said and replace "I can't—" with "I *won't—*" and take turns saying these sentences to your partner. Say exactly what you said before, except for this change, and then take time to be aware of how you experience saying each sentence. Is this really something impossible—or is it something possible that you refuse to do? I want you to become aware of your capability and your power of refusal. Then repeat this sentence that begins "I won't—" and immediately add any sentence that comes to you next. Take about five minutes to do this. . . .

Now take a few minutes to tell each other what you experienced as you did this. Did you experience any feeling of strength as you take responsibility for your refusal by saying "I won't"? What else did you discover? . . .

I Need—I Want—

Now take turns saying sentences to your partner that begin with the words "I need—" Take about five minutes to make a long list of your needs. . . .

Now go back to all these sentences you just said and replace "I need—" with "I *want—*" and take turns saying these sentences to your partner. Say exactly what you said before, except for this change, and then take time to be aware of how you experience saying each sentence. Is this something you really need or is it something that you want, but can easily survive without? I want you to realize the difference between something that you really need, like air and food, in contrast to other things you want that are very pleasant and nice, but not absolutely necessary. Then repeat this sentence that begins "I want—" and immediately add any words that come to you next. Take about five minutes to do this. . . .

Now take a few minutes to tell each other what you experienced as you did this. Did you experience any sense of lightness or freedom as you realize that some of your "needs" are really only conveniences and not necessities? What else did you become aware of? . . .

I'm Afraid to—I'd Like to—

Now take turns saying sentences to your partner that begin with the words "I'm afraid to—" Take about five minutes to make a long list of things that you are afraid to try. . . .

Now go back to all these sentences and replace "I'm afraid to—" with "I'd *like* to—" and take turns saying these sentences to your partner. Say exactly what you said before, except for this change, and then take time to be aware of how you experience saying each sentence. What is it that attracts you toward this risk, and what is the possible gain? I want you to realize that many of your fears hold back the satisfaction of important wants. Then repeat this sentence that begins "I'd like to—" and immediately add any sentence that comes to you next. Take about five minutes to do this. . . .

Now take a few minutes to tell each other what you experienced as you did this. Did you become aware of some of the wants and possible gains that your fears prevent you from reaching? . . . What else did you become aware of? . . .

Whenever I say "I have to" "I can't" "I need" or "I'm afraid to" I hypnotize myself into believing that I am less capable than I really am. "I have to" makes me a slave, "I can't" and "I'm afraid to" make me a weakling, and "I need" makes me helpless and incomplete. Whenever I say "I choose to," I affirm that I have the power of choice, even when I continue to choose in the same way as before. Whenever I say "I won't," I affirm my power of refusal, and often become aware of large reservoirs of hidden and disguised power to resist. Of course, it is possible for me to say "I won't" in a meek, small voice, so that it is clear to anyone that my real feeling is "I can't." When this happens, I can become aware of my tone of voice and take responsibility for this expression of myself as well. It is my willingness to identify fully with my experience and my actions, and be responsible for what I feel and do, that brings a sense of power and capability. When I say "I want," I can realize that although many of the things I desire might be very pleasant and comfortable, they are conveniences, not necessities. I can actually get along very well without them. I may even realize that the satisfactions of some of the things I try so hard to get are not worth half the effort I spend in trying to get them. When I say "I'd like to—" I can realize that I'm experiencing attraction as well as fear. I can then realize the possible gain as well as the possible loss in what I am afraid to attempt. I can realize that every risk has positive aspects as well as negative ones.

One aspect of growth is the discovery that many things are possible and that there are many alternatives in coping with the world and satisfying your wants. The real problem is that most people *believe* they are not capable and *believe* that there are no alternatives. We are in contact with our *beliefs,* and not in contact with reality. Rather than interact with reality and take certain risks, we hypnotize ourselves with our fantasies of what isn't possible, and the catastrophes that would happen if we tried alternatives, etc. Be aware of what you say and how you speak, and see if you can discover other ways that you hypnotize yourself into believing that you are less than you are—less capable, less feeling, less strong, less intelligent, etc.

We normally express our feelings and experiences through our body posture and movements. In some strongly emotional experiences, our entire body is involved. In joy, our whole body tends to be mobilized into activity—smiling, dancing, singing, etc. In fear, our whole body either becomes immobilized and tense, or explodes into actively running away. With other experiences, only parts of our body express what we are feeling. Perhaps only my mouth smiles, my nose wrinkles in disgust, my foot taps out my impatience, or tension in my neck or fist expresses my anger.

Most of us avoid experiencing certain feelings and other aspects of our experience which are uncomfortable or painful, or which might bring about an unpleasant response from other people in our environment. When I avoid awareness of what I am feeling, I also have to avoid awareness of how my body is expressing the feeling. Usually this involves partial or complete stopping of the movements that would normally express the feeling. If I feel angry and begin to make a fist and tense my arm and shoulders to hit, I can only stop this expression by tensing the muscles that oppose this movement. The resulting tension is still a signal to me that something is seeking expression, so I may also avoid being aware of this tension by directing my attention elsewhere and losing awareness of these areas of my body.

If I want to regain awareness of what I feel, it is often useful to reverse this process by deliberately focusing attention on the parts of my body that are tense or have very little feeling. By exploring the areas of tension or lack of sensation in my body, I can recover awareness of these feelings. The next experiment can give you some experience of doing this.

Face Awareness

Close your eyes, ... find a comfortable position, ... and become aware of your face. ... Be aware of the sensations coming from the different areas of your face. ... Where do you feel tension or tightness? ... What parts of your face can you feel distinctly? ... And which parts do you feel very vaguely or not at all? ... Notice what part of your face emerges most strongly into your awareness, ... and focus your attention on this part of your face. ... Become more and more aware of this part of your face, and see what feeling, expression or movement emerges as you do this. ... Let this part of your face do whatever it wants to do, and focus your attention on whatever develops out of this. ... What does this part of your face express? ... If this part of your face could talk to you silently, what would it say? ... Now imagine that you become this part of your face and identify with what this part of your face expresses. As this part of your face, what do you say? ... Really get into the experience of being this part of your face. ... What is your life like? ... And what do you do? ... How do you feel, and what is it that you are trying to express? ...

In a minute or so, I'm going to ask you to open your eyes and share your experience with the others in the group. Express your experience in the first-person present tense, as if it were happening now. Describe in detail what you are aware of in your face and show this in your facial expression. Go on to describe what develops as you focus your attention on a part of your face, intensify the expression, and then what you experience as you identify with this part of your face. ...

We meet and communicate with others mostly through the face, and the face is particularly important in communicating feelings and emotions. If you are willing to occasionally take a few moments to become really aware of your face, you can regain contact with what is going on in you at the time that is not being expressed. For instance, you might find your nose wrinkling in disgust, or your eyes holding back tears, or your mouth beginning to smile. Whatever you become aware of, realize that this is a part of your experience, another part of your life that you can regain and use—but only if you become deeply aware of what is held back.

You can become more aware of what is held back in any part of your body through this noticing and identification. You can also use a dialogue between parts of your body to deepen the experience of identification and discover how the different parts of your body are related to each other. The next experiment can give you an experience of this.

Hand Dialogue

Close your eyes, and keep them closed until I ask you to open them. Find a comfortable sitting position that allows you to use both of your hands. Get in touch with your physical existence. . . . Turn your attention away from the outside world and become aware of your body. . . . Notice which parts of your body emerge into your awareness, . . . and notice which parts of your body you are not very much aware of. . . .

Now bring your hands together in your lap in any way that is comfortable for you. Focus your attention on your hands. . . . Get in touch with your hands. . . . Become aware of the sensations that are coming from your hands. . . . What is the physical relationship between your hands? . . . Are your hands interacting in any way? . . . Let your hands begin to move a little, as if they were interacting or having a silent conversation. . . . How do your hands move, and how do they feel? . . .

Now I want you to give words to this silent conversation. Imagine that you become your right hand, and that you are silently speaking to your left hand. . . . As right hand, what do you say to left hand? . . . And what does left hand answer? . . . How do you feel as right hand? . . . How are you different from left hand? . . . Tell left hand how you are different. . . .

Now identify with your left hand. Become left hand, and continue this conversation. . . . Tell right hand how you feel as left hand, and how you are different from right hand. . . . What do you say as left hand, and what does right hand answer? . . . What is going on between you? . . .

Now become right hand again. Continue this dialogue between your hands for four or five minutes. Continue to focus your attention on your hands and find words for how they interact and relate to each other. Identify with one hand and feel how it is to be that hand speaking directly to the other hand. Switch back and forth between your hands whenever you wish. If you get stuck, say to the other hand "I'm stuck" or "I have nothing to say to you," and see what the other hand replies. Keep the interaction going and see what develops. . . .

Keep your eyes closed for a little while longer. Sit silently and absorb whatever you have just experienced. . . . What went on between your hands? . . . What did you experience while identifying with your hands? . . .

In a minute I'm going to ask you to open your eyes and share your experiences with the group. Express your experiences in first-person present tense, as if the dialogue were happening now: "As right hand, I am covering left hand; I feel confident and protective, and I say to left hand—" Really express your experiences in detail. Don't talk *about* your hands; *become* your hands. Don't talk in the past tense "I *was*;" talk in the present tense "I *am.*" Now open your eyes and tell your experiences to the others in the group. . . .

Almost everyone experiences some differences between their hands, and often these differences are quite impressive. Usually the right hand expresses what we think of as "masculine" aspects of personality—strength, activity, dominance, etc. Usually the left hand expresses what we think of as "feminine" aspects of personality—warmth, tenderness, weakness, etc. In some people the two hands are comfortable with their differentness: This differentness is a basis for interdependence and cooperation, as in a healthy relationship. In other people this differentness is mostly a source of conflict and disagreement. Sometimes the hands, or other parts of the body, express a continuing battle between the two sides of such a conflict. This continuing partial expression causes some parts of the body to be in continual or repeated activation and tension. This continued misuse of a body part without awareness often leads to distortion of its function, and if it is overlooked, can cause destructive physical changes and disease. We all misuse our bodies in some way, and we all suffer from some degree of such psychosomatic dis-ease. A great many difficulties—from "ordinary" aches, pains, and headaches to really crippling and killing diseases like ulcers, asthma, and arthritis— *can* be entirely a result of this unawareness and misuse of the body. Even when there is a distinct physical cause for a disease, our misuse of the diseased part is often a predisposing factor that makes this part break down, or that makes the disease much worse than it would otherwise be. See what you can learn about what is expressed in your own aches, pains, or other symptoms in the next experiment

Symptom Dialogue

Close your eyes and think of some physical symptom that bothers you. If possible, think of a symptom that you can feel right now. If you can't feel any discomfort right now, think of a symptom that bothers you regularly or repeatedly, and see if you can re-create the feeling of that discomfort. Focus your attention on this symptom and seek to be more aware of it in detail. . . . Exactly what parts of your body are affected, and what different sensations do you feel in these body parts? . . . Pay particular attention to feelings of pain and tension. . . . See if you can fully accept any discomfort you feel, and let it into your awareness. . . . See if you can increase this symptom. . . . Be aware of how you increase this symptom, . . . and now see if you can reduce it by letting go in some way. . . . Take a little more time to explore this symptom some more and become more aware of it in detail. . . .

Now *become* this symptom. As this symptom, what are you like? . . . What are your characteristics and what do you do to this person? . . . Now talk to this person and tell him what you do to him and how you make him feel. . . . As this symptom, what do you say to him? . . . What is your attitude, and how do you feel? . . .

Now become yourself again and talk back to this symptom. . . . What do you answer, and how do you feel as you answer? . . . What is going on between you? . . .

Now become the symptom again and continue the dialogue. . . . How do you feel now as this symptom, and what do you say? . . . Now tell this person what you do *for* him. . . . In what way are you useful to him, or make his life easier in some way? . . . What do you help him avoid? . . . What else can you say? . . .

Now become yourself again. What do you answer now? . . . Continue this dialogue for awhile and switch back and forth, so that you identify with whoever is speaking at the time. See what you can learn from each other as you continue this dialogue. . . .

Now keep your eyes closed and silently absorb this experience for awhile. . . . Now open your eyes and share your experience in first-person present tense, as if it were happening now. . . .

A symptom often has a great deal to tell you, if you take the time to pay attention to it and listen to the messages it sends you. At the same time that it is sending you messages, it is also sending messages to the people around you. A symptom is not just an expression of an alienated part of yourself, it also has powerful effects on others. See what you can learn about this from the next experiment.

Symptom-Other Dialogue

Close your eyes and again become aware of the same symptom that you worked with in the previous experiment. . . . Get really in touch with all the details of this symptom. . . . See if you can become aware of additional details that you didn't notice before. . . . Again see if you can exaggerate this symptom. . . . And be aware of how you exaggerate it—what do you do, and what muscles do you tense? . . .

Now *become* this symptom and identify with it. What are you like, and how do you feel? . . . What are your characteristics? . . . What do you do and how do you do it? . . . Now continue to be this symptom and talk to the people in your environment. Talk to parents, friends, boss, wife, children—anyone that you affect—and tell them how you affect them. . . . What do they do because of you? . . . Tell them what you do to them, and see what they reply. . . . Take some time to explore how you, as symptom, affect others. . . .

Now become yourself again and say the same things to these people *as yourself*. Take responsibility for what you do. For example, "I use my headaches to make you do things I don't want to do," or whatever your situation is. . . .

Now open your eyes and share your experience in first-person present tense as if it were happening now. . . .

Some symptoms are created or exaggerated primarily to influence others and manipulate them into certain responses. Some people suddenly get a headache whenever they don't want to face a chore or difficulty, so others have to help them. Even a symptom with a specific external cause, such as a broken leg, can be used to get more care and attention than is really necessary—and some people have an amazing ability to collect broken bones and other injuries. A symptom is an ideal way to manipulate others. It is something that I can't be held responsible for; it prevents me from doing certain things and it pressures others into doing them for me.

One of the most important things to learn about a symptom is what it does *for* you. Does it keep you out of trouble, give you a rest from overwork, take you out of unpleasant activities that you don't say "No" to, bring attention from others, give you "deserved" punishment, help you avoid unpleasant tasks, etc.? Whatever you find the symptom does for you, you might explore some means other than diseasing yourself that would achieve the same result. If you become ill in order to get a rest, perhaps you could be aware of your exhaustion, and take a rest before illness forces you to. If your symptom gets you care and attention from others, perhaps there is some other way that you could ask for this care and attention. Often when such an alternative is found, the symptom improves suddenly or disappears.

You can use a fantasy dialogue with *anything* in your life that gives you trouble, either in reality or fantasy. If you are trying to stop smoking, you can have a dialogue with a pack of cigarettes. If you find yourself angry at a car that keeps breaking down, you can have a dialogue with the car. If you discover a conflict or separation in a fantasy trip, you can have a dialogue between these parts, whatever they are. For instance, you could have a dialogue between your rosebush and anything that significantly affects it. Particularly important is anything that threatens or frustrates and anything that supports or protects in any way. Have a dialogue with the people who pick your roses, the fence that shuts you off from the sun's warmth, the bugs that eat your leaves, the greenhouse that protects you, or the grandmother that takes care of you. You can also have dialogues between parts of the rosebush that seem quite different— between the tiny fibrous roots and the thick stems, between the beautiful blossoms and the ugly thorns, between the half of the roots that are in soil and the half that are wiggling in the air, etc. Dialogues with things or qualities that are absent or vague can be particularly valuable. Have a dialogue with the roots you can't feel, the water that is missing from the dry soil, etc.

Every time you experience one of these dialogues you can discover a little more about your life and become a little less fragmented. You can discover more about your difficulties, especially what you gain from these difficulties and how much you contribute to them. As you deepen your awareness of your own functioning, you will feel more centered, and your life will become much simpler and less confusing. As you take more responsibility for what you do, you will gradually be able to act much more directly and honestly, and your actions will become much more effective and less destructive and self-defeating.

Stranger

Stranger, do not come one step nearer
do not reach out toward me
stranger
we must not touch our hands
to join your loneliness and mine

Abide by the regulation:
     no man shall approach a man
     no woman shall approach a woman
     nor man, woman, nor woman, man
Our life depends on it

You wear a red scarf
I wear a blue cap
there can be nothing between us

If you ask me the time, I must turn my wrist
If I ask you the way, you must point

The rules hang from every lamppost
above the basket of geraniums
they are nailed into the telephone poles
Though we scream to break the silence
who would conjecture the universality of his sorrow
who would confess at the streetcorner

Stranger, at the time of fire
     you will pass through the smoke to save me
Stranger, at the time of flood
     I will lift you from the water
At the time of the invader
     we will gather together

Guard us from our intimacy
now, as we stand adjacent on the endless belt
conveying us into the future
which, like the ancients' heaven
will justify the disaster of this hour

—Peter Goblen

Communication with Others

This poem *Stranger* moves me strongly each time I read it. I know that many of my contacts with others are superficial and dishonest. I also know the deep, solid satisfaction that comes with honest contact, when two people are willing to be themselves fully. The important question is *how. How* can we come together out of separateness and loneliness?

A great deal has been written about trust and love, and that if you can build a trusting, loving relationship, then people can be honest with each other. I believe this idea is exactly backwards. It is very nice if I feel trusting and loving toward someone, but if I don't feel this way, what can I do about it? Trust and love are my *feeling responses* toward another person, and these responses cannot be manufactured. Either I feel love or I don't. All the emphasis on trust and love results in many people *pretending* to feel trust and love "because it is healthy, and will bring about closeness, honesty, etc."—adding a new area of phoniness and dishonesty in their behavior.

Honesty, however, is a *behavior* and *is* something I can choose or not choose. I cannot decide to love or trust, but I can decide to be personally honest or not. And when I choose to be really honest and say what I experience and what I feel, I am showing that I can be trusted. In order to do this I have to first be honest with myself and get in touch with my experiencing, and take responsibility for it by expressing it as my experiencing. This is the *only* kind of behavior that can bring about a response of trust. Trust is my response to a person that I know I can believe. Even if I dislike a person, I can trust him if he is honest with me, and I can respect his willingness to be himself honestly. When I trust and respect myself enough to be myself honestly, others respond with trust and respect.

Likewise, honesty does not always bring a response of love, but it is absolutely essential to it. When I am honestly myself, and you respond warmly and with caring, then love exists. If I calculate and put on phony behavior in order to please you, you may love my *behavior*, but you cannot love *me*, because I have hidden my real existence behind this artificial behavior. Even when you love in response to my phony behavior, I cannot really receive your love. It is poisoned by my knowledge that the love is for the image I have created, not for me. I also have to be continually on guard to be sure that I maintain my image so that your love does not disappear. Since I have shut myself off from your love in this way, I will feel more lonely and unloved, and try even more desperately to manipulate myself and you in order to get this love. This is the tragic fallacy in all behavior that is based on fantasy and images, intention and manipulation. Whenever I manipulate myself in order to get a certain response from you, I know that your response is not directed toward *me*, so it gives me little satisfaction. All that effort to bring about a response that I can never really enjoy! In contrast, when I am honestly myself and you respond to me as I am in that moment, I can receive this fully and know the satisfaction of being really related with you. This honest relating is not always joyful or pleasant—it is sometimes sad, sometimes angry, etc.—but it is always *solid* and *real* and *vitally alive*.

Communication is very simple in terms of awareness. I have to be aware of my own experience, and be able and willing to make you aware of this experience: I have to send clear messages about my awareness—my experiences, my feelings, my needs, etc. I also have to be aware of the messages that you send: I have to be open to receive your expression of your awareness. Good communication is necessary because other people are often necessary to help me satisfy many of my needs and wants. Other people are often the source of my greatest joys and good experiences, as well as more ordinary basic needs such as food, shelter, etc. When you and I are really in touch with our experiencing and we both express this directly, there is no problem in communicating. Problems arise when our words are used for purposes other than clear communication of awareness. Words can be used to punish, soothe, manipulate, confuse, hypnotize, screen, drown, dominate, hang on, plead, beg, deceive, reject—the list is endless.

Scattershot*

Never believe them. Receive my words, my dear,
as the world seals up man's campsite scar, as air
accepts the air-age, as time endures its clocks.
I speak as a pouting child throws aimless rocks,
as a dog snarls at a wheel; my bullets flare
from a soldier raking the jungle night—for fear.

—Judson Jerome

When words are used for purposes other than direct communication of experience, they usually introduce further confusion into a situation that is often already difficult. Both you and I begin to believe the words, and we lose touch with our experience and what is actually going on between us. Many of our words serve to isolate us—both from contact with others and from awareness of our own experiencing. Because of this, it can be very useful to set aside a period of time during which words are absolutely prohibited, except for emergencies. When you need to communicate, do it non-verbally if at all possible. Use this silent time to take in and receive experiences that otherwise would have been drowned or pushed aside by

*From *Light in the West* by Judson Jerome, Golden Quill Press, Francestown, N. H., 1962, p. 18.

words. Notice how you experience this silence. Be aware of what you want to say, and what impulses impel you to speak. If you do speak through forgetfulness, notice what you say. Be aware of to what extent you actually do communicate something with these words, and to what extent they are useless noises. Begin by setting aside an hour or so during the day for silence. Try a silent meal, and see how much of the tastes, textures, and flavors of the food you have been losing as a result of the continuing chatter, and see what else the silence allows you to become aware of.

Often the content—the usual dictionary meaning of the words— is irrelevant to what is really being expressed. Often the real message, the honest expression, is in the voice itself: in the tone, the volume, the speed, the hesitations, etc. When a person is bragging, for instance, it doesn't matter if he talks about baseball, buttons, bumblebees, or bullfrogs. The real message is the demand that is conveyed by the tone of voice: "Look at me and respect how great I am—how much I know, and how much I've done!" The following experiments can help you to become more sensitive to what is communicated by the voice itself, irrespective of the words.

Voice Listening

Pair up with someone you would like to be with and get to know better. . . . Now close your eyes and sit together quietly. . . . I want you to keep your eyes closed to eliminate your vision, so that you are forced to use your other senses instead. Keep your eyes closed until I ask you to open them. I want you to silently get in touch with your experience of having your eyes closed. . . . Notice what you feel physically, . . . and notice any images or fantasies that come. . . .

In a moment I want you to tell each other about your experience of having your eyes closed, and as you do this, also focus your attention on your own and your partner's voices. I want you to be particularly aware of voices and what is expressed by the voice itself. See if you can learn to listen as if the other person were speaking a foreign language that you don't understand, so that the only way to understand the message is to listen to the emphasis, the tone, the hesitations, etc. Do this for about five minutes. . . .

Now express what you notice about your own and your partner's voices. Be very specific about what you are actually aware of in
the voice, and also say how you feel about it—your response to it,
and your impression of what it is like. For instance: "I'm very aware
of how softly you speak; I feel sleepy as I listen to your voice, like
listening to a lullaby." Take about five minutes to do this. . . .

Gibberish

Now open your eyes, face each other, and look at each other. In
a moment I want you to talk gibberish to each other. Make *any*
noises you like, that sound vaguely like language, but are *not* words
in any language you know. For example: Erah grool azt gronglek
gazel! That's *my* gibberish; I want you to discover what yours is like.
Don't try to carry on a meaningful conversation: Just gibber. Maintain eye contact with your partner as you do this. Go ahead now,
and talk gibberish to your partner. Be aware of how you feel as you
do this. . . .

Now stop the gibberish. Close your eyes, . . . and get in touch
with your physical experience. . . . Now open your eyes and tell your
partner what you are feeling: what you experience as you talk
gibberish to each other. . . .

Probably you experience some degree of unwillingness to talk
gibberish and some feelings of self-consciousness—feeling "silly,"
"stupid," or "foolish" when you do it. I'd like you to be fully aware
of this unwillingness to take the risk of appearing "silly," and to
silently take a couple of minutes to deliberately imagine what would
happen if you went ahead and really did become silly and foolish.
Imagine the worst thing that could happen if you did this. . . . Now
take a minute or two to share your catastrophic fantasies with your
partner. . . .

Probably you imagined someone else judging you, disapproving
of your being silly and childish. I'd like you to realize that you are
judging yourself in these fantasies. You are demanding of yourself
that you not appear silly and foolish. Another way of describing this
is that you are at least somewhat unwilling—even temporarily—to
give up your *image* of yourself as a sane, rational, stable person. Now

discuss these ideas with your partner to see if they make sense to you and fit with your experience. . . .

Now again talk gibberish to each other. See if you can get past your feelings of self-consciousness enough to enjoy it and really express yourself in gibberish. Tell your partner what you are experiencing—your uneasiness, how you feel about him, what you are aware of when you look at his face, etc.—but instead of telling him in words, tell him in nonsense noises. As you do this, be aware of how your and your partner's gibberish sounds. What is your impression of what is being expressed in these sounds? Occasionally close your eyes and really focus your attention on the sounds of your gibberish conversation, and notice what you feel physically. Talk gibberish to each other now for several minutes. . . .

Now take a few minutes to tell your partner in *words* how you experience your own gibberish, and how you experience his. What are these noises like, and what do they express to you? Try to really describe the characteristics and essence of these sounds. For instance, "My gibberish goes geeble, eeble, feeble. I sound weak and ineffectual, sort of bleating like a sheep," or whatever your experience is. . . .

Voice Identification

Now quickly decide who is *A* and who is *B*. . . . I want you to both close your eyes and keep them closed until I ask you to open them. I want *A* to listen to his own voice, identify with it, and to describe his voice and what it expresses *as if he were his voice.* For instance: "I am my voice. I am soft and slow and I waver up and down a little. I'm a little bit pleading—as if I'm asking for something—" If you get stuck, just repeat "I am my voice—" and listen to it and see what else you can discover about your voice. As *A* does this, I want *B* to be silent and *listen* very carefully to your partner's voice. Just listen. Be aware of the actual characteristics of the voice itself, and notice any feelings, impressions, or images that come to you as you listen to this voice. Do this for several minutes. . . .

Now switch. *A* listens silently now, while *B* identifies with his voice and describes himself for several minutes. . . . Now open your eyes, and take a couple of minutes to tell your partner what you noticed as you experienced his voice, and any images that came to you as you listened. Again try to express both the actual characteristics of the sounds, and also what these sounds, hesitations, etc. express to you. . . .

Parent-Child Dialogue

Now I want *A* to be a parent, and *B* to be a child. Talk to each other as if you were actually a parent and child. Make up anything you want. As you do this, be aware of what you say, what is expressed in the voice, how you feel, and how you interact with your partner. Take about five minutes to do this. . . .

Now switch: *B* is now the parent, and *A* is the child. Have another five-minute conversation between you, and be aware of what goes on as you do this. . . .

Now sit quietly and reflect on your experience. . . . Realize what *kind* of a parent and child you are. As a parent, are you cold, authoritative, shrewd, loving, scheming, etc.? As a child are you whining, apologetic, agreeable, rebellious, or sassy, etc.? Try to realize the flavor and details of how you played this parent and child. How did you experience your partner as he became parent and child? . . . Take about five minutes to explore this. . . .

Probably you got into some kind of power struggle in this dialogue. Usually the parent tries to control the child through threats and commands, while the child tries to evade this control through being helpless, forgetful, apologetic, etc. This evasion of control is also control. Since the parent is frustrated in his attempts to get the child to do things, he has to do many of them himself. Control is one of the most important factors in relationships, particularly in disturbed relationships with a lot of conflict. It is important to discover who controls who, and *how* this control is exercised. Are the attempts to control open demands or disguised manipulations? Does one person ask another to do for him what he can easily do for himself? Are the demands and control possible or impossible? Does one person ask another to provide him with something that no one else can possibly give him, such as peace or happiness? Are the demands clear and specific, such as "Shut the door after you," or vague, such as "Don't annoy me"?

Now recall the parent-child dialogue that you just had, and explore the control aspect of this dialogue. As a parent, how did you try to control your child? As a child, how did you try to evade this parental control, and how did you control the parent? Was this control struggle in the open, or somewhat disguised? Were your demands specific or vague, possible or impossible? What else did you notice about control in this relationship? Take a few minutes to discuss this. . . .

Whenever people are together, their actions or inactions will affect each other, and in this sense control always exists in a relationship. Nevertheless, there is a great difference between two people *responding* to each other and two people *manipulating* each other—it is the difference between a dance and a struggle. When I respond to you, I am in contact with you, and letting myself flow and happen without thinking. When I manipulate you, I am thinking about the future and straining to plan and control my actions in order to bring about the response I want from you. In order to control you, I have to control myself. I am the first victim in my struggle to control you. Whenever I hold myself back, I am interfering with my own functioning: manipulating myself in order to manipulate you. The more I do this, the more I disturb and distort my natural functioning.

When I try to control you, I also become controlled in another way: as soon as I want to control you, you can use this to control me. You can try to get what you want from me by withholding what I want from you, and you can disappoint me, frustrate me, and punish me if I don't give it to you. I get thoroughly caught and controlled through my struggle to control you.

Some demands pose a self-contradictory paradox that traps us both. If I say to you "Don't be so obedient," there is no way you can please me. If you comply with this demand you are being obedient, and if you ignore the demand you are continuing in the behavior that I dislike. Any such message that places both of us in an impossible situation is called a double-bind. Another example is "I want you to dominate me." If I try to comply with your request, your request dominates me. Common double-binds are demands for behavior that can only be spontaneous, such as "You should respect me," "Be spontaneous," or "You must love me."*

Some demands are actually completely one-sided, and take the form "What is good for me is bad for you." "Don't be selfish," really means "Let *me* be selfish; do it the way I want you to." "Don't be so stubborn," means "Give in so that I can stay stubborn."

The only way out of this destructive struggle for control is through awareness. I can become aware of all the details of the struggle itself, and my part in this control-madness. I can become aware of what I want from you, and how I am more concerned with my fantasies about your future obedience than with your present actuality. I can become aware of how I am tensing and holding back, by paying close attention to my awareness of my physical respond-ing. Physical discomfort is often a symptom of dishonesty—a signal that I am not expressing myself fully. By paying attention to my discomfort, I can discover how I manipulate and distort myself in order to control you.

I can best pay attention to myself if I pause to contact my experiencing, stay with it awhile to discover more about it, and then express it *as my experience,* and not as an accusation or some other veiled demand. For instance, I might discover that I am tensing my shoulders and arms and clenching my jaw, and as I focus on this, realize that I am feeling anger. If I say "You are a bastard," I accuse and blame you and demand that you change to make me feel better. I can take more responsibility for my feeling if I simply express it as *my* experiencing "I am angry about what you did."

If I stay with this feeling of anger, I can discover more details about it. I may discover that my anger in this moment has a solid, strong unyielding quality to it, as if expressing "I don't accept your doing that." Or I may discover that my anger in this moment has a helpless, wailing quality to it as if asking "Please help me: please don't do that again." If I continue to stay with my experiencing, I may notice that my shoulders are raised as if to ward off a blow, and

*See *An Anthology of Human Communication,* a book and audiotape by Paul Watzlawick, for extensive discussion and excellent examples of these and other important aspects of communication. Science and Behavior books, Palo Alto, 1964.

realize that I am afraid of your retaliation. Or I may get a strong image of a previous situation in my life, and realize that at least some of my anger is a response to this previous unfinished situation rather than to the present situation. By staying with my awareness of what I am experiencing, I can gradually become clearer and clearer about what is actually happening now in this situation.

The major obstacle to this process is the alienation of my experience through my making others responsible for it, instead of taking full responsibility for it myself. Again, it is the difference between expressing myself and manipulating you into doing something for me. Almost any behavior or emotion can be either an honest expression or a dishonest manipulation. Giving can be a free expression or an attempt to make you feel obligated. Crying can be a direct outpouring of grief or a wail for help. The next experiment can give you some experience of some of the different ways that people manipulate and control each other covertly instead of expressing themselves honestly.

Family Quarrel

Satir and Shostrom distinguish four basic types of manipulative role, each with countless variations and combinations:

1)PLACATING: Pacifying, smoothing over differences, being nice, protective, defending others gently, covering up. "Oh, it's not so bad, really," "We agree, basically."

2)AVOIDING: Being quiet, pretending not to understand, changing the subject, playing weak, playing helpless. "I can't help it," "I didn't hear you."

3) BLAMING: Judging, bullying, comparing, complaining, "It's always your fault." "You never—" "Why don't you—"

4) PREACHING: Lecturing, using outside authority, "You should—" "You must—" proving that you're right by explaining, calculating, using logic, etc. "Dr. Spock says—" "What you're actually doing is—"

Form groups of 4 or 5 people, and balance sex as evenly as possible. I want you to quickly form a "family." Imagine that you are a family, and decide who is Mother, Father, Son, Daughter, and *keep these familial roles throughout the experiment.*

Begin by playing the manipulative role (identified by number above) in the first row of the table below for about 5 minutes. After about 5 minutes, look at the next number in your column, and play that role for five minutes, and so on. For instance, for the first five minutes, Mother will be placating (1), father will be blaming (3), etc. For the second 5 minutes, mother will be avoiding (2), father will be preaching (4), etc.

	Mother	Father	Son	Daughter
First 5 minutes	1	3	2	4
Second 5 minutes	2	4	3	1
Third 5 minutes	3	1	4	2
Fourth 5 minutes	4	2	1	3

(I ditto the table above and the role descriptions, or at least put them on a blackboard.)

When you are assigned to be a blamer, start blaming: "Mom, it's your fault I got bad grades this semester, because you don't wake me up in the morning." "You never care about what I do anyway!" Make up any problems you like, and drop them when you want to move on to something else. Don't wait for someone else to stop talking—arguments aren't like that. Put a lot of energy into this and enjoy yourself. If you are a blamer or a preacher, don't let the avoider sit back and avoid without being challenged. Make sure that he has to actively avoid. O.K. Go ahead and play the role assigned to you in the first row of the table for about five minutes. . . .

(After five minutes) Everyone stop and go on to your next role. . . . (Repeat this until each person has played all four roles in the table.)

Now stop and enjoy the silence for a little while. Close your eyes and silently contemplate the last 20 minutes. . . . Which of the four roles was easiest for you to play and which was the hardest for you to play? . . . Which role was most comfortable and felt most spontaneous or energetic? . . . In which role were you least comfortable, feeling strained and uptight? . . . Now how about the other members of your "family." Which role do you think was easiest, and which was most difficult for each of them? . . . Now spend about five minutes discussing this with the other members of your "family." . . .

Now I want each person to play the role that you found *easiest* to play, for about two minutes. . . .

Now I want you each to play the role that you found *hardest* to play for about two minutes. . . .

It is no accident that some of these roles are easier for you than others. Some of them are easier for you because you have learned to play them well and they are familiar to you. Other ways of manipulating others are more difficult because you haven't used them so much. So now I'd like you to discuss to what extent you see your characteristic ways of dealing with others being expressed through these roles. Of the many possible ways of playing these roles, how did you express yourself, and how did others express themselves? What impressions do you have of each other as a result of this experience? Discuss this for five or ten minutes. . . .

Now I'd like to mention a few things about this experiment. I start out by asking you to play a phony role. And yet as you get into this role, you discover that it becomes somewhat real—you discover something about yourself: how you avoid confronting other people honestly and directly. Within each of these four basic kinds of role, there are hundreds of variations, and you can also discover your own personal style of playing a particular role. One person avoids by mumbling so that no one can hear, another avoids by being absent-minded, or looking away, and another avoids by keeping quiet, by being forgetful, or by talking continuously. When you observe yourself in your everyday behavior, you may find that you use different styles or even play very different roles with different significant people in your life. You may avoid with your father, blame your mother, placate your girlfriend, etc. Only rarely is a person so completely frozen into a single role that he has to use it with everyone in his life. Try this same experiment with your real family and see what you can discover.

I hope you got some concrete experience of the wide variety of styles of manipulation that are possible by watching the others in your group, so that you can begin to recognize when someone else is trying to manipulate you. Blaming and preaching are more open and active, and avoiding and placating are more passive, but all these roles pressure others to respond in certain ways. All of these roles are also ways of avoiding honest contact, ways of not openly declaring and taking responsibility for what I want or demand from others.

If I have a difference or dispute with another person, the real way to settle it is this: 1) to express clearly how I feel about it, what's important for me, and what I want from him. 2) to listen to the other person's feelings and demands. 3) and then either come to some kind of agreement or solution, or else decide to meet my needs and wants through some other person whose feelings and preferences are more compatible with mine. Most people are neither willing to compromise and agree, nor to let go of this person and find someone else with whom they could be happier. Most people are caught in their own net of continuing to demand something from another person what that person is not willing to provide. The blamer continues to try to push the other person into doing what he wants with "You should do it, and you are bad and wrong if you don't." The preacher tries to prove that you should do things his way. The avoider forces others to do things for him because he is "helpless" to do them himself, and the placater stops the open confrontation that might lead to a real exposure of the dispute and an end to his other avoidance manipulations. Honest confrontation risks disturbance of the status quo, and is often painful and disturbing—but the alternative is endless quarreling and unsatisfying and destructive manipulations. The more you can be aware of all the details of what is actually happening when you find yourself in quarrels and conflicts, the more you will be able to clear up confusion, and make communication direct enough to discover what the real problems are.

The experiments that follow will help you to recognize some important basic aspects of communication. In these, I want you to be aware of what goes on when you experience a particular kind of verbal interaction. Pair up with someone and sit facing each other.

(Or form groups of 4-6 people, balancing sex.) I'm going to ask you to talk to each other using different rules that restrict you to certain kinds of words and sentences. I want you to notice how you feel as you use these different kinds of sentences, and what you experience as you receive them. Also be aware of your partner as he uses these different kinds of communication. I want you to discover how your interaction with another person is altered by different kinds of messages. As you experience these different ways of talking I want you to be particularly aware of the amount of actual communication that exists: To what extent are you making the other person aware of something that you are aware of, and to what extent are you able to understand what the other person is experiencing? To what extent do you feel connected with this other person and involved in his experience?

Begin by talking with each other for about three minutes without any restrictions, to discover something about your usual way of communicating. Talk about anything you want, in any way you want. Be aware of what you and your partner do talk about, how you talk, and how you feel as you do this. . . .

Now silently review this discussion. What were you aware of during this time? What did you notice about your communication? . . . What did you talk about? . . . How did you talk? Did you really talk to each other, or did you just sit back and scatter words at each other? . . . Did you mostly maintain eye contact, or did you mostly avoid looking at your partner by staring out the window? . . .

"It" Statements

Now talk to each other for a couple of minutes with the following restrictions: Every sentence must be a statement that begins with "it." No questions are permitted, only "it" statements. . . .

Now briefly discuss your experience of making only "it" statements. How do you feel as you make "it" statements and how do you feel as you listen to your partner's "it" statements? . . .

"You" Statements

Now take a couple of minutes to talk to each other using only statements that begin with the word "you." No questions are permitted, only "you" statements. . . .

Now briefly discuss your experience of making only "you" statements. How do you feel as you make these "you" statements, and how do you feel as the receiver of "you" statements? Compare this experience of "you" statements with how you experienced sending and receiving "it" statements. . . .

"We" Statements

Now talk to each other using only statements that begin with "we." No questions are permitted, only "we" statements. . . .

Now discuss your experience of making "we" statements. Compare your experience of making "we" statements with how you experienced sending and receiving "it" and "you" statements. . . .

"I" Statements

Now talk to each other using only statements beginning with "I." No questions are permitted, only "I" statements. . . .

Again discuss your experience of doing this, and compare this with your previous experiences with "it" "you" and "we" statements. . . .

Questions

Now I want you to do nothing but ask questions. Ask each other any questions you wish, *but do not answer these questions. Every* sentence must be a question. Go ahead. . . .

Now discuss your experience of doing this. Don't get hung up on the fact that most of you probably wanted to answer the questions you were asked. Discuss other aspects of your feelings about asking, and being asked, questions. . . .

Changing Questions to "I" Statements

Now I want you to remember the questions that you asked each other, and to change every question into an "I" statement. For instance, if your question was "Why do you wear boots?" your statement could be "I notice that you are wearing boots," or "I like/dislike your boots," or some other statement about the boots that begins with "I." It is possible to transform *every* question into an "I" statement. If you have difficulty remembering your questions, perhaps your partner can help you recall some of them. . . .

Now discuss your experience of changing your questions into statements, and compare the experience of asking the questions and making the statements. How do you feel as the receiver of these questions and statements? . . .

Why-Because

Now talk to each other using only sentences that begin with the words "why" or "because." Every sentence must either be a question about something here and now that begins with "why" or an answer that begins with "because." . . .

Now discuss your experiences with these "why" and "because" sentences. What did you experience during this interchange? . . .

How-Thus

Now I want you to talk to each other with this restriction: Each sentence must either be a question about something here and now that begins with the words "how" or "what," or an answer to one of these questions. An answer to a "how" or "what" question does not begin with the word "because." Both "why" and "because" are forbidden, and "how come" is also not permitted; "How come?" is a substitute for "why." "How are you feeling?" might be answered with "I'm feeling excited and I can feel my shoulders tensing." "What do you like about me?" might be answered with "I like the way you smile and tilt your head as you talk to me." Do this now for about three minutes. . . .

Now discuss your experiences with "how" and "what" questions, and answers to these questions. Compare this with what you experienced with "why" questions and "because" answers. Which kind of question and answer really communicates information, and helps you contact the other person? . . .

But

Now make any statements you like, as long as the word "but" is somewhere in the middle of every sentence. You don't have to use "but" at the beginning; just make sure that you have one "but" in each sentence. . . .

Now discuss what you are aware of as you give and receive "but" statements. What do you experience as you do this? What effect does the "but" have upon the statement? . . .

And

Now make any statements you like, as long as the word "and" appears at least once somewhere. Every sentence must contain the word "and." The word "but" is forbidden. Try repeating some of the sentences you just made with "but," substituting "and" for "but" and notice what effect this has upon the message. . . .

Now discuss your experience of using "and" statements, and compare it with your experience of using "but" statements. What does the word "and" do to the statement? . . .

"I-You" Statements

Now use only statements that begin with "I" and that refer directly to your partner in some way, for instance, "I feel strange with you," or "I like the way your black hair curls and shines in the light." Every sentence must be an "I-you" statement. No questions are permitted. . . .

Now discuss your experience of this kind of communication with your partner, and compare it with the other modes of communication you have tried previously. . . .

Now take a few minutes to review your experiences, and summarize what you have learned about these different kinds of communication as you have experienced them. . . .

Now I'm going to discuss some aspects of these experiments to consolidate your experience and perhaps mention some things that you didn't clearly realize.

When I begin a sentence with "it," the subject is externalized. "It" is out there somewhere, neither part of me nor part of you. For instance, "It is strange that we are talking like this together." Where is this "it" that is strange? A sentence that communicates more directly is: "*I* feel strange talking with you."

When I begin a sentence with the word "you," this often tends to make the other person feel defensive. I may only be disowning my experience and my opinions by using the plural "you" instead of I. This "you" really means "anybody" or "everybody." "You know" usually means "Everyone knows" and "You feel funny in that situation" really means "Anyone would feel funny in that situation." When I am talking to a specific you, this is something of an intrusion into your existence. This is true even if my statement is neither attack "you are awful," nor flattery "you are wonderful." When I say "you," I am talking about something "out there" not something close to me. I can make "you" statements fairly easily, because I don't have to reveal or commit myself.

Most, if not all, "you" statements are actually "I" statements in disguise. "You are so wonderful" might mean "*I* like you; stay with me, and be nice to me." "You are awful" might mean "*I* don't like you and it's your fault; I want you to change so as to please me." "You" statements make the blaming game easy. If you and I have a difference or dispute, I can make it seem to be your fault. When I say "you," I avoid responsibility for my part in any difference between us. When I say "I," I acknowledge that I have a part in this difference between us, and it is harder to put all the blame on you. Perhaps your behavior is O.K. and my demand that you change is unreasonable. Perhaps you are not so wonderful, but your making life pleasant and convenient for me feels wonderful. Saying "I" means that I take responsibility for my end of the relationship. When I say, "I don't like you; I want you to change," this clearly identifies the dislike as *my* experience, and shows that I am making a demand for you to change in order to make life more pleasant for me. When I say "I feel wonderful when I'm with you," I am making a clear personal statement about my experience. When I say "I," I express myself; when I say "you," I stay distant and often manipulate you.

"We" statements have at least two aspects. They can bring people together by pointing out what we have in common: the things we agree on and the ways we are like each other. "We" statements also tend to diffuse experience—it is neither I nor you that feel or think, but the nebulous "we" that is somehow both of us, yet neither one of us. "We" can also whitewash and cover up the real differences between us, and try to trap you into my way. I may say "we agree" when I know that we disagree but I want to put over my point of view. "We" is often a disguise for an "I" statement. "We should fix dinner" may really mean "I'm hungry and I want you to fix dinner for me." "Let's go to the store" means "I want you to go to the store with me."

Questions also direct attention to the other person, and often tend to put him on the defensive and make him feel attacked. This is particularly likely if the question begins with "why?" A question like "Why do you wear boots?" often thinly conceals a criticism of wearing boots, and you will probably respond by being defensive—explaining and justifying the simple fact that you are wearing boots. Obsequious questions can also be used as flattery, making you feel important and intelligent, putting you at ease and making you like me.

If I change all my questions to "I" statements, then again I have to take responsibility for *my* position, *my* dislikes, *my* opinions and demands. Then I express myself, instead of hiding behind my question that asks *you* to express yourself. Very few questions are honest requests for information, and if a question begins with "why" you can almost be certain that it isn't honest. There are *some* real questions that can be asked using why. A "why" question that is a real request for information can be easily changed into a more specific question using the words how, which, what, where, when, etc. The "why-because" bit is the epitome of useless verbiage. Rather than increase your understanding, it leads you on an endless chain of futile questions and fruitless answers—rationalizations and explanations that take you farther and farther away from experiencing and awareness. If you eliminate "why" and "because" from your vocabulary, the only thing you will lose is some of your confusion.

> when man determined to destroy
> himself he picked the was
> of shall and finding only why
> smashed it into because
>
> —e. e. cummings*

*From "when god decided to invent" in *POEMS 1923-1954* by E. E. Cummings. Reprinted by permission of Harcourt Brace Jovanovich, Inc.

"How?" and "what?" on the other hand, are useful questions that can lead to deeper understanding. If I ask "how?" I am asking about the quality and process of what is occurring now, instead of leaving the present and guessing about the past. "Why do atoms react the way they do?" is a question for metaphysics, and there are a million useless answers. "How do atoms react?" is a question for physics and chemistry and there is only one very useful answer for each specific situation. "*Why* do you feel bad?" is at best a request for explanation and justification, and at worst a demand that you deny the fact that you feel bad if you can't justify it. "How do you feel bad?" or "What do you experience?" are real requests for information about your experience, and your answer "I feel tense in my stomach and my head aches," brings you into closer contact with your own experience. Your answer is a real communication that tells me more about yourself. When you ask "how" and "what" you request information about facts and processes. When you ask "why" you only ask for endless explanations—the cause of the cause of the cause of the cause of the cause.

Many questions are traps that ask you to commit yourself. Once you are committed, you can be punished, or argued into doing what you don't want to do. "When did you get back?" sounds like an innocent question. But if I already know you have been back for a week and I'm angry that you haven't called me, this question is actually bait that asks you to commit yourself. If you are honest, I can "legitimately" get angry at you, and if you lie, I can catch you in that. "I know you've been back for a week and I'm angry that you didn't call," is a statement that is much more honest. If I stay aware of my experiencing I can express myself even more honestly, for instance: "I wanted to see you right away, and I also want you to show that you care about me by calling me. So I didn't call you, and I'm disappointed that you don't seem to care about me." Statements express something; most questions are manipulations.

"But" is a word that can be useful to indicate contrast or difference, and it can also be used to cancel or negate the first part of a sentence. When I say "I like you, *but*—" the "I like you" is usually completely wiped out by the words that follow. A sentence with "but" in it can be so self-cancelling that it becomes completely meaningless and says nothing at all. Some people put a "but" in almost every sentence; they give the appearance of talking *but* everything they say is wiped out by something else that they say, and the result is zero. *But* is also a splitter. If I say, "I like your kindness, *but* I dislike your nervous laughter," it is almost as if the "but" put your kindness at one end of the room, and the nervous laughter at the other. This splitting is often a first step toward alienating and disowning part of your experience. If you say the same sentence, replacing "but" with "and," then your two experiences are joined rather than split. "And" keeps your experiences together, tends to prevent alienation, and perhaps leads you on to express other aspects of your experience. With "and" you can stay balanced with aware-ness of both sides, and realize that both are true: that my like and dislike are both part of my experiencing of you.

"I-you" statements are the most direct expression of my aware-ness to your awareness. I am taking responsibility for what I say, I say it directly to you, and by saying something about you, I reach out to you and tell you something about how I experience you. Explore these ideas further in your own everyday interactions with people in your life. Notice when you or others use these key words and these kinds of sentences, and become more deeply aware of how you feel and what is happening at the time. Notice under what circumstances you use these words, and how it affects your relation-ship. Try making "I" statements out of your own and others' questions. See what happens when you use "and" instead of "but," and "how" instead of "why." It is really amazing how much you can clear up your communication and deepen your understanding simply by changing some of your ways of expressing yourself.

You can practice using these ideas by keeping them in mind while you try the experiment that follows. Be aware of your commu-nication, and see if you can use these ideas to make what you say in the dialogue more direct and honest. If you do the experiment alone, talk out loud and act out the situation so that you can also be aware of what you express physically and bring this awareness into the dialogue.

Guilt

Close your eyes, find a comfortable position, and take a little time to get in touch with your physical existence. . . . Now remember a situation that you feel guilty about. . . . Put yourself back into this situation, as if it were happening now. . . . Recall all the details of this situation. Where are you? . . . Is anyone else there with you? . . . What happens in this situation? . . . What, exactly, do you do, that you feel guilty about? . . . How do you feel in this situation? . . . Where in your body do you feel tension or discomfort? . . .

Now think of the *one* person you would *least* want to tell about your guilt—the person who would be most upset or angry if he or she knew about it. . . . Now imagine that this person is here now, facing you. Try to visualize this person in detail. . . . How does this person look? . . . What clothes is this person wearing? . . . and what kind of facial expression does this person have? . . .

Imagine that you talk to this person and tell him exactly what you feel guilty about. Express yourself honestly and directly, and try to get the feeling that you are actually talking directly to this person. Say silently, "Mary, I'm going to tell you about something I did—" . . . How do you feel as you do this? . . .

Now change places with this other person. Become this person and talk to yourself as if you were this other person. What do you say in response to hearing about these things? . . . How do you feel as you reply to this guilty person? . . . Continue this dialogue for awhile. . . .

Resentment

Now become yourself again, and express to this other person the resentment that lies behind the guilt. For instance, if you acted in opposition to a parent's wishes, the resentment might be, "I resent you telling me what to do," or "I resent your treating me like a child," or something like that. So express your resentments in this situation that you feel guilty about. Speak directly to this person, and tell him honestly how you feel. . . . How do you feel as you do this? . . .

Again change places and respond to what you have said as if

you were this other person. How would this person respond to the resentments you expressed? . . . Try to really get the feel of being this other person. . . . What do you say? . . . How do you feel, physically, as you respond to these resentments? . . . Continue this dialogue for awhile. . . .

Demand

Now become yourself again and express the demand that lies behind the resentment. For instance, if the resentment is "I resent you treating me like a child," then the demand might be something like, "Treat me like an adult!" or "Leave me alone!" Express your demands to this other person clearly and strongly, as if you were giving orders. . . . How do you feel physically as you do this? . . .

Again change places. Become this other person and respond to the demands that you have just expressed. As this other person, what do you say? . . . How do you feel as this other person? . . . Continue this dialogue for awhile, switching back and forth between the two speakers whenever you want to. Continue to develop some honest communication between yourself and this other person for awhile. . . .

In a minute I'm going to ask you to open your eyes and tell each other about your experiences in this dialogue. Even if you are unwilling to reveal the specific situation that you felt guilty about, there is still a great deal that you can share about your experiences. How do you feel being each speaker, and how do your feelings and the interaction change as you express guilt, then resentments, then demands? What do you discover about your demands on this other person? Express your experiences in first-person present tense. Open your eyes now, and return to the group and share your experiences. . . .

A demand is a very direct kind of communication. When I say "Do this!" or "Don't do that!" I am expressing myself strongly and openly, and taking responsibility for my demand—*I* tell *you* what *I* want *you* to do. We all make many demands on each other, and we have the very real problem of dealing with them and finding an acceptable way of working out solutions to conflicting demands.

A far greater problem is that most demands are not expressed openly and directly. Usually I don't want to take responsibility for my demands, so I hide and disguise them in sweet requests, suggestions, questions, accusations, and countless other manipulations. I would like you to satisfy my desires without my having to ask you. If I demand directly, I run the risk that you might refuse, or you might point out that my demand is unreasonable or impossible, or that I can perfectly well do that for myself, etc. When I disguise the expression of my demands, they become unclear and often confusing—both to you and to me. We both lose awareness of what is going on between us. My demands may become so confusing that you can't satisfy them even when you are willing to.

When my demands are unsatisfied, I feel resentment and anger towards you for withholding this satisfaction from me. If I express this resentment and tell you how you displease me, then it usually becomes clear how you can please me. If I resent your talking incessantly, my demand is clearly to shut up once in awhile. By expressing my resentments, my demands can become clear. Even here, there is an opportunity for manipulation and misunderstanding. For instance, I can exaggerate your demand of me so that a reasonable demand appears to be an unreasonable demand. Since it is unreasonable, I now have a "reason" to refuse it, and I can blame you for making such an unreasonable demand, etc. In spite of such problems, any direct expression of resentments and demands results in clarification. When we know what we demand from each other, we have reestablished clear communication and contact. Now we can try to reach some agreement about a workable solution to the real problem of meeting these demands.

As we explore these demands, I may discover that you can't possibly satisfy some of them and that you are unwilling to satisfy others. Some of the things I demand from you I may have to do myself, and others I may be able to ask others to satisfy. Possibly we may realize that we are too different to get along, and that we will both be much happier working out our demands with someone else. In the real world, nothing can match your fantasy ideal, but whatever solution you can work out will be far preferable to the endless struggle that results from disguised demands, and continuing to demand what someone is not able or not willing to provide.

When I refuse to express my resentment, the resentment does not disappear. If I feel resentment, that is a fact I can't change. I only have the choice of expressing it openly, or in a disguised way with reduced awareness of what I am feeling and doing. The disguised, partial expression of resentment—nagging, criticism, and other kinds of annoyances and frustrations—actually preserves the feeling and keeps it going. Only the full acceptance and expression of a feeling allows it to become complete and make way for something else. Some people collect grievances and resentments in a large gunnysack and wait for a safe opportunity to dump them all on someone. And even then they don't fully express their resentment, because they usually don't really own the feeling and take responsiblity for it. They usually are still blaming others for their discomfort, which is a further manipulation and demand that the others should change to please them.

Any unwillingness to be honestly what I am and let you know what I feel and experience puts distance between us. The disguised expression of my feelings and actions adds additional confusion, resentment, and difficulty to whatever real problems exist between us.

Any demands on me to behave differently than I want to is a source of resentment. At the same time, I may agree strongly with these demands and *believe* that they are reasonable. My resentment is in conflict with my belief, and I tend to lose awareness of my resentment. Then when I fail to meet these demands I feel a sense of defeat and a fear of *the other person's resentment* and punishment. My own resentment at having to meet these demands is buried under this feeling of failure and fear of other's resentment that we call guilt. Some people (and many religions) are very good at creating guilt in others to manipulate them into satisfying their demands. So whenever you feel guilty or resentful, or have any difficulties with another person, see if you can express your resentments, and then seek out and clarify your demands on each other.

Ask everyone in your family to agree to try this experiment:

For a specified time (a day or an evening) insist that every communication be in the form of a clear demand. If someone says something that is not a demand, demand that the person change it into a demand. There is some demand in everything you say, even if it is simply "Hear me!" This experiment may seem extreme and artificial, but it can really alert you to the demands that you and others make on each other. If this seems too extreme, simply eliminate questions, and require that every sentence must be either a demand or an "I" statement. You can also find it helpful to explore your own special ways of covertly manipulating and demanding from others. See what you can discover in the next experiment.

You've Got It; I Want It

Pair up and face each other. In each pair, decide which person is *A* and which is *B*. . . .

Now be aware of how you decided who was *A* and who was *B*. Did one person take responsibility and decide, and if so, did he decide for himself "I'll be *A*" or did he decide for his partner "You be *A*"? Did one or both of you try to avoid responsibility, and force the other to decide by waiting, shrugging, or saying "What do you want," etc.? Discuss this briefly and reflect on how this expresses what you do when a decision has to be made. . . .

Now I want you to play a game called, "You've got it; I want it." I want you both to imagine that *A* has, and wants very much to keep, something that *B* wants very badly. *Do not discuss with each other what this desirable thing might be.* Just talk to each other *as if* you both knew what it was. You can imagine something specific if you want to, but *don't tell the other person what you're thinking of.* *B* might start off with, "I want it," and *A* answers, "I won't give it to you," etc. Continue this kind of a dialogue for four or five minutes. . . .

Now switch roles, so that *B* has it and *A* wants it. Again have a dialogue for four or five minutes. . . .

Now close your eyes, and spend several minutes quietly reflecting on what happened during this dialogue. What were you aware of in yourself and what did you notice in the other person? For instance, how did you and your partner try to get it? Did you demand and threaten, or try to bribe and wheedle? Did you complain, beg, or try to make the other person feel guilty? Did you use "logic" to convince him he didn't need it? How did you put off the other person's attempt to get it? How did you feel in each role? Did you enjoy refusing to give it away, or did you want to give in and please the other person, even at your own expense? Try to become really aware of all the details of the interaction that occurred between you. . . .

Now open your eyes and discuss all this with your partner for several minutes. Try to really bring out all the details of your interaction.

I'd like you to realize that this is not just a game; it brings out some of the characteristic ways that you deal with people—how you behave when you want something from someone else or someone else wants something from you. Take a few minutes to quietly absorb whatever you may have learned about yourself through this. For instance, you might say to yourself, "This is me. When I want something from you, I'll try to make you feel guilty for wanting to keep it," or whatever your way is. . . . Now take turns saying this out loud to your partner. . . .

Non-verbal Communication

Whenever I communicate with others, only part of the message is conveyed by the words themselves. A great deal is conveyed by my tone of voice and other non-verbal messages. When I am functioning and responding easily, all these messages combine to form a rich and clearly understandable whole. When I am feeling joyful and I express it, my voice sings and my body dances in confirmation and elaboration of what I say. When I am controlling and manipulating myself, the different messages don't all combine, and some of them conflict with others or contradict them. My efforts to control myself are never completely successful, so some of my expressions are direct and honest, while others are artificial and strained. When I am trying to show you a strength and confidence I don't feel, my words are betrayed by the quaver in my voice, the quick frightened movements of my eyes or my rigid, tense body, etc.

One fact that is not widely recognized is that *it is impossible not to communicate.* There is a Sufi story in which a man writes "I have written you seventy-one letters and have received no answer—this, too, is an answer." Another way of stating this is that every message has two aspects: 1) the content, or the factual information that is conveyed, and 2) a statement about the relationship between the two people who are communicating. Consider this simple factual statement: "The dishes are all dirty." A husband might say this in a haughty tone of voice that says "I'm so much better than you, you incompetent slob," or a friendly tone that says "I'll be glad to help you with this." A wife might say the same sentence in a heavy voice that says "I'm exhausted; please do the dishes for me," a hurt tone that says "Look what you've done to me!" or an angry tone that says "Damn you, I'm not going to clean up after you any more!" The possibilities are endless.

The factual content of a message is usually easy to get agreement on: either the dishes are all dirty or they aren't. The implied message about the relationship is more difficult to get agreement on. This is partly because it is somewhat hidden and unclear, and partly because it is usually part of a continuing battle for manipulation and control. A statement about relationship carries with it implications about control—who should do what for whom. "I am boss and you are employee, so you should listen to me and do it my way—even if you know more about it than I do." "You are my wife, so you should cook for me—even if you are sick and I have more time and energy." When you and I are responding openly and freely to each other, the relationship also changes freely with this happening together. It would be impossible to give a fixed definition of this changing relationship, and we have no need to define it.

When a person refuses to express himself directly in words, or when his words are used to disguise rather than communicate, his voice, body position, and movements often give a detailed statement. Anything that is not expressed openly seeks expression in other ways. We learn to lie mostly with our words, and to a much lesser degree with our non-verbal expressions. We learn to lie somewhat with voice tone and facial expressions, but these non-verbal lies are usually caricatures of reality, like the enthusiastic TV commercials for deodorants. Our non-verbal expressions are usually much more honest than our words, and often there is a large discrepancy between the two. A man might say "I'd really like to get to know you better," while his shoulders lean back and his hands make small pushing motions as if saying "Go away." A girl might say "I don't want to see you again," while her shoulders and hips wiggle in sexy invitation.

Smiles and laughter can be expressions of genuine love and joy. But when the smile becomes a smirk and the laughter becomes nervous, they send very different messages. Many people cannot even begin to express deep feelings without cancelling them with nervous titters that say "I'm not serious, I don't really feel that way." Others can't talk to anyone without maintaining their distance with a superior smirk. These smiles and laughter have changed from communications to cancellations. These are a few examples of how we cancel and disqualify our verbal messages with non-verbal messages. Try the next experiment to discover something about how you disqualify what you say.

Non-verbal Cancelling

Pair up with someone and sit down facing each other. I want you to deliberately cancel everything you say with a non-verbal disqualification. Whatever you say, cancel its meaning with a gesture, facial expression, tone of voice, laughter, or some other non-verbal behavior. Be aware of how you feel as you do this, and exactly what you and your partner do that cancels your verbal messages. Take turns doing this with your partner for about five minutes. . . .

Now sit quietly for a little while to absorb your experience. . . . How did you and your partner cancel your messages? . . . Do you recognize any of these ways of cancelling as things you have done before? . . . How did you feel during this message-cancelling? . . . What else did you notice during this? . . . Now take a few minutes to tell each other what you experienced during this experiment. . . .

When I say one thing with my words and another with my body, I am divided between my controlled expressions and my spontaneous expressions. The non-verbal message is usually much more honest and less distorted by fantasy and intention—shoulds, hopes, wishes, etc. Usually a non-verbal message expresses actuality, what *is*, while the verbal message expresses mostly fantasy, what *might be*—what I intend, or what I hope for, or try for, etc. To the extent that I am in touch with my intentions, I will be out of touch with my actuality and my non-verbal messages that express this. You, however, may be very aware of these non-verbal messages, or you may be responding to them without awareness. If so, I may be very puzzled—and perhaps angry and outraged—that your response to me is so totally unrelated to my words and intentions.

Sometimes the non-verbal message does not contradict what is said in words, but adds important information or modifies the verbal message in very significant ways. A man might say "I'd like to get to know you better," while leaning forward like a football tackle and making small grasping movements with his hands. In this case the posture and movements modify the meaning of his words and suggest *how* he'd like to get to know you better—probably with force and grasping, and probably without sensitivity and caring. You may be ignoring these non-verbal messages, or you may be responding to them without awareness. If you can become more aware of these important messages, you can bring them into the open, improve your communication, and move much closer to resolving the real problems in a relationship. You don't need a "dictionary" of movements and gestures to be able to understand what is expressed non-verbally. All you need is awareness of your own movements and what they express, and sensitivity to others. The next experiments focus on these non-verbal expressions.

Mirroring Body

Pair up with someone you don't know well, stand facing each other silently, and maintain frequent eye contact. . . . Now *freeze— don't move*! Take a minute or two to be aware of your own and your partner's physical position. Start with yourself. Be aware of how you are standing, what your body posture is like, how you hold your head, etc. Become really aware of your physical position. How do

you feel in this position? . . . How does this position express how
you feel right now in this situation? . . . Now look at your partner's
physical position. Be aware of how he stands, how he holds his arms,
the tilt of his head, etc. What is your impression of what his body
expresses about himself and how he feels? . . .

Now stay frozen in these positions and tell each other what you
are aware of in your own body position. Identify with how you are
holding your body and take responsibility for what you do. "I am
holding my arms tightly across my chest; I feel protected behind my
arms, as if I'm behind a wall," or whatever your experience is. . . .

Now tell each other what you are aware of in your partner's
body position. Be specific about what you are aware of—what you
actually *see*—and also express your *guesses* and *impressions* about the
other person's position. . . .

Mirroring Movements

Now unfreeze and let go. I want the taller person in each pair to
silently mirror the physical position and movements of the shorter person. Maintain eye contact as you do this. A mirror instantly reflects
exactly what is in front of it. If your partner has his left foot forward,
put your right foot forward in a mirror-image of his posture. If your
partner changes his position, change your position to mirror his. Begin
to do this now—the taller person mirroring the shorter one. As you do
this, be aware of all the details of your partner's position, and be aware
of how you feel as you mirror him. How does this position feel to you?
. . . What does this position express? . . . In what kind of situation might
you stand like this and what would you feel in such a situation? . . .

I want the shorter person to be aware of how you feel as you
see your position reflected in the person who is mirroring you.
Notice what you do when you see some aspect of your mirrored
posture that you don't like. . . . Do you immediately change it and
cover it up? . . . If you do this, realize that you are more interested in
your appearance—maintaining your *image* of yourself—than you are
in becoming more aware of yourself as you actually *are*. The next
time you notice something in your mirrored movements that you
don't like, see if you can become more aware of it. Instead of

covering up, keep doing it or even exaggerate it and discover what this movement or posture expresses about you. If you make this experiment into "just a game," you lose a real opportunity to become more aware of your own and your partner's posture and what this posture expresses. . . .

Now continue this mirroring and at the same time tell each other what you are aware of as you do this. Express all the details of your awareness of yourself and the other person. . . .

Now switch, so that the shorter person mirrors the position and movements of the taller one. Again begin with silent mirroring, and then in a minute or two also tell each other what you are aware of as you do this. . . .

Mirroring Gibberish

Now I want you to focus your attention on what is expressed by sounds without words. I want the shorter person in each pair to speak gibberish: gibberish is any noises you want to make that are not words in any language you know. I want the taller person to listen carefully to this gibberish and be aware of all the details of these sounds, and to repeat these back to him as quickly and as accurately as you can. Don't wait for him to finish a set of noises; immediately mirror these sounds—repeat them with the same loudness, tone of voice, hesitations, etc. (Demonstrate with someone.) Do this for a couple of minutes. . . .

Now switch, so that the taller person speaks gibberish, while the shorter person immediately mirrors all the sounds he makes. Do this for a couple of minutes. . . .

Now take a few minutes to tell each other what you experienced as you did this. Say how you felt and what you were aware of as you mirrored the other person's gibberish, and as you listened to him mirroring your own. What were these noises like, and what do they express? . . .

Mirroring Body

Now *freeze—don't move!* Stay in whatever position you were in when I told you to freeze. Take a minute to be aware of your own position and what it expresses, and also be aware of your partner's position and what it seems to you to express. . . .

Now I want the shorter person to stay frozen in your present position, while the taller one mirrors his frozen posture. Copy all the details of the way his body is positioned. As you do this, be aware of how you feel in this position. . . . Close your eyes briefly and feel what your body is like in this position you have copied. What would you be expressing if you took this position yourself? . . . Now stay in this position and share your awareness and impressions. Tell him what you notice about his posture as you copy it and get into the feel of it, and find out what he is aware of—both within himself, and as he sees you mirroring him. . . .

Mirroring Speech

Next I want you to mirror speech and facial expressions in the same way that you mirrored gibberish. I want the taller person to say anything he wants, while the shorter person immediately repeats whatever he says as quickly and accurately as you can—with the same loudness, tone, hesitations, etc. As you do this, also mirror all the expressive movements of the speaker's face and head. Try to really get the feel of being this other person and be aware of how he expresses himself. (Demonstrate with someone.) Do this for a couple of minutes. . . .

Now switch, so that the shorter person speaks, while the taller one immediately mirrors everything he says and all his facial expressions and movements. Do this for a couple of minutes. . . .

Now take about five minutes to share your experience of doing this. What did you become aware of in yourself and in your partner as you mirrored each other's speech and facial expressions. . . .

Mirroring Body

Now *freeze—don't move!* Stay in whatever position you were in when I told you to freeze. Take a minute to be aware of your own position and what it expresses, and also be aware of your partner's position and what it seems to express. . . .

Now I want the taller person to stay frozen, while the shorter one mirrors his frozen posture. . . . As you copy his posture, be aware of how your body feels in this position. . . . Close your eyes briefly and feel what your body is like in this position. . . . What does this posture express? . . . Now stay in this position and share your awareness and impressions. Tell him what you notice about his posture as you copy it and get into the feel of it, and find out what he is aware of in himself, and as he sees you mirroring him. . . .

Mirroring Simultaneously

Now unfreeze. Next I want you to both mirror each other's position and movements at the same time. Begin by taking the same position and move very slowly so that you are not sure whether you are mirroring him or he is mirroring you. Let it become a slow dance—a dialogue of movement and interaction between you for the next five minutes or so. . . .

Now sit down with your partner and take at least five minutes to review what you have discovered through these experiments, and summarize what each of you expresses about yourself through your body postures, movements, tone of voice, etc. . . .

Now I want you to explore how these non-verbal expressions affect others. Even if you are not aware of them, these non-verbal expressions often have powerful effects on others. A person whose depression is expressed in slumped shoulders, downcast head and eyes, slow dead tone of voice, etc. usually also depresses anyone nearby. What did you feel and how did you respond to your partner's position and movements? For instance, if your partner frequently kept his hands in his pockets, turned away and kept distant from you, how did you respond? Did you tend to respond by giving up getting to know him, or did you feel protective and try to make him feel safer and more comfortable? Take a few minutes to tell each other how you responded to your partner's non-verbal expressions. . . .

As you pay more attention to non-verbal communication, you can regain awareness of what is actually going on in others and in yourself. In most situations people try to achieve agreement or confluence. Confluence means "flowing together," as two streams join together into a single stream. When you and I agree, when our activities flow together without conflict, this confluence is very convenient, very comfortable, and can also be very beautiful. When I have been feeling alone, separate, and different from others, and then find someone with whom I agree, this experience can be overwhelmingly beautiful. But I can only be fully aware of this agreement and sameness as it exists in contrast to disagreement and differentness. As my memory of my previous experience fades, I quickly lose awareness of the areas of agreement between us and I begin to take them for granted. Then the inevitable areas of differentness and conflict between us emerge into our awareness, and appear to be very large and important because I have lost awareness and appreciation of our areas of agreement. This is what happens in most friendships, most love affairs, and most marriages.

Differences and disagreement have to be dealt with, and most people will try to achieve agreement. If real agreement is not possible, most people will then try to achieve the *appearance* of agreement by manipulating themselves or the other person into changing so that the difference disappears. If these efforts fail, the differentness is fought—rejected and pushed away, walled off, or destroyed. At best there is that uneasy truce that is called tolerance.

Confluence is the absence of difference, and conflict is the rejection of difference. The acceptance of difference is called contact, and this provides a third alternative in relationships. Contact is the appreciation of difference: the willingness to become more deeply aware of difference and explore it without trying to change it. Contact is the willingness to be aware of areas of difference, as well as areas of sameness. When I am willing to contact you fully I have no need for dishonesty—either to falsify myself, or to manipulate you. Explore these ideas further through your experiences in the experiments that follow.

Resentments

Pair up with someone with whom you have differences and disagreements, and sit facing this person. . . . Maintain eye contact, and also maintain some kind of physical contact with this person. In a moment I want you to take turns expressing your resentments to each other. Begin each sentence with the words "I resent—" and express clearly exactly what you resent about your partner. When you have finished with a resentment, be silent while your partner expresses a resentment of you. Continue to alternate expressing resentments for about five minutes. If you get stuck, just say "I resent—" and see what words come to you next. Go ahead. . . .

Appreciations

Now I want you to go back over all the resentments you expressed and to cross out the word *resent* and substitute the word *appreciate*. Take turns saying these new sentences to each other. Try them on for size as if you were trying on a shirt. Pause after each sentence to get in touch with how you feel as you say it. Is there some truth in this sentence that begins, "I appreciate—"? For instance, one of my sentences might have been "I resent your pouting and avoiding me when I say something you don't like." When I change this to "I appreciate your pouting and avoiding me when I say something you don't like" I may realize that I do appreciate your avoiding me: I don't have to face your anger and displeasure directly. When you do get some realization of your appreciation, repeat the sentence that begins "I appreciate—" and then add a sentence or two that elaborates on your appreciation. . . .

There is almost always some appreciation of what you resent. If you can discover this appreciation and bring it into the foreground, you will be much more balanced in outlook, and be more aware of both sides of a difficult situation. If your appreciation is quite strong, you may be actually encouraging the behavior that you resent without realizing it. For instance, often the wife of an alcoholic wants to feel superior to someone and really appreciates having a helpless alcoholic spouse much more than she resents the inconvenience. If the alcoholic stops drinking, she may sneer and nag him back into drinking so that she can feel superior to him again. Likewise, most of us resent our parents' advice or meddling in our affairs, but we may not trust our own judgment, so we appreciate letting them make difficult decisions for us—and then we can appreciate blaming them if the decision turns out badly!

Often the major problem is simply the fact that a minor resentment is not expressed. Just expressing resentments and appreciations can often bring you back to balance, or open up communication enough for one or both of you to adjust easily to suit the other. If a resentment remains very strong, it is often more useful to work it out first in dialogue with yourself in fantasy, than with the other person in reality. Then when you are less confused and conflicted with yourself, you can return to the other person and continue to work things out with him. There are also some other things you can do to help open up communication about a problem area of disagreement and conflict.

Differences

Sit facing each other and maintain eye contact. Tell each other all the ways that you differ and disagree, and how you *feel* about these differences. Don't blame, justify, or argue, etc.; just state the differences between you as you see them. Be as clear, as specific, and as detailed as you can about these differences, and also be very detailed about your feelings about these differences. Do this for at least five minutes. . . .

Stating the Other's Position

Many difficulties are caused not by the actual differences between people, but by the imagined differences that result from misunderstanding. Now I want you to go over your important areas of disagreement again. I want you each to clearly state your understanding of your *partner's* position and feelings *until he is satisfied that you understand him.* If he is not satisfied with the way you have stated his position, listen carefully while he tells you again. Then restate your understanding of what he has said in your own words until he agrees. Take about five minutes to do this. . . .

Responding to Feelings

Now I want you to see to what extent you can accept and respond to your partner's feelings and experiences, even if you still disagree with his opinions and actions that result from his experiencing. These feelings and experiences are facts, and if you can accept, explore and deepen your awareness of these facts, you can get quite a lot of understanding of each other. Take some time now to really explore the feelings and experiences that underlie your disagreements. See if you can express your acceptance of at least some aspects of your partner's position in these disagreements between you. . . .

Now share your experiences in these experiments with each other. What did you become aware of in yourself and in your partner? Take another five minutes to explore your experiences. . . .

When you really explore the feelings and experiences that you have in a disagreement, you often find that the real difficulty has little to do with what you are arguing about. An argument about where to go on a vacation might be only a symptom of two people's assumptions: "If you loved me, you'd do it my way," and "If you respected me, you'd do it my way." The fears behind these assumptions are quite similar: "I'm afraid you don't love/respect me." The feelings beneath these fears may be even more similar: feelings of inadequacy, emptiness, loneliness, etc. At this deeper level, you will often discover that you and your partner actually have a great deal in common. Your surface disagreement may be only an expression of the differences in the way that you each avoid or cope with very similar feelings and experiences.

No decision about the vacation can be really satisfactory unless these deeper levels of experience are recognized, expressed, and listened to. When I get in touch with my experience and express it to you and you really listen to me, I probably won't care where we go on vacation! On the other hand, sometimes significant and disturbing differences remain between us, even after this deeper exploration. In this case we can at least accept that these differences exist. We can stop trying to change each other to eliminate these differences, and stop blaming each other when these manipulations aren't successful.

The real world of contact and awareness sometimes has pain, conflict, and other unpleasantness. It also has pleasure, satisfying activities, joy, and participation. If I stay in contact with whatever my own reality and my surroundings offer me, I can make the most out of my living. If I reject reality because it is not perfectly ideal, I only add confusion to my pain and lose whatever satisfactions and pleasures I do have. Loss without gain is a bad bargain.

To the Group Leader or Teacher

The methods described in this book are powerful tools for self-exploration and self-expression. Any tools can be used skillfully or clumsily, or they can be unused or misused. A hammer can be left on a shelf, where it is only a piece of junk, or it can be put to good use driving nails. A hammer can also be used to knock a hole in a board or to smash someone's thumb. I am particularly concerned with pointing out some of the ways these tools can be misused.

The aim of all these experiments is to help people rediscover their own awareness of what they are actually experiencing, *whatever that experience may be.* Sometimes people will discover pleasant experiences—comfort, joy, love, etc., and sometimes relatively unpleasant experiences—anger, grief, confusion, etc. Whatever a person discovers, *his experience must be respected.* There are many ways that a person's experience can be disrespected. Here are a few of the commonest ways: *judgment, helping, shoulds,* and *explaining.*

Judgment Some of the experiences and images that people have will seem strange, unfamiliar, or even bizarre to some people. Any judgment, scorn, jeering laughter, etc., is a condemnation of the experience and will not encourage people to explore themselves more deeply. The leader must be open enough to accept and acknowledge a person's experience, however strange it may seem. The leader must also be able to stop judgment by others, whether it is verbal or non-verbal. If someone judges the experience of another, there are two things you can do. First, you can point out that this person is judging and that this is a "mind" or fantasy activity, and not awareness. Secondly, you can explore the *experience* of the person who judges. He might experience fear, puzzlement, disgust, etc., and this is *his* valid experience. "I feel uncomfortable" is an experience, while "You are crazy" is a judgment. In judging, I blame and condemn you for my experience.

Helping One of the commonest (and also widely accepted) ways of not respecting a person's experience is to rush in with help when a person is feeling "bad" or uncomfortable. Being "helpful" with reassurance, jokes, comfort, etc., prevents the person from fully experiencing his grief, anger, aloneness, etc. Only through experiencing it fully can he accept it, assimilate it into his total life experience, and grow into a more complete and integrated human being. Almost always the "helper" actually helps *himself* by helping others. By rushing in with a band-aid, he stops the expression of feelings which are painful for *him* to feel. He also convinces himself and others that he is capable of helping others and doesn't need help himself. Almost every "helper" has strong feelings of helplessness which diminish temporarily when he helps someone else. This is true of a great many people in the "helping" professions: teachers, psychologists, and especially social workers. If you have this symptom, you will have to explore it in yourself and accept your own feelings of helplessness before you can really help others. Try a fantasy dialogue with someone you help, and play both roles to discover how you help yourself by helping others.

There is a widespread assumption that a person who is in difficulties is weak and needs help. In one sense this is true, because so much of his energy is spent in manipulation of himself and manipulation of others that he has very little energy left for direct coping with the world. If you "help" such a person, you encourage him in his delusion that he needs you to help him, and you increase his investment in manipulating you to come to his rescue. But if you insist that he get more in touch with his own experience, he can come to realize the tremendous energy and power he expends in manipulating both himself and others in order to get support from others. As he assimilates this energy, he can learn to use it more directly for his own self-support. He can realize that he can do many things for himself that he previously thought he needed others to do for him.

Everyone has a great deal of unused potential. Most people are much more capable, more intelligent, stronger and more able than either they or you believe. A great deal of the weakness, stupidity, and craziness in the world is not real; it is playing weak, playing stupid, and playing crazy. Think of the strength in playing weak so that everyone else runs to your rescue and does your work for you! Consider the intelligence in playing stupid so that others will do your thinking for you and be there to take the blame when it doesn't work out! Realize the sanity in the crazy behavior that manipulates others drastically, yet appears to be incomprehensible and beyond control and responsibility!

If you set yourself up to help someone, you also set yourself up to be manipulated in these ways. If you take responsibility for yourself and insist that others also do this, you become immune to these manipulations. Fritz Perls used to begin his seminars by saying "If you want to go crazy, commit suicide, improve, get 'turned on,' or get an experience that will change your life, that's up to you. I do my thing and you do your thing. Anybody who does not want to take the responsibility for this, please do not attend this seminar."

Although many people try to take responsibility for others, it is actually impossible. I can only be responsible for myself and for what I do. Even when I "take responsibility" for a small child, I can only be responsible for what *I* do and not for what he does. A lot of "taking responsibility" for someone else is actually a thin disguise for strong demands on him, an investment that must be repaid with compound interest: "After all I've done for you, surely it's not too much to ask—"

The way to really help someone is not to help him do anything but become more aware of his own experience—his feelings, his actions, his fantasies—and insist that he explore his own experience more deeply and take responsibility for it, no matter what that experience is. Often this means pointing out how the person is avoiding his experience, and frustrating his avoidance. If a person is sad, he must explore it and experience it more deeply before he can assimilate it and grow. If a person is angry, he must really feel and express this anger before he can admit it into his life. The only way out is *through.*

Shoulds If you in any way say or imply that a person "should" have a particular kind of experience in any experiment, this image will obscure experience. If you try to counteract the artificial "shoulds" of society with new "shoulds" of your own, all you do is create an additional layer of artificiality and phoniness. Then the individual has two "shoulds" to contend with, putting him even farther away from his own experience, and making his life even "shoulddier." For instance, I have seen leaders who have said or implied that people should enjoy experiments in which people touch each other. Touching is an important human need, and many people do enjoy these experiments and discover how important this experience is for them. Other people feel distaste or disgust during touching experiments, and this is their valid experience.

There is no "right" or "correct" response to any of these experiments. There is only one "should" in this book—and expecially in this section—and that is that you should get in touch with your own experience, whatever that is: that *you should be what you actually are* at the moment. If you are experiencing something, experience it; if you are avoiding something, realize that you are avoiding it; if you are lying, be aware that you are lying; if you are imagining, realize that you are occupied with a fantasy.

Whatever your experience is, you have to begin where you are and start your journey of self-discovery there. There is an old story that illustrates the futility of trying to start from anywhere else: A man gets very lost in the winding country roads of Vermont, and finally stops at a field to ask directions from a farmer. "How can I get to New York?" The farmer chews on his grass-stem thoughtfully for awhile and then says, "Mister, if I was you I wouldn't start from here!" No matter how lost and confused I am, I have to start from here—with my experience of being lost and confused. It may be a *poor* place to start, but there is no alternative—it is the *only* place to start.

Explaining Seeking causes and reasons, interpreting, explaining, etc., are all widely-accepted ways of "understanding" your experience. In fact, these are actually all ways of *avoiding* your experience, which may account for their popularity. Explaining, interpreting, justifying, etc., are all fantasy activities—*talking about* experience and not *expressions of* that experience. As soon as you begin to explain your experience, you start to lose contact with the experience itself, and get lost in a jungle of whys, becauses, ifs, and buts. If you want to lose yourself in this jungle, that's your responsibility, but don't drag others into your morass by interpreting and explaining what is happening to them.

Your interpretations are your own projections, whether they are "correct" or not. And even if they are "correct," they are irrelevant to the person's own experiencing and can only reduce his awareness of himself. This is the major defect of all but a very few encounter groups. A great deal of time is spent in all sorts of interpretations, opinions, blaming games, guessing games, etc. Often any genuine encounter or awareness is drowned and lost in these interpretations. To help a person get more in touch with his own experiencing, seek the details of that experiencing, not the "reasons" for it. "How do you feel?" "What are you experiencing?" "What is going on in you now?" "What do you feel physically?" are all useful questions that can help a person get more in touch with the specific details of what he is experiencing.

The whole approach presented in this book is the value and importance of experiencing and becoming aware of what *is*. As a group leader you can't take responsibility for the group or anyone in it but you can do what you can to keep people's attention focused on awareness, and try to eliminate anything that interferes with this. It's valuable if you have some experience of working with people and responding sensitively to what is happening in them and between them, so that the experiments you use are most fruitful. If a group is feeling fairly good about each other, an experiment involving touching and physical expression of feelings can help people to open up even more. But if a group is very nervous, defensive, or antagonistic, you have to acknowledge this and work with clarifying and making explicit whatever is going on at the time.

If a group is very scared and you try to bring them together with a touching experiment, either it won't work at all or you will only succeed in covering up the fear with an artificial closeness. Often there is a good deal of nervous laughter, giggling, deadness, or other symptoms of avoidance and fear at the beginning of a session. One way to work with this is to take some time to express these feelings and the fantasies that generate them. Another way is to spend some time in quiet withdrawal and contacting the feelings and sensations of physical experience, etc. If some giggling persists—for example during the beginning of a fantasy trip—I ask people to leave the room if they can't stop their giggling or otherwise disturbing others. There are some people who have no willingness to explore their awareness, and I have no objection to that as long as they don't interfere with the others in the group.

An ideal size of group for many of these experiments is about fourteen to sixteen people. This is large enough to provide a good variety of people, and is still small enough to allow plenty of contact. If a group is larger than eighteen or twenty, there is more likelihood that it will be scattered and that contacts will be shallower and more diffuse. With groups larger than twenty, spend a lot of time in smaller sub-groups so that each individual has opportunity for direct contact with a smaller number of people at a time. You can start with some pairs experiments, and then move to experiments involving four, six or eight people, and then conclude with the whole group together for sharing experiences and discussion. This is particularly useful if you ask that people initially pair up with people that they don't know well, or pair up with people they resent or feel uncomfortable with, or use some other method of pairing that will increase the likelihood of contact between people.

It would be ideal if each person had exactly as much time as he wants for each experiment. When you are working with a group of people, you can only hope to arrange the timing so that most people have enough time or a little more. Inevitably some people will finish early and have "nothing to do," while others will still be incomplete long after everyone else has finished. You can keep track of how far along people are, and adjust the time accordingly. You can usually tell pretty well what is happening by looking at postures and listening briefly to the sounds that people are making in the different groups. The times given in this book are only suggestions. The size of the group makes a big difference, and some people take much more time than others do. Sometimes one talker will take as much as half of the group's time. If you see this happening, ask him to send telegram sentences for awhile. You can also give an advance warning near the end of a sharing period: "I want you to finish up in the next couple of minutes."

Some groups really invest themselves deeply in an experiment and have a rich experience that will take more time to share and explore. Other groups will be much less involved and will have only a little to share. If you see this happening, you can ask the uninvolved group to get in touch with their uninvolvement and express it. As they do this, they will become at least somewhat more involved. If you see that some groups are moving more slowly than others, you can visit each group briefly to ask the slower ones to speed up a bit, and ask the faster ones to take a bit more time and go into more detail. If a group finishes quite early, you can give them another short experiment to do while the other groups are finishing.

When you are working with several groups or pairs at once in the same room, it's convenient to have some way of getting everyone's attention at the end of a discussion period when you want to go on to another experiment. Clapping your hands is the easiest way, but many people object to this. A small bell works well, and fewer people object. If someone objects to this, ask them to take the responsibility for finding a better way of getting attention.

The experiments in this book are written in a form that I have found most useful, and they are gathered into sections of similar experiments so that you can find them more easily. When you use several experiments in one session, choose different kinds of experiments so that you involve people with different aspects of their experiencing. You can begin with less threatening experiments and gradually move toward experiments that involve more personal risk. You can begin with a quiet period of turning inward, and a fantasy in which people can explore their own private world without fear of rejection. Then later each person can decide how much of their personal world they are willing to share with others. Be sure that you allow time to absorb an experience before going on to something else. There are countless variations and combinations of these experiments. I have presented mirroring as a pair activity. It can also be useful to have a whole group mirror an individual at once, although in this case only one person can see himself mirrored at a time. Most of the fantasy journeys are presented as group activities so that people can also share their inner experiences with others, but the fantasy itself can of course be done in pairs, or by an individual alone by himself.

Although all these experiments are written for adults, most of them are also applicable to children of all ages. The instructions will have to be simplified to communicate clearly with younger children. Many of these experiments will work better with children. Small children are usually much more in touch with their own experiencing, much more aware, more spontaneous, and less confused than adults.

These experiments can be used in any classroom exactly as presented here, or as a separate activity to bring the class together and establish open communication. Establishing good communication and working through some personal difficulties will result in much better comprehension and retention, *whatever the subject matter*. A few classes can be spent in some of these experiments at the beginning of the year, with other experiments every couple of weeks during the year to maintain and continue to develop good communication. A few days spent in these experiments will be more than regained, because so much less time will be wasted in disruptions, fruitless struggles and arguments, student-teacher infighting, etc.

Many of these experiments can also be integrated into the

subject-matter of the class. Many of the basic awareness experiments exemplify the scientific method of observation, hypothesis, testing against reality through experimentation, etc. There are even more opportunities to use this approach in social studies and government classes. Role-playing of historic conflicts can bring understanding of history, as well as understanding of conflict and experience with alternative methods of conflict resolution between groups or individuals. Instead of *talking about* different forms of government, you can ask your students to form themselves into different kinds of government and *experience* them. Let them discover what these different kinds of social organization are like, and let them realize the difference between the democracy that you preach and the tyranny (benevolent or not) that you probably teach through your actions in the classroom. A lot of time is usually spent teaching about the mechanics of democracy—voting, legislatures, levels of government, etc. Usually much less time is spent on the really fundamental process of democracy: that everyone has a say in the government, and that all these different views are respected as they come together to work out some kind of solution through open and reasonable discussion. Usually almost no time at all is spent in actually *practicing* democracy. Democracy is based on the idea of communication instead of merely power, authority, and fighting. Anything you can do to increase communication in your class will reduce your need to impose order by authority, and reduce the student's need to rebel against that authority. The class will become more a place for listening and learning, and less a place for fighting and antagonism.

The experiments that deal with anxiety, self-consciousness, and the fantasies that cause these symptoms are very useful in developing simple self-confidence. Drama, public speaking, or any other class that requires a performance in front of others can be made much more productive and creative by using these experiments.

Many of these experiments can be used directly in art classes to let self-expression blossom into artistic expression in different media. Our society tends to focus on technical competence in the arts. Letting feelings and images flow into expressive media is the basic and fundamental *process* of artistic expression. Learning to focus on and become aware of the "shoulds" and rules that block expression can do a lot to release this process.

The humming and sound experiments can be used in music and singing classes, both to reduce tension and self-consciousness, and also to let inner feeling resources flow into musical expression and composition. Fantasy journeys and many of the other experiments are excellent stimuli for creative expression through writing. I even know a typing teacher who had all his students do the rosebush fantasy trip with their arms folded on their typewriters. Then he asked them to type out their experiences. He graded the papers for typing errors, etc., just as he would any other assignment, and he also got a very personal statement from each of his students. The ten minutes he spent with this fantasy gave him more understanding of his students' existence and feelings than an entire semester of being with them. This understanding spontaneously brought many changes in his attitudes and behavior toward many of his students. Even if you use only a few of these experiments in a small way, you can see definite results. The more you work with these experiments yourself, and become familiar with this approach, the more creative you will be in seeing ways of adapting these methods to your situation— inventing new experiments, and using these methods in whatever you do.

Anything can be done with awareness or without awareness, and the experiments in this book are no exception. You can turn every one of them into superficial party games by insisting that everything be fun. You can make them all into grim drudgery if you attempt to force unwilling people into them or insist that it is all very serious. If you are on a self-improvement program, you can grind diligently through them like a boy scout collecting merit badges and gold stars.

But if you do these experiments with awareness, you can discover more and more about your experiencing and functioning, and this approach can become more and more an integral part of whatever you do.

Fantasy Journeys

Each of the fantasies in this section will be much more effective if they are preceded by instructions to take a comfortable position with eyes closed and focus attention on inner experience: get in touch with physical sensations, breathing, etc. It is impossible to get fully involved with your inner fantasy life if you are tense and still preoccupied with recent memories and thoughts about external reality.

These fantasy journeys will also be much more valuable if they are immediately told to someone else in the *first-person present tense, as if they were happening now.* This telling deepens the feeling of identification with the fantasy experience and helps you realize that this is not "just a fantasy" but is an important expression of yourself and your life situation. As you tell your experience in the present tense, you often become aware of important details that you were only dimly aware of during the fantasy experience itself. Also, a listener can notice details or aspects that you overlook or ignore, and notice omissions and avoidances that you don't notice. In this way it is possible to explore the fantasy further and become more aware of whatever is slighted, avoided, or omitted.

Another value in immediately telling someone else your fantasy is that you are communicating directly to another person. As you tell him about your feelings and experiences in this fantasy existence, you will often find that what you say is far more honest and personal than your usual way of speaking to others. You will often reveal quite a lot about yourself and your existence, and you can experience how others respond to your honesty. It is valuable to become more aware of yourself, and it is also important to communicate your awareness to someone else so that your life is connected with others in honest contact.

These fantasy journeys may seem somewhat repetitious—especially if you just read them quickly without experiencing them. In a way they are repetitious; they all use the same means—projection into a fantasy situation and then re-identifying through role-playing and dialogue. At the same time, the different fantasy settings *do* make a difference—you will make different discoveries in the different fantasy situations. And you will also discover that some of your main feelings and themes reappear again and again despite the different settings. This is another confirmation that what you experience in these fantasies is a real expression of your existence—how you actually live and feel and function.

These fantasies are most effective if you can become comfortable and close your eyes while someone else reads the instructions to you slowly and with pauses, so that your attention is not divided between your involvement in the fantasy experience and the task of reading the instructions. When you want to take one of these journeys alone by yourself, I suggest that you read over the instructions once or twice so that you remember the overall structure of the fantasy. Then close your eyes, and take your own journey without being too concerned about whether you follow the instructions in detail. There is nothing magic or sacred in these instructions. I have written them out in detail to help you learn what you can discover with the tools of identification, role-playing, and dialogue with your fantasies. After you have had a range of experience with the potential of these methods, you can take your own fantasy journeys and work with whatever you encounter in them on your own.

Immediately following the first fantasy is a verbatim transcript of the responses of a small group and my comments on these responses.

Stump, Cabin, Stream

Now I'd like you to imagine that you are a tree stump in the mountains. *Become* this tree stump. Visualize yourself and your surroundings. ... Take some time to get the feel of being a tree stump. ... It might help to describe yourself. What kind of a stump are you? ... What's your shape? ... What kind of bark and roots do you have? ... Try to get into the experience of being this tree stump. ... What is your existence as a tree stump? ... What kinds of things hapen to you as this stump? ...

Fairly near this stump, there is a cabin. I'd like you now to become this cabin. ... And again, I'd like you to get the flavor of the experience of being this cabin. ... What are you like? ... What are your characteristics? ... Explore your existence as a cabin. ... What do you have inside you, and what happens to you? ... Take some time to get in touch with being this cabin. ...

Near this cabin, there is a stream. I'd like you now to become this stream. As a stream, what kind of existence do you have? ... What kind of a stream are you? ... How do you feel as a stream? ... What kinds of experiences do you have as a stream? ... What are your surroundings like? ...

As this stream, I would like you to talk to the cabin. What do you say to the cabin? ... Talk to the cabin and imagine that the cabin answers back, so that you have a dialogue, a conversation. ... As this stream, what do you say to this cabin and what does the cabin answer back? ... Now become the cabin again and continue the conversation. What do you have to say to the stream? ... Continue this dialogue for awhile. ... (You can also have dialogues between the stump and cabin, or between the stump and the stream.)

Now say goodbye to the mountains. Say goodbye to the cabin, the stream, the stump, and come back here to this room and your existence here. ... Open your eyes when you feel like it. ...

Now I'd like each of you to express your experience of being the stump, the cabin, and the stream. And I want you to do this in the *first-person present tense:* "*I am—*" "As a stump, I am old and twisted. I am sawed off level and chipmunks sit on me and crack nuts," or whatever *your* experience of being a stump is like. . . .

Don't read the responses and discussion that follows until you have experienced this fantasy yourself.

Responses and Comments

Rene: (vigorously) I *loved* it. I really had a nice time. I am a very tall stump, very tall and thin. I am cut—when they cut me off I was left very high and was growing, branches were—branches *are* growing on me and leaves are coming out and I know that I'll grow up very tall and be a very tall tree very soon.

And I am a cabin. I have a nice rug inside the cabin. I have a warm, orange rug inside of me, and I have warm furniture, and I like—sometimes in me—the cabin feels empty and lonely and I like it more when I have a lot of people, nice people inside the cabin. And I sometimes like the noise of children. But I usually like the noise of friends inside me more.

And I am a stream that starts out very strong, and then I get softer and I stay there, and I want to stay in this one place. I don't want to just run and keep going. I don't want to be a very long stream and keep going. I like being near this cabin and I am very warm, uh, I started being cold and I didn't like it being cold and I feel that I like being warm, and I want all the people in the cabin to come and enjoy the warmth of the stream. And I really liked—oh, I *really* liked it, it was really—it felt really nice.

Leader (L): Did you have any conversation between the—

Rene: Yeah, you know, that's what I was saying—the stream was saying, "I'm warm and I want to stay here," and the cabin was saying, "I like it here, I like it warm and full." It was a very nice trip.

Abby: (rapidly) I am a short, fat, sawed-off stump, charcoal burned—for some reason I was in a fire and I'm all black. And I have eyes and the eyes are looking around, and I see a cabin. I'm a log cabin, all—

L: Is there any more to your stump?

Abby: No, there's—nooo.

L: How did you feel as a stump?

Abby: I wanted to get out of there.

L: You didn't like being a stump.

Abby: I felt like I was in there and I wanted to get out very badly and those eyes were poking out, seeing, looking around for some way to get out of there—a *horrible* place to be stuck. And then I saw this cabin, and it was a tremendous relief because the minute I heard that, I jumped up and ran over and became the cabin and I'm very rough logs, very rough wood, very rustic and I have bear rugs on the floor. And on my left side I have a fireplace and it's very warm. And I have people in me. I like it when the people are there. I don't like it when the people leave. (short laugh)

Then I became the stream, and I like it because I'm moving very fast, and I like to move fast. I like the feeling of the motion, but it's lonely being a stream, 'cause there aren't people. Once in a while someone will fish into me, jab me with one of those hooks. And once in a while somebody'll bump over me in a boat, and I feel kind of abused—except that I'm going so fast. Even though I don't quite know where I'm going, it's nice to be going so fast.

Then I talk to the cabin and I say, "Hah, hah, you're stuck over there and I'm moving, hah, hah, hah. You know, here you're just stuck there all by yourself, and I'm just really going someplace."

And the cabin says back—I say "Yeah, but look at all the groovy people I have here that are talking by the warm fire, having a good time, and I get to take this all in. It's better being here."

And the stream would say "Yes, but the people will leave and you'll be lonely, and you won't be getting anywhere."

L: I'm curious—you said the fireplace is on the left side of your cabin. /Abby: Uhuh./ What's on the right side?

Abby: I don't know. . . . Nothing.

L: Close your eyes and take a look.

Abby: Ohh. . . . toward the front, on the right, there's a kitchen, and a sink. And as the cabin I'd say, "Yes, and I have water in me, too, flowing in the sink." But there's nothing on the right side until you get to the kitchen up toward the front.

L: How do you feel about the right side?

Abby: I feel very different from it. I'm closer to the left. /L: Yeah./ (short laugh) That means something? Does that mean I'm a "leftist?" (laughter) Oh! it's funny, because—*Hey!* that's amazing because when you first said get aware of your body, my left contact lens was bothering me, and my left leg was itching, and *Yes!* /L: You were aware of your left side, but not of your right./ I was aware of my left side. *Yes.* What does that mean?

L: It means that you're not in touch with your right side. (laughter) /Abby: Is that all?/ Well, there's probably more to it than that. I don't know what's there. But you can discover what's there— either by exploring your cabin further, or by just getting in touch with your right side.

George: Well, I'm a very large stump—I think a redwood. I'm very high up overlooking a valley, cut off rough on top with a saw. I'm very concerned—my roots are long roots that are exposed, trying to get into the rock. I have a very hard time being a stump because I'm not sure if it's my arms or my legs that are the roots that are trying to hang onto this rock. And yet I'm not particularly aware that I'm going to slip off the mountain, either, and in fact I think I really want to be off the mountain. I don't want to be a stump just sitting there.

As a cabin I'm very concerned with how my shape as a cabin is. Am I standing up on all four legs or am I lying down, being a comfortable cabin? But not very much about what kind of cabin.

And as a stream, I don't know if I'm a stream that—something that's going from here in the mountains all the way to the ocean, or if I'm just a piece of the stream, or if I'm water in the stream. . . . And the cabin and the tree keep telling me, "You're lucky because you get to see the sea." And yet I'm not really sure that I do get to see the sea. And the parallel that goes through all of these is unsureness: Exactly how am I what I am, and how am I?

Jean: I'm a stump, and I'm—I'm in a forest. And I realize that all the forest has been burned, and I was burned and keep thinking that's not what I want. I have all these things inside me—I think that's what I'm not—and then I say, "No, that's what I really am—you know, a burned forest." And I don't have any particular feelings about myself as a stump, so I try, and I'm a cabin and I can't be a cabin—I just can't, uh, I try to think of being a cabin and nothing comes, as a cabin. I have logs—I'm a log cabin. The first thing I got when you said cabin was I was a log cabin, but I couldn't do anything about it. I couldn't be in it, and I couldn't be it, and I couldn't feel. /L: You went into the past tense. Tell it in the present./

And then I become a stream, and I like being a stream. I was real happy as a stream. I had fish in me and I had a deer—and a bear came down and had a drink. I visited with the bear and the deer. /L: Present tense./ I feel really free being the stream and I tried to talk to the cabin and I couldn't get anything. I couldn't even talk to the cabin. I didn't know anything about the cabin. . . .

L: You feel good as the stream. /J: Yes./ The others you couldn't get into. /J: No./ You went back to the past tense repeatedly. That's a way of putting distance between you and your experience. You have a lot to discover still.

Jean: (joking) A cabin.

L: Your "cabinness" and your "stumpness."

Mary: (softly) I'm a short stump and there are trees all around me; they're looking down on me, and I see a little tiny patch of sky wayyy up there someplace. And I have absolutely no feelings whatsoever. I can't feel anything—being a stump or a cabin or a stream—I don't actually feel anything. And I'm not a stump very long.

And when I become a cabin, it's kind of bad, because I'm empty, and I've got a lot of windows, but there's no curtains up or anything. There's no furniture. I think I enjoy being a stream most of all, because I'm bubbly and there's some pebbles in me, but at least that's better than not having anything in me at all. We can't talk together, there's no dialogue at all between my stream and my cabin. I guess that's it.

L: O.K. You say you have no feelings about this, and yet you say that you enjoy being a stream, and that being a cabin was "bad."

M: Well, I have kind of a bad feeling, thinking about it after it was all over with.

L: So you did have some feelings about that.

M: Yes, but not while I was actually being a cabin.

L: You didn't like being this cabin, later.

M: I don't think so.

L: Could you elaborate?

M: I think it's that I don't like the idea of being empty and not having any curtains or anything. There are all those windows and everybody can look in at me. (short laugh)

L: And when you were a stump, the other trees were looking down at you too.

Virginia: (thoughtfully) I'm an old gray weathered stump. There's some kind of disintegration, because I can see myself as having lines and darkness where the wood is worn away. I'm on a mountain-top, and there are no other trees around me. But out of me, in spite of my age, comes a very green, sturdy shoot, with the kind of green leaves I can see on me that signify a very healthy tree. And I'm aware, in my fantasy, of lots of peaks and bright blue sky and exciting views. And I have the thought, "Why, out of an old stump like that, in an exposed situation, would I have such a healthy-looking shoot?" But that's just the way it is and I don't care about questions anyway.

So then I shift to a cabin and I see a very new cabin and I see the exposed edges of the cabin where the logs are cut, being painted with some kind of sealer that makes them sort of shiny and very new. And I don't see any people in this cabin. There may be animals coming around but it's very new and it's very bare and it— /L: Instead of "it," say "I."/ *I* am very new and very bare and I don't have any sheltering trees, but I don't seem to need them particularly.

I then shift to the stream. I'm an extremely happy stream, I feel the essence of being a stream is the essence of all kinds of experimentation. I leap *way* up in the air and I *dash* against rocks, and then I deliberately go and coil into placid little eddies, and then I meander here and there. I have lots of animals coming and lots of people. Sometimes I'm broad like the Russian river, with lots of little children, and sometimes I'm narrow, and people are fishing.

And I call up to the cabin, "Why don't you be free and experimental as I am? Why are you so new, and just sitting there?" And the cabin answers, "I don't know what I'm built for, and I'm very new, but I'll find my way in my way." As a cabin, I didn't feel any need to be the stream. And the stream seemed to be satisfied with that.

L: O.K. What do any of you get from this?

Virginia: I got a split, for myself. And I saw it in other people, too. I get some left—I don't know what significance it has, but I get some left and right handedness. I see my cabin here on my left and my stream here on my right as I visualize it. I noticed that when it was pointed out that Abby's fireplace was on the left. I thought, "Well, where's mine?" I see the push-pull—the stability and rooted-ness of the cabin and the expressive freedom of the stream. And I see in my cabin—which interests me—the loneliness, the newness, the lack of knowing where it was going. The lack of people in the house and the joyous abundance of people with the stream shows a split.

L: You notice there didn't seem to be any split in yours, Rene. /Rene: A split?/ Yeah, Virginia is saying she was quite different as the cabin and as the stream. And you felt much the same in all three. Isn't that right? /Rene: Yeah./ There was warmth, vigor and enjoyment and things happening, no matter what I asked you to become.

Mary: I could only see one little part—one little part of my cabin, of myself as a cabin inside. And I don't know whether it was left or right. That didn't come through at all, but it was just sort of over to a side, but I don't know which side. I guess it would have to be the left side, because (gesturing) this was the wall and there was everything over here, but all I could see was just this part—/L: A little bit of the left side./ At the time it didn't occur to me that it was the left side, but now that I think about it, I guess it must have been.

L: And what do you see there on the left?

Mary: Not much of anything really—all those windows! (laughs nervously) I don't like that cabin *at all!* (continues to laugh) And I'll probably never *forget* it, either. . . . It's very significant to me—everybody looking in at me, and that bare room—I don't like that. I like being the stream the best, it makes me feel the most comfortable.

L: Most people enjoy the stream. It has the freedom and spontaneity. It hops and jumps, and so on.

Mary: You can do your own thing as a stream.

Rene: I was thinking—I really feel that if I had done this a month ago, I would have been a different stump.

Jean: You were a tall stump?

Rene: (strongly) I was tall, and I saw those *green* leaves and I—you know, I *feel* those green leaves. You know, they're gonna come out and it's gonna grow and nothing is gonna stop them.

L: Do you hear the "green leaves" in her voice? (several agree).

Rene: Yeah, they're *there.* My dreams are like that, too!

L: Well, there are two basic ideas behind this. One is that if you let go and just be with yourself and get in touch with yourself, everything is there. You can find yourself just by staying with yourself and listening. The other idea is that of saying "I" to identify with your own experience. Identify with your fantasy, identify with your physical experience, identify with your feelings. Every time you say "I," you get a little bit closer, a little more in touch with yourself. This is why I ask you to identify with your fantasy, both while you have it and as you report it. And I don't mean the "I" that says, "I am such a wonderful person, I do all these things so much better than others." That I is the "ego trip" comparing game that takes you away from yourself. I mean simply that you identify with your experience. "I am having this experience, I am thinking these things, feeling these feelings, doing these actions." "I am a bare cabin, with many people looking in," or "I am an old decaying stump with one very healthy shoot growing up," or whatever your experience is.

There is no right or wrong to such an experience, it simply *is.* Society or parents say "This is right, this is wrong, you should be this and not that," and if we comply with this we lose touch with what we *are*. Identifying with your fantasy is one way of regaining contact with yourself as you are now. At another time your experience may be quite different. And as you talk about your experiences in this fantasy, it comes through very clearly, particularly for some people, that *this is you*. When you identify with your fantasy it is no longer "just a fantasy" but an expression of *yourself*. It might be hard for you to realize this for yourself, particularly if your experience is unpleasant. But as others expressed their fantasies, I'm sure some of you could see that this really expressed the person.

Rene: Yes, I really feel like I got to know some people through this.

L: When we are asked to introduce ourselves to other people, what we usually say is mostly bullshit. We give our "name, rank and serial number"—what kind of work we do, how many kids we have, etc. But if you take a little fantasy journey like this and identify with it, you *really* introduce yourself; you really begin to get in touch with what is going on in you. I simply ask you to be a stump—and look at the variety of things that different people discover through being a stump. For many people, being a stump brings out feelings of being a cut-down tree—feelings of lost or reduced potential. Yet here we have two examples of stumps that are full of life and vigorous growth. What you find in your stump is so much you, that this is an excellent way of discovering what is going on in you—or at *least* a way of discovering that you are *not* in touch. Several people here had some difficulty in getting in touch with their fantasy. Jean, you had difficulty in being the stump and the cabin; you didn't feel much, and you didn't have any dialogue between the cabin and the stream. Mary, you were only in touch with a little bit of the left side of your cabin, and others had varying degrees of contact with different parts of your fantasies.

Most people have some degree of left-right division. Usually the left side has to do with characteristics that our culture defines as being feminine: sensitivity, receptivity, taking in, warmth—Abby's fireplace is on her left side. The right side usually has to do with "masculine" things: activity, strength, aggression, being outgoing, etc. Several women here were much more in touch with their left side, the feminine aspects of their presonality, and mostly out of touch with their right side. For men it is usually the reverse. To be a whole person, you have to be in good contact with both aspects of your personality, so that you can be both open and sensitive to the world *and* able to take action in the world.

I'd like to say one more thing. If you encounter unpleasantness in your fantasy experience, that doesn't mean that you are stuck with this unpleasantness for the rest of your life. It does mean that you have something unpleasant to deal with, something to work through and experience more fully. What we usually do is to *avoid* unpleasantness—*and then avoid the fact that we are avoiding.* This is the *alienation* process. This is how we push away problems: these painful experiences are not dealt with and continue to influence our lives outside our awareness. What we did here is just the reverse of alienation: *Identification.* And you can all discover more on your own. You can go back to that same cabin, or to your tree stump, and discover more about your life. If you are willing to stay with any unpleasantness that comes up and really identify with it and get in touch with it, then the dead, chopped, burned tree stump will begin to sprout and grow and you will experience more movement and energy in your life.

Thoughts

Be aware of whatever thoughts, words or images are going through your mind. ... Now imagine that you are in a good-sized room with two large doorways in opposite walls. Imagine that your thoughts and images come into this room through one doorway and then go out of the room through the other doorway. Just watch your thoughts as they move into the room, stay for awhile, and then move out of the room again. ... What are they like? ... What do they do while they are in the room? ... How do they come in, and how do they go out? ... Are they in a rush, or do they stay awhile so that you can see them clearly? ...

Now be aware of what happens if you close the *exit* door. ... Now open it again. ... Now close the *entrance* door, and notice what happens. . . . Now open it again. . . . Now close both doors at once, and trap some of your thoughts in this room with you. . . . Examine them as carefully as you can. What are they like, how do they act, and what do they do? . . . How do you feel towards these thoughts, and how do they respond to you? . . . Talk to them now, . . . and let them answer you. . . . What do you say to them, and what do they reply? . . .

Now become your thoughts, and continue the dialogue. . . . As thoughts, what are you like, and what do you do? . . . How do you feel as thoughts, and what do you say to yourself? . . .

Now become yourself again and continue this dialogue. Be aware of the relationship between you and these thoughts, and bring this awareness into the dialogue. For example, if you feel frustrated, tell thoughts "You frustrate me" and see what thoughts answer to this. Switch places whenever you want to, and continue this dialogue. See what more you can learn about each other. . . .

Resentment-Appreciation

Think of someone you really resent—someone who annoys and disturbs you, or someone with whom you have some difficulty. Imagine that this person is in front of you, facing you and looking at you. Visualize this person in detail. What is he wearing? . . . How does his face look, and how does he look at you? . . . Now express your resentments directly *to* this person: "Bob, I resent—" Be very specific, and say exactly what you resent about this person. Try to get the feel of actually communicating with him. . . . Take some time and express a long list of resentments to this person. . . .

Now go through this same list of resentments and cross out the word *resent* and substitute the word *appreciate* and say this to this person. Pause after you have said it, as if you were trying on a shirt for size. Notice how you feel as you say the sentence, and see if any realization come to you. For instance, if my resentment is "I resent your weakness, because I have to do things for you," when I go back I might say, "I appreciate your weakness; it makes me feel strong and capable in comparison." Take a few minutes to do this and see if you can discover some appreciation of what you resent. Go ahead. . . .

Weakness-Strength

Close your eyes and turn your attention inward. . . . Get in touch with your physical existence. . . . I want you to have a silent conversation between weakness and strength. I would like you to start by being weakness talking directly to strength. You might start out with something like "I'm so weak, and you're so strong, you can do so many things," etc. Be weakness and talk to strength for a little while, and be aware of how you feel, physically, as you do this. . . . Go into some specific details about how you are weak, and how he is strong. . . .

Now switch roles and become strength replying to weakness. . . . What do you say as strength, and how do you say it? . . . How do you feel in this role? . . . And how do you feel toward weakness? . . . Now tell weakness what it does *for* you to be strong. . . . What do you gain by being strong? . . .

Now switch roles and be weakness again. . . . What do you reply to strength, and how do you feel as you do this? . . . Now tell strength what it does *for* you to be weak. . . . What do you gain by being weak? . . . Tell him about the strength in your weakness. Tell him all the advantages of being weak—how you can use your weakness to manipulate others and get them to help you, etc. . . . Go into specific details about the strength of your weakness. . . .

Now become strength again and reply to weakness. . . . What do you say as strength, and how do you feel now? . . . Now talk about the weakness in your strength. Tell about the disadvantages of being strong—how others lean on you and drain your energy, etc. . . . Go into specific details about the weakness of your strength. . . .

Now become weakness again and reply to strength. . . . How do you feel now and what do you say? . . . Continue this dialogue for awhile on your own. Switch roles whenever you want to, but keep up this dialogue between weakness and strength for awhile and see what you can discover. . . .

(This kind of internal dialogue can be immensely useful for pointing out and clarifying the relationship that exists *within the individual,* between any pair of complementary people, roles, qualities or aspects. It can be particularly useful in working toward understanding between conflicting groups of people: teachers and students, blacks and whites, straights and hippies, etc. All our relationships with other people are cluttered by our *images* of each other. If you can identify with the opposition between your own images, and get some clarification and reduction of this opposition, then you can begin to see the real people behind your images and begin to respond to the real people instead of to your images of them. You can also do this kind of experiment using two people to play the opposites and switch back and forth between them. Several examples of this are given in the *Pairs* section. Some other productive sets of opposites are: husband-wife, parent-child, planner-spontaneous person, strange-familiar, helper-helpless, honest-dishonest, boss-employee, neat-sloppy, male-female, responsible-irresponsible, mind-body, stupid-smart, etc. Notice what you have difficulty with in your life, and then reduce this difficulty to a particular person, behavior or quality. Then think of the *opposite* of this person, behavior, or quality and work with it in dialogue. If you really invest yourself in this dialogue, you will discover the symmetry and similarity that lies beneath the apparent opposition. In the example above, there is the strength of weakness and the weakness of strength, and also that both sides are using different means to do the same thing—control each other.)

Communication Reversal

Now focus your attention on my words—which originate in my brain somewhere, are spoken by me, travel through the air until they come to your ear and then go to your brain, where you understand them. ... Now *reverse* this. Imagine that my words, right now, originate in your mind, ... go to your ear, ... out of your ear, ... through the air to my mouth, ... and then to my brain where I understand them. ... Stay with this reversal for a little while, ... and now switch back. ...

Tree Reversal

Now visualize a tree and watch it change through the seasons. Imagine the water and substances from the soil moving into the roots in the spring, ... and up the trunk and into the branches, ... becoming buds, ... and growing leaves and shoots. ... Watch the leaves grow bigger and more mature as they move with the summer breeze, ... and then become older, and perhaps more colorful as fall approaches. ... Then the leaves drop to the ground and slowly wither and rot, and become part of the soil during the winter, ... and then are absorbed by the roots again as the tree comes to life in the spring. ...

Now reverse this cycle, and imagine the old dry leaves on the ground rising to the branches, ... becoming greener and greener, ... then becoming smaller as they are absorbed into the branches, ... and traveling down the trunk to the roots, ... and into the soil and rotting leaves. ... Continue with this reversal for awhile. ...

Now identify with this reversed tree. Become this tree as it changes with the reversed seasons. ... Feel your leaves being absorbed into the upper part of your body and moving down toward your roots, where they move into the soil. ... Continue to be this reversed tree for awhile, and notice how you feel as this tree. ...

Now continue to be this tree, but reverse the cycle back to normal. ... Feel your roots drinking moisture from the soil, ... feel it move up your trunk and into your branches. ... Continue this for awhile and be aware of how you feel as this tree. ...

Dominant Characteristics Reversal

Now think of two or three adjectives that you would use to describe what you are like—two or three words that best express your sense of yourself as a person. ... Take a little time to decide on your words. ... Now think of the *opposites* of these words. ... Now become a person who has these opposite characteristics. ... Describe yourself. ... What are you like? ... How do you feel being this person? ... What is your life like? ... What do you like and dislike about being this person? ... Take a little time to really get in touch with what it would be like to be this kind of person. ... Now become yourself again and compare the experience of being these two people. ...

Statue of Yourself

Now I want you to imagine that you are in a very dark building.

You can't see anything at all yet, but you know that it is some kind of art museum or art gallery for sculpture. Directly in front of you, there is a statue or sculpture of yourself as you really are. It might be realistic or abstract, but this statue somehow expresses your basic existence. Look into the darkness, and as the light gradually increases you will be able to see what this statue is like. . . . Slowly the light will increase, and you will be able to discover more about this statue. . . . What is its shape and form? . . . How large is it, and what is it made of? . . . As you are able to see it more clearly, discover still more details. . . . Walk around it and look at it from different angles. . . . Go close to it and touch it with your hands. . . . How does it feel? . . .

Now I want you to *become* this statue. Imagine that you are this statue, and change your posture and position to fit the form of the statue. . . . How do you feel as this statue? . . . What are you like? . . . Describe yourself as this statue, "I am—" . . . What is your existence like as this statue? . . . What happens to you, and how do you feel about this? . . .

Now bring this statue to life in your imagination. . . . As a living statue, what do you do and what is your life like? . . . Take a little time to discover more about your existence as this living statue. . . .

Now become yourself again and look at this statue. . . . Does the statue seem any different to you now? . . . Has anything changed? . . . How do you feel now toward this statue? . . . Slowly get ready to say goodbye to this statue. . . . Say goodbye now, return to your existence in this room, and quietly absorb what you have just experienced. . . .

In a minute or two I'm going to ask you to open your eyes and return to the group. Then I want each of you, in turn, to become your statue physically, and tell about your existence as this statue— take a posture that fits your statue and tell all the details of your experience as this statue and what you do when you bring the statue to life. . . . Now open your eyes, and come back to the group. . . . Who is willing to begin? . . .

Companion

Find a quiet place where you can spend at least ten or fifteen minutes alone with yourself. Sit quietly, look around at your surroundings, and take a little time to really get in touch with them. Even if this is a familiar place, really contact it now, and see what more you can discover about it. . . .

Now close your eyes and really get in touch with what is going on inside your body. Take some time to really contact your inner physical sensations and feelings, and discover what you are experiencing within yourself. . . .

Now imagine that you have a companion there with you, and gradually get to know this fantasy companion. . . . What is your companion like? . . . What kind of clothes, body, and posture does he or she have? . . . What does your companion express about himself with his posture, movements, and facial expressions? . . . How does your companion feel? . . . Discover even more about this companion. Ask questions and listen and watch for replies. . . . Tell your companion how you feel toward him or her and discover how your companion feels toward you. . . . Take some more time to discover more about your companion, and see what you can learn from him. . . .

Now become this fantasy companion. . . . As this person, what are you like? . . . How do you feel, physically—what is your body position like, and how do you move? . . .

Actually move your body into a position that is appropriate for you as this companion. . . . How does this position feel? . . . Begin to move a little, and get more into the feel of being this companion. What kind of a person are you? . . . What kinds of things do you do and how do you interact with others? . . . Move around more now. . . . Continue to be your companion and slowly open your eyes. . . . Get even more into the feeling of being this person. . . .

Motorcycle

Now imagine that you are a motorcycle. . . . What kind of motorcycle are you? . . . What is your life like as a motorcycle? . . . Where do you spend most of your time, and what is it like there? . . . Where is your home and where do you go? . . . How do you feel as this motorcycle? . . . Continue to explore all the details of your existence as this motorcycle for awhile. . . .

Now start up and go somewhere. . . . How do you get started,

and what kind of sounds do you make when you're running? ...
What are your surroundings like, and what is the ground beneath
your wheels like? ... Be aware of how you function, and how your
tires feel as they contact the ground. ... Where are you going? ...
Look back now, and see who is riding you. ... What is your rider
like? ... How do you feel towards your rider? ... What kind of
relationship do you have with your rider? ... Let your fantasy
develop for a few minutes, and get even more in touch with all the
details of your existence as a motorcycle. ...

(You can also go on to have a dialogue with the rider.)

Mirror

Now imagine that you are in a very dark room. You can't see
anything yet, but there is a large mirror in front of you. As the room
gradually becomes lighter, you will be able to see an image of
yourself reflected in the mirror. This image might be quite different
from the image you usually see, or it might not be. Just look into the
darkness and let this image emerge as the light grows brighter. ...
Eventually, you will be able to see it quite clearly. ... What is this
image like? ... What do you notice most about this image? ... What
is its posture like? ... How does it move? ... What is its facial
expression like? ... What feeling or attitude does this image express?
... How do you feel toward this image? ...

Now talk silently to this image, and imagine that the image can
speak to you. ... What do you say to the image and what does the
image answer? ... How do you feel as you speak to this image? ...

Now trade places, and *become* the image in the mirror. As this
image, what are you like, ... and how do you feel? ... As this
image, what do you say to yourself as you continue the dialogue
between you? ... Comment on the relationship between you two.
... See if you can discover even more about your experience of
being this image. ... Continue this conversation between the image
and yourself for awhile, and see what else you can discover from
each other. Switch back and forth between the two whenever you
like, but continue the dialogue and interaction between you. ...

Now become yourself again, and look again at the image in the mirror. . . . How do you feel now toward this image? . . . Are there any changes now, compared with when you first saw this image? . . . Is there anything you want to say to this image before you say goodbye? . . . Now slowly say goodbye to this image, . . . and return to your existence in this room. Just stay quietly with your experience for awhile. . . .

Abandoned Store and Swapshop

I want you to imagine that you are walking in a city at night in the rain. You are warmly dressed, and you can see the lights of the city reflected in the wet streets. . . . Just walk along for awhile and explore your city. . . . What do you see? . . . What is your city like? . . . What happens in your city? . . . How do you feel as you walk through this city? . . .

Just ahead there is a little neglected side street. Walk down this side street, and soon you will see an old abandoned store. . . . The front display window is dirty, misty, and spattered with rain, but if you look closely, you can see some dim shapes behind it. . . . What has been left abandoned in this store window? . . . Move closer and try to see what is there. . . . Wipe away some of the mist and moisture so that you can see more clearly. . . . Examine this abandoned thing closely. . . . What is it like? . . . Notice all the details of it. . . .

Now *become* this thing in the abandoned store. What is your existence like as this abandoned object? . . . Why were you left here? . . . And how do you feel as this thing? . . . Get even more into the experience of being this abandoned thing. . . .

Now become yourself again and look closely again at the abandoned thing in the window. . . . Do you notice anything about it that you didn't notice before? . . . Slowly say goodbye to this store window and what is in it, and walk on through the city streets. . . . Continue to explore your city for a while. . . .

Just ahead there is another strange little side street. As you walk down this street, you will see one store window that has an incredible variety of things in it—some old, some new, some very ancient. Some of it is junk and some is treasure, and you'd never expect to see all these things in the same window. . . . As you stand there looking at this window full of things, a friendly little old man walks out of the door and invites you into his shop. He explains that this is no ordinary shop. Within this apparently small shop there is *everything in the world*. Anyone who finds his way to this shop can choose one thing from the shop and take it with him. You can only take *one* thing. You cannot take money, and you cannot sell what you take for money. Aside from this, you can have any one thing from the shop. Take some time now to look around the shop and see what is there. . . . There are all sorts of little nooks and side rooms, with things that you might like to have. . . . Eventually you will have to decide which of these many things you want to take with you. . . . When you have decided what you want to take with you, take some time getting to know it better. Look at it carefully, and notice all the details about it. . . . Touch it with your hands, . . . handle it and smell it. . . . How do you feel about this thing? . . .

As you start to walk out the door with it, the storekeeper speaks to you again and says: "You may have this, as I said before. There is only one condition—you must give me something in return. It can be absolutely *anything* you have, and you need not have it with you now, but you must give me something in return for what you take. What will you give to the old man? . . . Take a little time to decide. . . . Now tell the old man what you will give him. . . . Now walk out the door, and take a last look at your city. . . . Slowly say goodbye to this city. . . . Now return to this room and bring with you whatever you decided to take from the shop. . . .

Now *become* this thing that you found in the shop. . . . As this thing, what are you like? . . . What are your characteristics? . . . What is your life like? . . . And what happens to you? . . . What is your function or use? . . . Try to really get into all the details of the experience of being this object. . . .

Now become yourself again, and look again at this object. . . . See if you can discover still more about it. . . . Do you understand it better now? . . . Slowly say goodbye to this object, and put it away somewhere in your memory, . . . and now just rest quietly for a little while. . . .

(A fantasy like this with a city setting is particularly good if you are in a place where there are loud traffic noises, etc. These noises would disrupt or intrude into some fantasies, but they will *add* to this fantasy since the noises are appropriate to the city setting, and they will become part of the fantasy experience without disturbing it. The fantasy that follows is another example of how to include and use noises that might otherwise tend to disrupt a fantasy.)

Undersea Cave

(I have written three alternatives for the middle part of this fantasy; each alternative uses the same beginning and end. Use only one of the three alternatives.)

(Beginning.) Imagine that you are skin-diving in a tropical sea near the shore (on another planet). Listen to all the sounds that you hear, and look around to see what is making each sound in your undersea world. . . . Swim around in this undersea world and explore it. . . . What is it like, . . . and how do you feel about being there? What do you see? . . . And what can you feel with your hands and skin? . . . Explore some more, and discover more about this experience of being a skin-diver. . . .

(Alternative One.) Just ahead, you can see the opening of an undersea cave. As you swim toward it, you can see it is quite large and deep. There is something hidden in the back of this cave, where the light is very dim and it's difficult for you to see. Slowly explore this cave and see what you discover when you come to the back of it. . . . When you find something, look at it carefully and see what it is like. . . . How do you feel toward it? . . . Now talk to it, and imagine that it can reply. . . . What do you say to it? . . . And what does it answer? . . . Tell it how you feel toward it. . . . Now switch places. Become the thing in the cave and continue the conversation. . . . How do you feel as this thing? . . . Look at the skin-diver in the cave with you. . . . How do you feel toward the skin-diver and what do you say to him? . . . What else is going on between you as you talk? . . . Switch places whenever you wish, and continue to interact and speak with each other for awhile. . . .

(Alternative Two.) Of all the things in your underwater world,

what is it that attracts your attention most? ... What one thing demands your attention? ... Whatever it is, move closer to it and see what you can discover about it. ... What is it about this thing that attracts your interest? ... Really look at it carefully.... Touch it if you can, and see what it feels like. ... Move around it so that you can see it from other angles. ... Now talk to it. Tell it what it is about it that attracts your attention. ... Tell it how you feel about it, ... and imagine that it can answer you. ... What does it say back to you? ... Now switch places and become this thing and continue the conversation. As this thing, what are you like? ... How do you feel? ... What do you say to the skin-diver? ... What else is going on between you as you talk? ... Switch places whenever you wish, and continue to interact and talk to each other for awhile. ...

(Alternative Three.) Now look far to your left in your undersea world and you will see something indistinct and far away, slowly moving toward you. ... As it gradually comes closer to you, you will be able to see it more and more clearly. ... Now look far to your right and you will see something different moving toward you. It will also be unclear at first, and then become clearer as it comes closer to you. ... Keep watching these two moving things. As they come closer to you, you will be able to see more and more of what they are and how they move. ... Eventually they will meet in front of you, and when they do, be aware of how they meet and interact with each other. ... Now become the one that came from your left. What are you like? ... And how do you feel being this moving thing? ... How are you interacting with the other moving thing that came from the right? ... Talk to this other one. ... What do you say? ... And what does it answer? ... How are you different? ... And how do you feel about these differences? ... Now switch and become the other moving thing and continue the conversation. What are you like, now? ... And how do you feel? ... As this moving thing, how do you feel about the other? ... And what do you say to it? ... Switch places whenever you like, and continue to interact and talk to each other for awhile. ...

(Ending.) Now become yourself as the skin-diver and get ready to say goodbye to your undersea world. ... Take a last look around, ... and then return to your existence in this room. ...

Seashore

I want you to imagine that you are at the seashore somewhere. . . . What is your seashore like? . . . Walk around a bit. . . . What is the beach under your feet like? . . . Reach down and touch the beach and get to know it better. . . . Go down to the water's edge and feel the salt water. . . . Walk along the shore and see what has drifted in on the tide. . . . What can you smell? . . . What is the weather like? . . . How do you feel being there? . . . Explore your seashore on your own for awhile, and see what else you can discover. . . .

Now I want you to look out at the ocean. . . . What is the ocean like? . . . Look up and down the coast. . . . Now look straight out to sea. Quite far out there is something gradually moving toward you, coming in with the waves. At first you will be uncertain about what it is and how large it is, but as it slowly comes closer you will be able to see what it is. . . . Watch it closely as it comes closer and eventually comes up to the beach. . . . When it does come in, go over to it and examine it carefully, and discover all you can about it. . . . Walk around it and look at it from the other side. . . . What is it like? . . . Touch it and see how it feels. . . . Can you guess anything about its past and what events brought it to this beach? . . . How do you feel toward it? . . .

Now I want you to *become* this object that came in to your beach. As this thing, what are you like? . . . What are your characteristics? Silently describe yourself: "I am—" . . . How do you feel being this thing? . . . What has happened to you that brought you to this beach? . . . Take a little time to get even more into the experience of being this thing. . . .

Now become yourself again, and look again at this object on your beach. . . . Do you see anything that you didn't notice before? . . . How do you feel towards this thing now? . . . Take a last look around at your seashore, . . . and notice if anything else has changed. . . . Now slowly say goodbye to your seashore, . . . and to whatever came in on your beach, . . . and return to your existence in this room. Just stay quietly with your experience for a little while. . . .

Dark Room

Now imagine that you are at one end of a large dark room. It is completely dark, but you may slowly get some feeling about what kind of room it is. . . . Imagine that you reach down to feel the floor, . . . and reach over to touch the wall to see what it is like. . . . What are the wall and floor like, and what kind of room is this? . . . Now you can just barely hear something moving at the other end of the room. . . . As you listen carefully to these sounds, they will become clearer, and you may get some idea of what is making them. . . . As you listen to the sounds, the light in the room will slowly increase, so that you can gradually see what it is that is making the sounds. . . . As you are able to see it, look at it carefully. . . . What is it like? . . . Examine it in detail. . . . Eventually you will be able to see it quite clearly, and be able to discover more details that you didn't notice at first. . . . What is it doing, . . . and how do you feel toward it? . . .

Now trade places and imagine that you become this moving thing. Identify with it and become it. . . . What are you like as this thing? . . . What is your existence like? . . . What do you do, and what are your characteristics? . . . How do you feel as this moving thing? . . . What is your experience of being this thing? . . . As this moving thing, talk to yourself. . . . How do you react toward yourself? . . . As this thing, what do you say to yourself, and what does yourself answer back? . . . What else is going on between you as you talk to each other? . . .

Now become yourself again, and continue the dialogue and the interaction between you. . . . How do you feel now as yourself? . . . And how do you feel toward the moving thing? . . . Now look carefully at this moving thing. Do you notice any change, or anything new that you didn't see before? . . .

Now slowly say goodbye to your room, and to whatever you found in the room, and return to this room and your existence here. . . . Take a little time to absorb your experience. How do you feel about your room and what you found there? . . . How did you feel about saying goodbye to this fantasy? . . .

Wise Man

I want you to imagine that you are walking up a trail in the mountains at night. There is a full moon which lets you see the trail easily, and you can also see quite a lot of your surroundings. . . .

What is this trail like? . . . What else can you see around you? . . . How do you feel as you walk up this mountain trail? . . . Just ahead there is a small side trail that leads up higher to a cave that is the home of a very wise man who can tell you the answer to any question. Turn off onto this side trail and walk toward the wise man's cave. . . . Notice how your surroundings change as you move up this trail and come closer to his cave. . . .

When you arrive at the cave, you will see a small campfire in front of the cave, and you will be able to faintly see the silent wise man by the light of the dancing flames of the fire. . . . Go up to the fire, put some more wood on it, and sit quietly. . . . As the fire burns more brightly you will be able to see the wise man more clearly. Take some time to really become aware of him—his clothes, his body, his face, his eyes. . . .

Now ask the wise man some question that is important to you. As you ask this question, continue to watch the wise man, and see how he reacts to what you say. He might answer you with words alone, or he might also answer you with a gesture or facial expression, or he might show you something. . . . What kind of answer does he give you? . . .

Now become the wise man. . . . What is your existence like as this wise man? . . . How do you feel, and what is your life like? . . . What is your attitude toward this visitor who questions you? . . . How do you feel toward this visitor? . . . What do you say to your visitor—whether in words, gestures or actions? . . .

Become yourself again and continue this dialogue with the wise man. Do you understand what he is saying to you? . . . Do you have any other questions to ask him? . . . How do you feel toward the wise man? . . .

Now become the wise man again, and continue this conversation. . . . Is there anything else you can say to your visitor? . . .

Become yourself again. You will soon have to say goodbye to the wise man. . . . Say anything else you want to before you leave. . . . Just as you are about to say goodbye to the wise man, he turns and reaches into an old leather bag behind him, and searches in the bag for something very special to give to you. . . . He takes it out of the bag and gives it to you to take home with you. . . . Look at the gift he gives you. . . . How do you feel toward the wise man now? . . . Tell him how you feel, . . . and slowly say goodbye to him. . . .

Now turn away, and start walking back down the mountain trail, carrying your gift with you. . . . As you walk back down the trail, look at the trail carefully, so that you will remember how to find your way back to the wise man when you want to visit him again. . . . Be aware of your surroundings, and how you feel. . . .

Now keep your eyes closed, and bring your gift with you as you return to this room. . . . Take some time now to examine this gift in more detail. . . . What did he give you? Really discover more about it. . . . Touch it, . . . smell it, . . . turn it over in your hands and look at it carefully. . . .

Now *become* this gift. Identify with it and describe yourself. What are you like as this gift? . . . How do you feel as this thing? . . . What are your qualities? . . . What do you do, or how can you be used or appreciated? . . .

Now become yourself again and look at the gift and see if you can discover even more about it. . . . Do you notice any change in it, or anything that you didn't notice before? . . . Now put this gift away carefully and safely in your memory, . . . and say goodbye to it for now. . . .

The Search

I want you to imagine that you are searching for something that is very important to you. You may have some idea of what it is that you are looking for, or you may not. You do know, however, that what you are searching for is very important to you, and that your life will be somehow incomplete until you find it. Where are you now, as you begin this search? . . . Where do you go? . . . And how do you search? . . . What happens to you? . . . Notice what obstacles or delays are in your way. . . . And be aware of how you encounter these obstacles and how you deal with them. . . . What alternatives do you try? . . . Continue on this search for awhile. Discover more about it, and see how close you can come to your goal. . . . You may find that the search changes in some way as you proceed. What do you find as you continue your search? . . . Even if you have not yet reached the goal of your search, you may have discovered more about what you are searching for. You may even be able to see it in the distance, even though something prevents you from reaching it. Whatever your situation, try to discover more about the object of your search. Whether you have found what you are looking for, or can only see it, or can only imagine what it is like, examine it carefully, . . . and be aware of your feelings toward it. . . . What is your goal like? . . . And what would reaching your goal do for you? . . . Is it this goal itself that you want, or is it a *means*—a way of getting something *else* that you want? . . . If this goal could speak to you now, what would it say to you? . . . And what would you say to it? . . . Talk to it for awhile, and see if you can learn more from it. . . .

Now return to your existence in this room and stay quietly with your experience for a while. . . .

Crazy

Close your eyes and turn your attention inward. . . . Now I want you to imagine that you go crazy. Become completely insane in your fantasy, and discover what insanity is like for you. . . . What kinds of things do you do, now that you are crazy? . . . Where are you? . . . How do you feel? . . . Take some time to get in touch with all the details of your experience of being crazy. . . . How do you interact with other people? . . . How do others respond to your being crazy? . . . What does being crazy do *to* you? . . . And what does being crazy do *for* you? . . . Explore this being crazy a bit more. . . .

Now become the exact oppostie of crazy. Whatever *your* experience of being crazy is like, now imagine that you become its reverse. For instance, if you go completely out of control when you are crazy, now become completely *in* control, and experience what this is like. . . . Really explore what you experience as the opposite of being crazy. . . . What do you do now? . . . How do you interact with other people now? . . . And how do others respond to you? . . . Explore this opposite of being crazy some more. . . .

Left-Right Person

There is someone standing to your right and behind you. Turn your head to the right and look over your shoulder to see who is there and notice all the details about this person. . . . What clothes is this person wearing? . . . How does this person look? . . . What does this person's posture and facial expression express? . . . What else do you notice about this person? . . .

There is also someone standing to your left and behind you. Turn your head to the left and see who is there, and what this person is like. . . . What clothes is this person wearing? . . . How does this person look? . . . What does this person's posture and facial expression express? . . . What else do you notice about this person? . . .

Now let these two people move forward and toward each other, until they meet in front of you. . . . Notice how they move, and how they act toward each other as they meet. . . . Watch them closely and see what they do. . . . How do they interact, and what do they say to each other? . . . Be aware of all the details of what is going on between them. . . .

Now become the person on your right. . . . As this person, what are you like? . . . And how do you feel? . . . What are you saying to this other person? . . . And how do you feel toward this person? . . .

Now switch, and become the other person in this dialogue. . . . How do you feel as this person? . . . And what are you like? . . . What are you saying to the other person? . . . And how do you feel toward this other person? . . . Continue with this dialogue for a while. Switch back and forth between being each of these two people whenever you like. Keep the interaction going and see what else you can discover about being each of these two people. . . .

Now become yourself again, and watch these two people. . . . Have they learned anything from each other? . . . Is their interaction any different now then it was at the beginning? . . . Slowly say goodbye to these two people and return to your existence here. . . .

Other Possibilities

There are endless possibilities for fantasy journeys. The best thing to work with is whatever fantasy occurs to you at the moment. Invest yourself in it through identifying with your awareness in the present. Last week, I watched my two-year-old boy struggle to open the front door without letting go of the large newspaper he was carrying. I thought, "What if this were a snapshot that I am looking at ten years from now?" As I imagined that what I was seeing was ten years in the past, I got in touch with feelings of warmth and caring for my son that I had been bypassing in the moment. What follows are brief suggestions for fantasy journeys that you can develop and experience on your own through identification and dialogue. If you just "go on a trip" or only think *about* or analyze your fantasy, it will be a waste of your time. A fantasy is only useful if you stay with your awareness as you experience it and own this experience as part of yourself now.

Go back to an earlier year of your life that comes to mind easily, and experience what it is like for you to be this age again. After you have really invested yourself in this, have a dialogue between yourself at this age and yourself at your actual age. What does it do *for* you to be this younger age?

Re-experience your earliest memory in detail. Now, at this age, do you have any memory of earlier events? If so, re-live these and discover what you have invested in them.

You are cleaning out an attic or unused storeroom full of old things in some house you once lived in, and re-discovering old things that were important to you once. Find an old photograph album and look through the pictures. Invest yourself.

Go back to your childhood. There is something missing in your life now, that you left behind in childhood. Go back and discover it and encounter it: See if you can assimilate this into your life now.

You are sitting quietly on a river bank. Be aware of the events that occur there, and what the river brings you.

You are in a valley. Discover what your valley is like and what happens there. Then look up, and see something far away moving toward you. Discover it as it moves closer to you, and you encounter it.

You are in a dim, smoky room and behind the smoke is something very important to you. As the smoke gradually clears, you will be able to see what it is, and then discover it and encounter it.

You are looking at a blank screen, and some representation of your inner feelings will appear on this screen. Invest yourself in this and become it.

Your mind is like a big trunk with lots of little compartments. Imagine that you lift the lid and look inside. What things and events do you find?

It is a dark night, and you are running away from something or someone. Discover what it is that is pursuing you, then turn and face it through interaction, dialogue and identification.

You have just crash-landed on another planet. Explore this new planet, and discover it. Then find a native. Encounter him, and then become him.

You are in a costume room at a theater or opera. Look through the clothes and accessories and choose something to wear. Then make up a new name and identity for yourself and explore this new existence. What does this new existence do for you, and what do you avoid?

You are in a long hallway with a locked door at the end. Find the key to this door, and open it. Discover what is behind it, and then become what you have discovered.

You and your family are picnicking in the country. Imagine that each person turns into some kind of animal, yourself included. Discover how you relate to each other.

Imagine a male animal, and then a female animal. Put them both in a clearing and watch them encounter each other. Then identify with each as they interact.

Think of someone you hate, and imagine that both he and you are transformed into animals. Discover how you interact with each other, and what you can learn from each other.

Invent an animal you would like to become, and then become it and explore your existence as this animal. How are you unique?

Pairs

Most of the experiments in this section are written for you to experience while sitting facing another person. It is very important to maintain eye-contact with your partner—not staring, just seeing each other. If you are willing to also maintain some kind of physical contact as well, this will usually deepen your involvement and make it more likely that you will learn something about yourself and your partner, and how you intereact. Each experiment should be followed by at least a few minutes of sharing your experiences and discoveries during the experiment itself.

If you do several of these experiments with the same person, you can deepen and broaden your relationship by exploring and re-exploring different aspects of your experiencing each time with the same person. However, you will not be exposed to as wide a range of experience as if you did the same experiments with several different people, and you will miss quite a lot. Different people will respond differently to the experiments and you can learn from these differences. Also, you will respond differently with different people, and if you do the experiments with only one person, you will not discover aspects of yourself that only emerge when you are encountering another kind of person. Do some of these experiments with a partner of the same sex, and others with someone of the opposite sex. On the other hand, if you always change partners, you will not have the time to develop substantial communication with any of them. Try to do a number of the experiments with one person, and also try to do some of them with others to give you more experience of the range of possibilities.

In the *Couples* section there are a number of experiments for pairs which are particularly useful for couples or other pairs who have known each other for some time, and who have an ongoing relationship. However, many of these experiments can also be used by people who are not couples.

It is Obvious to me That—I Imagine That—

Face each other and maintain eye contact. . . . Now I want you to tell each other about your awareness from moment to moment. Begin every sentence with the words "It is obvious to me that—" and complete the sentence with something that you are actually aware of at that moment. This might be awareness of something outside that you can point to and your partner can verify, or it might be a private experience inside your body that he may not be able to verify. As you do this, point out to each other when you say something that is fantasy—imagining what will happen next, or guessing what your partner is thinking, etc.—and is not actually awareness of present reality. Do this for about five minutes. . . .

Now I want you to focus on your fantasies and guesses from moment to moment. Begin every sentence with the words "I imagine that—" and complete the sentence with some impression or guess that occurs to you at that moment. Express what is going on in you now that is *not* awareness of the present. Do this for about five minutes. . . .

Now I want you to compare your experience of expressing your awareness and your experience of telling your fantasies to your partner. How did you feel as you did this, and what did you become aware of? Which was easier for you? Where do you spend more time—in fantasy, or reality? Take about five minutes to share your experiences. . . .

Next I want you to bring fantasy and reality together. I want you first to make an observation that begins with the words "It is obvious to me that—" Then immediately follow this with an impression that is based on this observation. For instance, "It is obvious to me that your hands are crossed tightly over your chest, and I imagine that you are nervous and defensive." Take about five minutes to do this connecting of your awareness and your fantasies. . . .

Now discuss what you were aware of as you did this, and what you noticed about yourself and your partner. . . .

This is a very important and very basic experiment. The ability to distinguish awareness from fantasy and to bring the two together in the moment is fundamental to all the other experiments in this book. Do this experiment repeatedly whenever you have a few minutes free.

Working With Imagination

Continue to look at each other, and imagine what your partner is feeling and experiencing right now. . . . Do you think he is comfortable or nervous, scared or confident, etc.? . . .

Now tell your partner your guesses about how he is feeling. Begin each sentence with the words "I imagine that you feel—" and complete the sentence with your guesses. Don't discuss these guesses yet, just express them. When you are through doing this, sit silently facing each other. . . .

Now recall exactly what you guessed about how your partner felt. Instead of saying *"I imagine that* you feel—" say *"I am deliberately making* you feel—" and say this sentence to your partner. Pause to absorb this sentence and be aware of how you feel as you say it. Then repeat this sentence, and say any words that come to you next. After you have done this, take a few minutes to share your experience of doing this. . . .

Maintain eye contact and tell your partner your guesses and impressions about what he is experiencing. Begin each sentence with the words "It is my guess that—" and finish the sentence with whatever you guess about him in that moment. Do this for about three minutes. . . .

Now recall your guesses about your partner, and *identify* with this guess by saying "I am—" For instance, if you said "It is my impression that you are nervous and tense," now say *"I am nervous and tense."* Pause to absorb this sentence, and be aware of how you feel as you say it. Then repeat this sentence and add any words that come to you next. After you have both done this, take a few minutes to share your experience of doing this. . . .

Now face each other and silently imagine several things that you think your partner sees as he looks at you, but does not say. . . . What do you think he has noticed about you, but has not expressed for some reason, and why do you think he does not express this? . . . What is he avoiding by not telling you about these things that he sees? . . .

Now tell your partner what you imagine he sees, but does not say, and why you think he doesn't say it. Find out if he had noticed these things before you mentioned them. . . .

Now recall the things that you thought your partner noticed and preface each thing with the words "I want you to notice my—" and say this sentence to your partner. Pause to absorb this sentence and how you feel as you say it. Then repeat the sentence and add any words that come to you next. After you have both done this, take a few minutes to share your experience of doing this. . . .

Now imagine what your partner dislikes about you. . . . How do you think you irritate him? . . . Imagine in detail what he dislikes or resents about you. . . .

Now express these guesses to your partner. Begin each sentence with the words "I imagine you dislike—" and finish it with your guess. After you have both done this, do some reality-testing with your partner, and find out if your guesses are correct or not. . . .

Back Conversation

Pair up with someone about the same height and size as you are, and sit back to back. . . . Close your eyes and silently contact your partner with your back. Sit still at first, and just be aware of your physical sensing of your body. ... Now focus your awareness on your back, and let your back begin to move a little, and interact with your partner as if you were having a silent conversation. This experiment might seem silly to you, but if you make it into a "silly game," you lose the possibility of discovering something from it. ... What is your partner's back like, and how does it move? ... How do you feel as you do this? ... Explore some other possible ways of moving with your partner. Continue to interact with your backs and gradually bring your head, arms, and hands into this interaction. ... Let this movement flow into a dance that expresses what is going on between you. ...

Now silently, and very slowly, say goodbye with your body, and bend slightly forward. ... Pause to absorb what you have just experienced and to get in touch with how you feel, now that you are by yourself again. ... Now turn around and face your partner and share what you experienced during this back conversation. ...

I Am—I Play—

Face each other and keep in touch with your partner's eyes. I want the shorter person to spend about three minutes describing himself in terms of his most prominent characteristics. Begin every sentence with the words "I am—" and make a long list of your characteristics, while your partner listens silently. ...

Now switch, so that the taller person describes himself for about three minutes while his partner listens silently. ...

Now I want the shorter person to repeat all the things you said about yourself, but instead of saying "I *am*—" say "I *play*—" After each sentence, pause to aborb it and be aware of how you feel as you say it. To what extent is this actually a description of what you *play*, rather than what you *are*? Then repeat this same sentence and add any words that come to you next. When you have finished, it is your partner's turn to do the same thing. ...

Now take a few minutes to share your experience of doing this. ...

Desert Island

Pair up with someone you'd like to know better, and sit silently facing each other. . . . Take some time to really look at each other. . . . Notice all the details of this other person's face. . . . Become aware of this person's eyes, . . . nose, . . . mouth, . . . chin, . . . jaw, . . . cheeks, . . . ears, . . . hair, . . . forehead, . . . and return to the eyes. . . .

Now close your eyes and take this person with you as an image. . . . Look at your image of this person. . . . How complete is your image? . . . Notice where your image is unclear. . . . Now open your eyes again and look at the parts of your partner's face that were unclear in your image. . . . Really look at them, so that you can complete the image. . . .

Now close your eyes, and again take this person with you as an image, . . . and now go to a desert island together. The two of you are alone on this desert island. . . . Look around and see what it is like to be there. . . . What is the island like? . . . What is the ocean and the weather like? . . . How do you feel about being on this island? . . . What do you do there? . . . What does your partner do? . . . How do you interact, and what happens to you? Just continue this experience for a few minutes and see what develops. . . .

Now get ready to leave your desert island. . . . Is there anything you want to do before you leave? . . . Do anything else you want to do. . . . Now take a last look around your island. . . . Say goodbye to it. . . . Return to your existence in this room, and sit quietly for a little while and absorb this experience. . . . In a minute I want you to open your eyes, and return to your partner. Maintain eye contact, and tell each other about your experiences on your desert island in first-person present tense, as if they were happening now. . . .

Gibberish

Pair up with someone that you have difficulties with. Sit facing this person silently and look at each other. . . . In a moment I want you to express yourself in gibberish—any sounds or noises that are not words in any language you know. By talking in gibberish, you can express your feelings fully without getting stuck in causes, reasons, justifications, arguments, etc. Be aware of all the things that you resent and dislike in this person, as well as what you like, what interests or excites you, etc. As you get in touch with your feelings, let them flow into the nonsense noises of gibberish. Be aware of how you and your partner express yourselves, and how you interact in this gibberish conversation. Do this for several minutes now. . . .

Now stop. Sit quietly and absorb your experience for awhile. . . . How did each of you express yourself? . . . Were there any changes in your gibberish and interaction as this conversation continued? . . . How did you feel doing this? . . . Now share your experiences with your partner, and then tell him in words at least some of the things that you expressed in your gibberish. . . .

Opening

I want the taller person to close your eyes, silently bring your body together into as closed a position as you can, . . . and get in touch with how you feel in this closed position. . . . In a little while, I'm going to ask your partner to open you up very slowly and gently, as if he were opening a flower. Continue to be aware of how you feel as your partner very slowly and gently opens you up until you are open to the world. I want the opener to also be aware of how you feel as you do this. . . .

Now switch, so that the shorter person takes a very closed up position and gets in touch with how he feels there, and is then very slowly opened up by his partner. . . .

Now take a couple of minutes to share your experience of doing this with your partner. . . .

Face Drawing

I want the shorter person to sit still and close your eyes. . . . I want the taller person to look at your partner's face and become aware of all the features and details you can see there. . . . Now, without talking, and *without touching his face,* begin to move your finger over his features as if you were drawing a sketch of him. . . . As you do this, notice which side of his face seems *less* dominant. . . . Continue this sketching motion on this less dominant side of his face. Now begin to stroke this side of his face very lightly as your fingers move. . . . Imagine that the touch of your fingers draws out these features and brings them to life. . . . Now slowly withdraw your hand and give your partner some time to absorb his experience. . . .

Now switch roles without talking, and do the same thing. . . . Now the taller person sits with eyes closed while the shorter person first looks at his face and becomes aware of his features and details. . . . And then draws these features with his finger without touching them, . . . and notices which side of the face seems less dominant, . . . and then begins to touch this less dominant side of the face gently, . . . drawing out these features and bringing them to life. . . . Now slowly withdraw your hand and give your partner some time to absorb his experience. . . .

Now tell each other what you experienced during this face drawing. Tell your partner what you see when you look at his face and describe what makes one side seem less dominant to you. Tell what you experienced as he drew out the less dominant side of your face, etc. Take about five minutes to do this. . . .

Telegrams
Sit facing each other and tell your partner your awareness of yourself and your awareness of him for about a minute. . . .

Now express your awareness using only phrases or very short sentences for about a minute. . . .

Now communicate with only single words for about a minute. . . .

Now don't use any words. Express yourself only through sounds for the next minute. . . .

Now express yourself in gibberish nonsense noises for the next minute. . . .

Now again use sounds to express yourself for the next minute. . . .

Now again use only single words to communicate your awareness. . . .

Now use phrases or very short sentences for the next minute. . . .

Now use complete sentences again, and take about five minutes to share your awareness of what you experienced as you expressed yourself in these different ways. . . .

Voids

Now sit facing each other silently and try to become aware of what is *missing* in your partner. . . . What qualities or capacities seem to be absent? . . . Does your partner lack warmth, confidence, anger, gentleness? What seems to be missing? . . .

Now tell your partner what you miss in him and how you feel about these missing qualities, and then discuss this for a few minutes. . . .

Next

Now I want you each to imagine what I will ask you to do next. Imagine it in detail. . . . Now tell your partner what you think I will ask you to do next. . . .

And now I want you to both go ahead and actually do whatever it was that you thought I would ask you to do. See what you can learn from this. . . .

Hand Dialogue

Maintain eye contact with your partner without talking. . . . Bring your hands up near your face and touch your partner's hands. . . . Focus your attention on your hands as you continue to look at each other, and use your hands to interact with your partner in any way that feels comfortable. Have a silent conversation with your eyes and hands for the next three or four minutes. . . .

Now very, very slowly bring this conversation to a close, . . . and then silently say goodbye with your hands and eyes, . . . and close your eyes and stay with your experience for awhile. . . .

Now return to your partner and take a few minutes to share your experience of this eye and hand conversation and goodbye. . . .

Secrets

Close your eyes and think of three secrets about yourself that you would *least* like your partner to know. Think of things that you think would most damage your relationship with him. Take some time to decide on these three secrets. ... Now be aware of what went on in you as you decided on your three secrets. What things did you think of and then reject? ... How do you feel about these three secrets? ... Now imagine that you silently tell these secrets to your partner, and imagine what his response is. ... What is your catastrophic expectation? What is the worst thing that could happen? ... Now open your eyes and *without telling your partner what your secret is*, tell him in detail what you think his response would be by completing this sentence for each secret: "If I told you my secret, you would—"

Now tell your partner what it does *for* you to keep these secrets—what do you gain by keeping these things hidden? As you do this, be aware of how you feel and how you speak. Are you simply stating facts, or are you apologizing, bragging, enticing, etc. ...

Now tell your partner what it does *to* you to keep these secrets. What do you lose by keeping these things hidden? Again be aware of how you feel and how you speak as you do this. ...

Now *brag* about your secrets and your ability to keep these secrets. ...

Now silently contemplate how secrets affect the relationship between you. ... For instance, how do you feel about your partner's keeping secrets from you? ... How do your secrets manipulate the other person and create distance and distrust in your relationship? ...

Now I want you to take a few minutes to tell each other how your secrets affect your relationship. If you feel like taking the risk of telling one or more of your secrets, do this and see how your partner responds in reality. Compare this actual response with your catastrophic expectations. ...

Good Boy-Bad Boy

Pair up with someone you'd like to know better, ... and quickly decide who is *A* and who is *B*. ...

Now I want *A* to be a bad boy or bad girl, and *B* to be a good boy or good girl, and talk to each other. Tell each other all about yourselves—what you are like and the specific things you do. For instance, "I'm a good girl; I always wipe the mud off my shoes before I come into the house, and I never get angry. I'd *never* do the awful things you do." As you carry on this conversation, be aware of your own and your partner's voice—be particularly aware of voice tone, hesitations, volume, expressiveness, etc. Take about five minutes for this conversation. . . .

Now switch. *A* is now the good boy or good girl, and *B* is the bad boy or bad girl. Again have a conversation for about five minutes. . . .

Now silently absorb your experiences. How did you feel in each role? . . . Which role felt more comfortable and easy? . . . What kinds of things did you say in each role? . . . How did you interact with the opposite role played by your partner? . . . Did you discover anything about yourself as you played these roles? . . . Think of these same questions applied to your partner. . . . What were you most aware of in your partner's expressions? . . . Now tell each other about your own experiences, and your impressions of each other. . . .

(There are *many* other polarities, or sets of opposites, that can be productively experienced in the same way: parent-child, black-white, helper-helpless, teacher-student, employer-employee, husband-wife, strong-weak, emotional-unemotional, master-slave, sane-crazy, honest-dishonest, etc. This can also be done with blindfolds, to help people to notice more about voice tone, etc. Some people express much more while blindfolded, and some express less.)

Shoulds

Now I want *A* to say sentences to your partner that begin with the words "I should—" After each sentence he says, I want *B* to answer a clear, firm, even "No." Don't say anything else. Continue this for four minutes, and be aware of what you experience as you do this. . . .

Now switch, so that *B* says sentences that begin with the words "I should—" and *A* answers a clear, firm, even "No." Be aware of what you experience as you do this for the next four minutes. . . .

Now share your experiences for a few minutes. What did you learn about your "shoulds," and how did you feel when your partner said "No"? How did you feel as you said "No" to your partner's "shoulds"? . . .

Teacher-Student

Close your eyes and think of one of your students. (If you are a student, think of one of your teachers.) Pick a particular student and visualize him clearly. Now I want one of you to *become* your student and speak out loud as if you were talking to your teacher. As this student, talk about yourself. Tell what you are like and what your life is like, and what you do and how you feel toward your teacher, etc. I want your partner to just listen to what you say. Listen with your body and your feelings as well as your mind, and notice how you respond to what this "student" says. . . . Do this for about four minutes. . . .

Now switch, so that the one who has been listening becomes *his* student talking to his teacher about his life, feelings, and how he relates to him, while his partner listens. Again take about four minutes to do this. . . .

Now take five minutes to share your awareness of your feelings and impressions about what your partner's "student" said and how he said it. What did you realize about your own "student's" experiences and responses through this experiment? . . . How much of this can you recognize as your *own* feelings and experiences? . . .

(This can also be done with any other relationship pair: husband-wife, employer-employee, parent-child, social worker-client, etc.)

Parents' Chat

Pair up with someone and sit together. I want you each to imagine that you are one of your parents. Decide now which of your parents you will become for this experiment. . . . You and this other parent have met and are each talking to the other about your child—yourself. In other words, you are talking about yourself as you imagine your parent might talk about you. Take at least five minutes to talk to each other about your child—what your child has done with his life, how you feel about him, how well he has met your expectations, how he compares with any other children you have, or whatever else occurs to you. . . .

Now take another five minutes to discuss what you have discovered through this experience. How did you feel doing this? What did you notice about your partner's "parent," and what did you discover about your own, or about yourself? . . .

Now become your other parent and repeat this experiment. . . .

Sentence Completions

(*Alternate one.*) In a moment I am going to say the first part of a sentence, and I want you to complete the sentence silently with the *first* words that come to you. (Or complete each sentence three times as quickly as possible.) Then say your complete sentence to your partner out loud, and then discuss this for a couple of minutes.

Complete the following sentence: "If you really knew me—" . . . Now tell each other how you completed the sentence and discuss this for a few minutes. . . .

(There are a number of incomplete sentences which are useful in facilitating encounters in pairs or small groups. Only one or two should be used at a time, usually in between other experiments, or when the sentence seems particularly appropriate in terms of what appears to be going on between two people at the time. See the list below for some other good ones.)

"Now I'm avoiding you by—"

"I'm trying to give you the impression that—"

"I won't—"

"I control you by—"

"What I'm not saying now is—"

"I'm pretending—"

"If I took a risk with you, I'd—"

"To please me, I'd—"

"I refuse to—"

"I feel excited by your—"

"I'm afraid you'll think I'm—"

"I'd like to give you—"
"If I told you what I am feeling now—"
"The game I am playing now is—"
"If I acted on impulse right now, I would—"
"I am sabotaging our relationship by—"
"I'm avoiding—"
"It is obvious to me that—"
"If I were honest with you right now, I'd say—"
"What I want from you is—"
"If I went crazy right now, I would—"
"I give you permission to—"
"Right now, I'm—"
"I'd like you to—"
"Right now, I'm afraid that—"
"If I get angry with you—"
"Don't—"
"I could shock you by—"
"I want to tell you—"
"If I touched you—"
"I expect that you'll—"
"I try to please you by—"
"I keep you from getting close to me by—"
"I'd be willing to let you know me if—"
"My expectations of the next few minutes are—"
"I refuse to face—"
"I refuse to feel—"
"I'm rehearsing—"

(*Alternate two.*) Pair up and face each other, and look at each other. Quickly decide who is *A* and who is *B*. For the next four minutes I want *A* to ask *B* "What do you pretend?" *B* will reply with a complete sentence beginning with "I pretend—" such as, "I pretend to be more confident that I feel." Then *A* says "Thank you" and repeats the question "What do you pretend?" Continue this for the next four minutes. Do *not* say anything else and do not talk *about* what you are doing. O.K. Go ahead. . . .

Now switch, so that for the next four minutes, *B* asks *A* "What do you pretend?" and *A* replies "I pretend—" Go ahead. . . .

Now share your experiences with your partner. . . .

(These sentence completions can be made more or less productive and/or threatening by specifying what kind of person in a group to pair up with in the beginning: Pair up with someone you like, dislike, feel distant from, feel close to, trust, distrust, fear, are attracted to, etc. See the list below for some other key sentences that can be used in this way.)

"How do you avoid me?"

"What do you fear in me?"

"What do you resent in me?"

"How do you control me?"

"What are you not telling me?"

"What would you like from me?"

"How do you keep distant from me?"

"What do you see when you look at me now?"

Not-Self

Sit facing your partner, looking at each other, and also make some kind of physical contact. . . . I want you both to take about five minutes to repeatedly complete the sentence "I am not—" Say "I am not—" and then say whatever words come to you next. Then say it again and see what words come next this time. If you get stuck just repeat "I am not—" until some words come to you. Take turns saying these sentences to each other, and make a long list of things you are not. . . .

Now stop talking and silently go over what you and your partner have just said. . . . Let a kind of summary of what you are not emerge from this list. . . . Now give each other a summary of what you are not. If your partner omits something that you remember, remind him of what he said so that he can include it. . . .

Now repeat this summary, but omit the "not" in each sentence and then give an example. For instance, if you first said "I am *not* cruel," now I want you to say "I *am* cruel," and then to give an example of your cruelty, such as "I make my wife feel stupid and miserable when she makes a mistake." Take about five minutes to do this. . . .

Blind Walk

We usually depend so much on vision that we tend to ignore our other senses: hearing, touch, smell, and our body senses. I want you to pair up and take each other on a silent "blind walk," so that you can get more in touch with these other senses. One of you will put on a blindfold (Closed eyes is O.K. if no blindfolds are available.) for about twenty minutes while your partner guides you around. Then you will trade places for another twenty minutes. Decide now who you would like to be with for the blind walk, and pair up. . . .

The guide's job is to provide the "blind" person with as wide a variety of experience of touching, smelling, hearing, etc. as possible. The guide must also lead the "blind" person past obstacles and protect him from anything that could possibly be dangerous, frightening, or really unpleasant. While you are leading the "blind" person around, use this way of holding hands. (Demonstrate.) The guide holds his hand as if he were holding a short, fat drinking glass, and the "blind" person hooks his hand over the guide's hand with his fingertips touching the center of the guide's palm. This is a very flexible way of holding hands, yet the guide can easily support the "blind" person if he happens to stumble or lose his balance.

Neither of you may talk. Communicate by the strength and direction of your hand movements. Lead the person slowly up steps or over obstacles, and use your free hand to indicate direction by touching, and to guide his free hand or his head, etc. to whatever you want him to experience. When you come to a large object like a tree trunk, place both his hands on it, and wait quietly until he is through sensing it before leading him on to something else. Allow enough time for him to fully experience whatever he is in contact with. Be aware of how hesitant he is and don't rush or push him. If you go slowly at first, he'll become more trusting as he gets more used to the situation.

Lead the person to a wide variety of objects, both natural and man-made, to give him a rich sensory experience. At some time during the walk, be sure to include another person in what the "blind" person touches. Another nice experience is to roll slowly down a gentle grassy slope, if one is available. Later in the walk, try walking faster and faster, and then, *if* you're *both* willing, try running slowly. This is a fantastic experience, but *only* if you *both* feel confident enough to try it. You can tell when a person resists by his hand-pull and body movements. *Don't force the "blind" person into doing anything he doesn't want to do, even if you're sure it's harmless.* Any questions? ... O.K. One of you put on the blindfold and begin your walk. Remember: No talking. ...

(Do this on a nice day, outside. If you're trapped in a city or bad weather, try the *Blind Object Exploration* experiment in the *Group Activities* section.)

Personal Space

Pair up with someone and stand facing them silently. Don't talk until I ask you to. Bring your hands up and join palms and fingertips with your partner, so that your hands are gently pressing against your partner's. Now I want you to look into each other's eyes, while you interact with your partner through your hands. Begin to move your hands and fingers, and see how much you can learn about your partner through this interaction. ... Be particularly aware of what you feel in your hands, but also be aware of how you feel and what you observe in your partner as you do this. ... Do some experimenting with your hand movements. ... What do your partner's movements express? ... Let your hands move lightly, and play some games with your partner. ... Now let your hands flow and dance with your partner's hands. ... Which of you is more active in beginning movements and exploring your interaction? ... How else could you learn about your partner through this hand dialogue? ...

Now explore the size and shape of your partner's personal space—the area around his body that he is reluctant to let you enter. Move your hands toward your partner in different ways and see how close he will let you come. ... How do you feel as you reach into his personal space? How far are you willing to go, and to what extent does he reach into your own personal space? ... Be aware of when your partner resists your movements, or retreats even slightly. ... How do you feel as your partner comes close to your own personal space? ... How close are you willing to let him come to you? ...

What is the size and shape of your own personal space? ... In a moment I'm going to say the beginning of a sentence. I want you to finish the sentence with the *first* words that come to you, and say this out loud to your partner. "If I let you get close to me—" ...

Now close your eyes and continue this silent hand interaction for a while longer and see what else you can learn about each other. ... Now keep your eyes closed, and very slowly break contact. ... Bring your hands back to yourself, and stand quietly by yourself for a little while. ...

Now open your eyes and sit down with your partner and share your experience of this hand dialogue. Tell your partner what you felt, and what you noticed about him, yourself, your personal spaces, and the interaction between you as you did this, etc. Take about five minutes to do this. ...

Yes-No Pushing

Pair up with someone who is about your size and strength. (Or someone you feel antagonistic toward; or someone with whom you feel some kind of struggle or competition.) Stand facing each other and place your hands flat against your partner's hands without interlacing fingers. In a minute I'm going to ask you both to look each other in the eyes and begin to push with your hands. I want one of you to shout, "Yes! Yes! Yes!" ... and the other to shout "No! No! No!" ... When you begin to shout, push as hard as you can. After you have done this for about a minute, switch words and continue to push for about another minute. ... Any questions? ... Go ahead. ...

Now stop. I'd like you to reflect on this silently, and be aware of whether you pushed harder when shouting "Yes!" or "No!"—or did you push about the same with each word? ... Did you really push as hard as you could, or did you hold yourself back to protect the other person, or keep him from "losing"? ... Did you notice any difference in your partner's efforts with the two words? ... If you notice a difference in yourself, think about whether this has any meaning in your life. For instance, if you pushed harder with "No!" it might mean that most of your efforts are in opposition to something, rather than in affirmation of something, or whatever your experience is. Take a couple of minutes now to share your experiences with your partner and discuss this. . . .

Again stand facing each other and place your palms flat against your partner's palms without interlacing fingers. In a minute I'm going to ask you to look each other in the eyes and begin to push. As you do this, I want you to be aware of how you feel, and to shout words or very short sentences with each push and with each breath you exhale. Use any words that you want to, that express your awareness of that moment. Push as hard as you can for a couple of minutes. . . .

O.K., now rest silently and stay with your awareness of the last couple of minutes. . . . What did you experience as you pushed against your partner? . . . Now share your experiences with your partner for a few minutes. . . .

Couples

The pair experiments in this section are particularly useful for married couples or for *any* two people who have an ongoing relationship and spend a good deal of time together. Couples can also benefit from the experiments in the preceding pairs section, and many of these couples experiments—particularly *Resentment-Appreciation*—can also be quite useful for any two people who want to explore their relationship.

Meeting

Sit down facing each other. Imagine that you have just met, and that you have never seen each other before. Try to see each other as you are right now at this moment. I want you to get acquainted, and be aware of how you do this—what you talk about and how you go about discovering this new person you have just met. Take about ten minutes now to get acquainted with your partner. . . .

Now I want you to tell each other what you were aware of as you got acquainted. How did you get to know each other, and to what extent did you really meet and honestly contact each other? How much did each of you reveal about yourself and your feelings, and how much did you keep hidden? Who took the most active part in this getting acquainted? Take about five minutes to explore all the details of what went on during this last ten minutes. . . .

Proverbs

Sit facing each other silently and look at each other. . . . Continue to do this and notice the *first* proverb that comes to your mind. . . . Now each tell your proverb to your partner. . . . I want you both to do an experiment with the same proverb, so I want you to take a minute or two to decide which of these proverbs you will use for this experiment. . . .

Now share your awareness of what happened as you made this decision. How did you decide, who took the most active part in making the decision, and how do you feel about it? For instance, one of you may have shrugged and let your partner make the decision, and then felt resentful when he didn't choose your proverb. Try to be aware of the exact sequence of actions and events that resulted in the decision. . . .

Now take a couple of minutes to discuss to what extent this decision is an example of how the two of you often arrive at decisions. Does this illustrate a common pattern of interaction between you? . . .

Now both close your eyes and think of this proverb you have chosen. . . . Say it to yourself several times with different emphasis, and then invest yourself in it by experiencing the content of the proverb directly. For instance, if your proverb is "A rolling stone gathers no moss," become the rolling stone, and see what you experience. How do you feel as this stone and how do you roll? Do you want to stop for awhile and get some moss, or do you like rolling and hate moss, etc.? Take a little while to become aware of how *you* experience this proverb. . . .

Now open your eyes and tell your partner in detail what this proverb means to you in terms of your own experience. After you have both done this, take some time to point out any differences in what the same proverb expresses to each of you. Then discuss how these differences are reflected in your relationship and your life together. . . .

Now close your eyes again and think of the proverb that you decided not to use earlier. . . . Silently repeat it to yourself several times with different inflections and then take some time to identify with it and see how you experience it. . . .

Now open your eyes and tell each other in detail what this proverb means to you in terms of your own experience. Again be aware of differences between you and discuss how these differences are reflected in your relationship. . . .

Assumptions

While facing each other and maintaining eye contact, alternate saying sentences to each other that begin with the words "I assume that you—" Don't discuss these assumptions or say anything that doesn't begin with the words "I assume that you—" Do this for about four minutes. If you get stuck just say the beginning of the sentence again and see what words come to you. . . .

Now tell each other what you experienced as you did this, and check out your assumptions. What did you discover about your own and your partner's assumptions? To what extent were you each already aware of these assumptions, and to what extent were you wrong about your assumptions about each other. Take about five minutes to discuss this. . . .

(A useful variant of this is "I assume you know—")

Appreciation

One assumption we often make is that others know when we appreciate them. We take it for granted that they know when we are pleased, so we don't bother to express our approval directly. Even if I know that you appreciate me, I like to hear you say it now and then. Now I want you to take turns stating your appreciations of each other. Begin each sentence "I appreciate—" and go on to state your appreciation specifically and in detail. Use examples to be certain your partner knows exactly what you appreciate about him. Take about five minutes to do this. If you get stuck, just start with the words "I appreciate—" and see what words come to you next. . . .

Now take some time to share your experience of doing this.

Express how you felt as you gave and received appreciation, and what you became aware of as you did this. . . .

Indirect "No"

I want one of you to ask for something that you know your partner doesn't want to give to you. Continue to ask for this same thing repeatedly. Each time you ask, I want your partner to say "No," *without actually saying "No."* Be aware of *how* you evade your partner's demand without actually refusing it openly. Do this for about four minutes. . . .

Now switch places, so that the one who has been asking for something now has to refuse his partner's repeated request without actually saying "No." Again do this for about four minutes. . . .

Now share your experience of doing this. What did you learn about your own and your partner's ways of saying "No" indirectly. . . .

Role Reversal

Now I want you both to reverse roles, and take each other's place. Speaking *as if you were your partner,* express "your" feelings about your relationship and what is wrong with it. For instance a husband, *playing his wife,* might say "I really get angry when you come home tired and go to sleep right after dinner—I just don't feel like I'm married to you at all." Express all your irritations, dislikes, annoyances, unhappinesses, etc. Try to really become your partner; get into the experience of being him, seeing things from his point of view, and expressing this viewpoint. Take at least five or ten minutes for this, and then take another five or ten minutes to share your experience of doing this. . . .

Hurting

I want you each to express how you feel *hurt.* Face your partner and take turns saying sentences that begin with the words "I feel hurt by—" Make a long list of hurts. If you get stuck, repeat these beginning words, and see what words come to you next. Do this for about four minutes, and be aware of your posture and tone of voice as you do this. . . .

Now I want you to go back over this list of hurts and make each one into an accusation. Instead of saying "I feel hurt by—" say "You hurt me by—" Be aware of how you feel, your posture, and your voice tone as you say these new sentences. . . .

Now I want you to express the anger and wish to retaliate that lies behind these accusations. Go back over this list of accusations and instead of saying "You hurt me by—" say "I want to hurt you for—" Again be aware of your posture, your voice tone, and how you feel as you say these sentences. . . .

Now share your experiences with your partner for at least five minutes. . . .

Whenever someone says he feels "hurt," you can translate this into the word *vindictive*. Feeling "hurt" disguises a wish to retaliate and hurt someone in return. Instead of expressing this anger openly, he advertises the injustice that has been done to him so that you will feel bad and take care of him. The phoniness of feeling "hurt" can be easily demonstrated by asking the person to say where in his body he feels this "hurt." As long as he searches for "hurts" he will be stuck. If he really gets in touch with his physical sensations, what he will discover is smoldering anger.

Expectations

Now I want you to alternate telling each other your expectations. I want you to begin *every* sentence with the words "I expect you to—" One of you say a sentence, and then pause for your partner to say a sentence. Be very specific about your expectations. Don't be vague and just say, "I expect you to please me." Tell him in detail exactly how you expect him to please you, and what he can do to please you. Don't reply to these expectations or discuss whether they are reasonable or not—just express them and get them out in the open. Do this for about five minutes. If you get stuck, just say "I expect you to—" and see what words come to you next. . . .

Now quietly reflect on the last five minutes, and silently summarize what you expect from each other. . . . In a minute I want you to share your summaries with each other and clear up any misunderstandings or disagreements about what you expect from each other. *Don't* discuss them or argue whether they are reasonable or not, etc.

Just be certain that you understand each other's expectations clearly. Before you can discuss anything sensibly, you have to get agreement on what it is that you're discussing. Go ahead. . . .

Now that you are clear about what you expect from each other, take about ten minutes to express how you *feel* about these expectations. Which of your own expectations are really important to you? Which of your partner's expectations are you happy to meet or willing to meet, and which are you reluctant or unwilling to meet. Don't confuse each other with reasons, rationalizing, whining, blaming, judging, etc. Just state your own position: how you feel about your expectations of each other. Go ahead. . . .

Now take five or ten minutes to discuss your expectations of each other in any way that you like. Be aware of how you feel and what is going on between you as you do this, and bring this awareness into your discussion. If you notice that you are feeling tense, or that your partner is whining or threatening you, etc., tell him this. Every time you reveal more of your awareness it will help to clarify what is going on between you. Go ahead. . . .

Now I want you to pause and silently reflect on what happened during the discussion you just had. Did you begin to clarify your relationship and your demands on each other, or did you start some kind of blaming game "Look what you're doing to me," "It's all your fault," etc.? . . . In what ways did you make honest, direct contact with each other? . . . And in what ways did you try to evade your partner's expectations and try to impose your own expectations? Take about five minutes to discuss this now. . . .

Now take turns telling your partner how he doesn't live up to your expectations. Be specific and tell him in detail all the ways that he doesn't meet your expectations. Tell him one of these ways that he disappoints you, and then listen while your partner tells you one of the ways in which you don't meet his expectations. Take about five minutes to do this. . . .

Demand-Spiteful Response
Now make each of your expectations into a demand, and take turns making these demands on each other. Express these demands

clearly and firmly as if you were giving orders. After you have made a demand, I want your partner to respond very spitefully. Spite is a sneaky way of retaliating. For example, if the demand is "Keep the kitchen clean," a spiteful response could be "No, I won't keep it clean, I'll deliberately leave it even messier than I like it just to bug you," or "O.K., I'll make a lot of noise washing dishes while you're trying to watch TV, and get so tired cleaning the kitchen that you'll have to put the kids to bed." Really let go and put yourself into this spiteful response. Take about five minutes now to express these demands and spiteful responses. . . .

Now take a few minutes to discuss what you were aware of as you did this, and what you discovered. To what extent could you really get into your spite and enjoy it? Was it "just a game" or did you express some of the actual ways that you retaliate against each other? . . .

Now make this retaliation explicit. Take turns telling each other how you sabotage your partner's demands. Be very specific about what you do to evade your partner's demands on you, and exactly how you frustrate many of his wishes, goals, and actions. Begin each sentence with the words "I sabotage you by—" For example, "I sabotage you by putting off fixing things around the house until the stores are closed and I can't buy parts." Take about five minutes to do this. . . .

Now tell each other how you're stuck with each other in these demands that you're not willing to satisfy. Really get into all the details of your deadlocks—what you continue to demand, and your partner continues to refuse. For instance, "I'm stuck with nagging you to fix things and getting more and more frustrated as you delay and avoid doing it," etc. Take about five minutes to express all the ways that you are stuck with each other. . . .

Now face each other and look at each other and also make physical contact. Say the following sentence to each other, and pause to absorb what you experience as you do this: "At this moment I cannot possibly be any different than what I am." . . .

Now switch to: "At this moment, you cannot possibly be any different from what you are." . . .

Now take some time to share your experiences in these experiments. . . .

Life-Script

As you grow up and learn ways of coping with difficulties, you develop a kind of "life-script." Like a script for a movie or a play, this life-script is a ritualized scheme of roles, goals, images, and demands that guides your actions and describes what will happen in your life. One person develops a life-script that describes her as a helpless waif who requires someone to come to her rescue. Another person's life-script requires that every attempt at meeting people result in disappointment so that he can continue to stay in his safe isolation. Now I want the shorter person to take about five minutes to describe your life-script to your partner. Begin with the words "My life-script requires—" and tell all about your present life-script. Don't discuss it, just express it in detail. When you are through, it is your partner's turn to describe his life-script for about five minutes. . . .

Now take a few minutes to discuss your life-scripts—how you feel about them, what you discovered about each other, etc. . . .

When two people establish a relationship, it is because each person can gain something from the other. Now I want you to take turns telling each other what it does *for* you to be in your relationship with your partner. What do you gain by being his spouse, parent, friend, lover, or whatever your relationship is? Begin each sentence with the words "By being your wife, I gain—" or something similar, and then express what you gain in detail. If you get stuck, just repeat this incomplete sentence, and see what words come to you next. Take about five minutes to do this. . . .

Now take a few minutes to share your experience of doing this. How did you feel as you did this and what did you become aware of? . . .

Relationship-Script

Every relationship quickly develops many unexpressed rules and assumptions about what is permitted, who does what, what is avoided, etc. A relationship develops because the two partners' life-scripts somehow fit together, and then they tend to develop a joint script that describes their relationship, what their roles are, and what will happen within this relationship. Each person's role requires certain things and behaviors from the partner. There can be no husband without a wife, no mother without children, etc. Now I want you to take turns telling each other what your own role in your relationship demands of your partner. Begin each sentence with "In order for me to be a good wife (or husband, friend, lover, mother, etc.) you must—" Go into all the details of what your roles demand of each other. Take about five minutes to do this. . . .

Now take five or ten minutes to share how you felt and what you became aware of about your relationship as you did this. See if you can clarify your relationship further. If you think of any other "ground rules" that describe your relationship-script, discuss these too. . . .

Name Contacting

I want you to sit facing each other silently. Now I want the taller of you two to try to contact your partner by saying your partner's name. When your partner doesn't feel contact, he shakes his head, and you have to try a different way of saying his name until you reach him. Be aware of how you feel as you do this, and notice which ways of saying your partner's name don't reach him. When your partner does feel contact, he nods his head. Pause for a moment so that you can both become aware of how you said his name when you did reach him. Then it is your partner's turn to try to reach you by saying your name. Don't say anything except your partner's name. . . .

Now I want you to tell each other what you became aware of during this experiment. How did you try to reach each other, and how did you feel as you did this? What ways of saying your partner's name did you try, and which ways did and didn't work? How did your partner reach you—by a demand, sweetness, pleading, etc.? Take a few minutes to share your experiences. . . .

Needs-Wants-Lacks

Now I want you to take turns expressing what you need from each other. Be very specific and detailed as you tell your partner what you need from him. Begin each sentence with the words "I need—" Take about five minutes to make a long list of needs. . . .

Now take turns saying exactly the same things you just said, but replace "I *need*—" with "I *want*—" Be aware of how you feel as you say this new sentence. Is this really a need—something you must have and can't live without? Or is it a want—something that you might desire quite a lot but which is not really necessary to your survival? Is this "need" actually just something that spares you the inconvenience of doing something for yourself? Then repeat this sentence that begins "I want—" and immediately add whatever words come to you next. . . .

The word "wanting" has two basic meanings: to *desire* and to *lack.* I want you to go over this same list of wants and needs again, and express the feeling of *lacking or absence* that you feel in yourself that lies behind the want or the need. For example, if my want is "I want you to approve of my housekeeping," then the lack might be "I feel a lack of approval for what I do," or possibly "I lack a feeling of confidence in my own work." Try to be really honest in expressing and taking responsibility for your own feelings of lacking. . . .

Now take five or ten minutes to share your experiences as you did this, and discuss what emerged in this experiment. . . .

Yes-No Dialogue

I want you to spend the next four minutes communicating *only* with the words "yes" and "no." Look at each other as you use these two words to communicate by changing your tone of voice, speed, volume, inflection, etc. Be aware of how you feel as you do this, what you communicate, and how you interact. . . .

Now take about five minutes to share your experiences. How did you feel while doing this, and what did you express about yourselves and your relationship? . . .

Now do exactly the same thing, except use only the words "I" and "you" (instead of yes and no) for the next four minutes, and then share your experiences. . . .

Gestalt Prayer

Fritz Perls' Gestalt Therapy prayer is:

I do my thing, and you do your thing.
I am not in this world to live up to your expectations
And you are not in this world to live up to mine.
You are you and I am I
And if by chance we meet, it's beautiful.
If not, it can't be helped.

I want you each to say this slowly to your partner, while making eye contact and physical contact with him. Be aware of what you experience as you do this. . . .

Now I want you each to paraphrase the Gestalt prayer: Tell your partner what it means to you in your own words. . . .

Now again tell your partner what the prayer means to you in your own words, but this time expand on what you mean and be very specific in terms of the two of you and your relationship. Say in detail what your own and your partner's "things" are and be detailed about what your expectations are that you are not in this world to meet, etc. . . .

Now take some time to share what you experienced as you did this. To what extent do you agree or disagree with the Gestalt prayer, and to what extent can you actually live by it? . . .

Group Activities

In this section there are instructions for a wide variety of group activities: demonstrations, verbal and non-verbal experiments, role-playing, fantasy identifications, trust experiments, rocking, massage, etc. These are further opportunities for becoming more aware of yourself—opportunities that will be lost unless you explore your awareness as you do them, and allow time to absorb and reflect on your experiences, and go on to share them with others.

Rehearsing and Anxiety

Close your eyes, and keep them closed until I ask you to open them. In about three minutes I am going to call on one of you to stand up and tell this group of strangers about yourself honestly and in some detail. . . . Between now and then I want you to imagine that you are the one that I will call upon. I'm giving you a chance to rehearse and decide what you will say. . . . Actually imagine yourself standing in front of the group facing the people here. . . . What will you say about yourself? . . . Now get in touch with your physical existence. What is going on in your body? . . . What tension, nervousness, or excitement do you feel? . . .

Now stay in touch with your physical existence and notice any changes that occur as I tell you that I am *not* going to ask anyone to stand up and tell the group about himself. . . . Be aware of what happens in your body now. . . .

O.K. Open your eyes. Now I want to give you some words which may be useful to you in understanding this experience. I deliberately threatened you with a situation in the *future.* I asked you to jump into the future and prepare for this task of telling the group about yourself. Your energy and excitement increases in order to meet this challenge, and you feel some symptoms—your heart beating faster and certain muscles tensing or trembling. If the task were actually present here, all this excitement could flow into activity—moving your body, speaking, gesturing, etc. But since the challenge is in the future, all your excitement has nothing to do, so it piles up and you experience what is called anxiety or stage fright. You will also get this experience if the task is actually present and waiting for you, but you don't dare attempt it yet, so you are still rehearsing for the future. Most of you probably not only rehearse for the task itself, but in addition imagine all kinds of failure and dreadful consequences. As you become more excited and agitated about these awful catastrophes that only exist in your imagination, your being upset will interfere with the task itself and may even bring about the failure that you fear. I want you to realize that this kind of difficulty occurs when you leave the now of ongoing reality and jump into the imaginary future which doesn't exist.

There is a story that illustrates the waste of this involvement with the future. A young man has just made a date with an attractive girl for this evening. It is now noon, and tomorrow morning he has a very important exam that he has to study for. So what happens? All afternoon, his mind is so occupied with thinking about the date this evening, that he can't study. Then in the evening when he is with the girl, he is so worried about the exam next morning that he can't enjoy being with the girl! I'm sure you can recognize yourself in this story. Any preoccupation with the future reduces your contact with what exists now, and may wipe it out completely.

"Remembering," or thinking about the "past" does the same

thing. Almost all remembering is useless fantasy activity: basking in sentimental replays, thinking about events you wish had gone differently, rehearsing other ways you could have acted, torturing yourself for the actual outcome, etc. None of this can be of any use to you, yet most of your energy is bound up in these fantasies so that you can't experience anything or do anything *now*.

Identification Demonstration

(*Beforehand,* take a used piece of paper—or a polystyrene cup—and make it more interesting by tearing off a corner, folding it, and scratching or marking it a little.)

I want you all to focus your attention on what I am holding in my hand, and to call out very brief descriptions of it—a word or two, or a short phrase. (Take time to get a large number of responses—white, damaged, being held, flexible, thin, sharp, marked, etc.)

Now I want you to notice that although you all looked at the same object, different people were aware of very different things. If I did this experiment with each of you individually, you would each mention only a few of the many aspects that have been mentioned here in this group. Some of you would never notice characteristics that are obvious and significant to others. The fact that some of you notice some aspects and others notice other details is no accident. What you notice in the world is not simply a result of what exists "out there," but is somehow connected with who you are and what is important to you at the time. Your memory is also selective, according to your life and your interests. Most of you have already forgotten several of the descriptions of this object that were mentioned only a few minutes ago.

Take a few minutes now to recall which descriptions come easily to your mind and contemplate what connection these descriptive phrases might have with your life. . . . If you noticed that the paper is thin and sharp, see if thinness or sharpness have any special meaning to you. Are you thin or would you like to be? Are you sharp or do you fear the sharpness of others, etc.? . . . Particularly focus on the things you noticed, or remember clearly. . . . Now close your eyes and try describing yourself with these same words. If you noticed that the paper (or cup) had a piece missing, try saying "I have a piece missing," and see how you feel as you say this. If you sense some truth in this, stay with this experience and see if you can discover what is missing from you. Take a little time to do this. . . .

Now open your eyes. Did any of you discover anything through this experiment? Did any of you feel anything as you tried identifying with these descriptions? I'd like to hear of your experience if anyone is willing to talk about it. . . .

Now I want you all to be silent and try this identification again. Look at the paper I am holding and imagine that you *are* this piece of paper. Say to yourself silently "I am being held. . . . I am white, . . . written on, . . . folded. . . . I have a piece missing." . . . Really *become* this piece of paper. . . . (After about 15 seconds or when everyone is into the experience, suddenly crush the paper in your hand.) What happens? Stay with whatever you are experiencing now. Stay with whatever feelings you have now. . . . Now I'd like you each to briefly express what went on in you as I did this. . . .

I promise that I won't play this kind of nasty trick on you again. I did it because I don't know a better way of showing you how the process of identification can bring you in touch with your feelings. In this case I have rigged the situation—I decide what you identify with, and I arrange for the paper to be crushed. The feelings that you feel are in response to me and what I have done. If you identify with something of your own choosing, or with your own fantasy, or with something from a dream of your own that is crushed, then you can regain awareness of *your own* buried feelings. Even in this rigged situation, you can learn something about yourself, namely, how do you react when I "crush" you? Did you only feel crushed, or did you feel anger and an urge to retaliate? Take a minute to recall your response to this situation in detail, and contemplate how this experience might be characteristic of how you respond to injury. . . .

This experiment also shows how easily we can lose ourselves by identifying with things and events outside ourselves. When I crush the *paper,* you react as if *you* had been crushed. If you identify strongly with your country's flag, you will be enraged if someone burns it. You will react as if *you* had been burned instead of only a piece of colored cloth. If you identify very strongly with your job, you may respond with a suicidal depression when your job disappears—reacting as if your life had ended instead of just your job. When you work through your fantasies and identify solidly with your own awareness and your own experiencing, you will be able to respond appropriately to real injuries and be immune to the imagined injuries and imagined dangers that occupy so much of most people's attention.

Forming Groups

Usually it is best to form groups with about the same number of males and females, to take advantage of their different viewpoints. Sometimes it is good to form groups who know each other as little as possible in order to get people to know each other and feel more comfortable. At other times, it is valuable to form groups on the basis of bringing together people who already like or dislike each other so that they can explore these relationships further. If at all possible, use the process of group formation itself as a focus for deepening awareness. Here are some possibilities:

Form groups of *exactly* five people, and balance sex as evenly as possible. As you form your groups, be aware of what you and others do, and how you feel as you do this. As soon as you have formed your group of *exactly* five people, sit down in a circle and don't talk until I ask you to. . . .

Now I want you to express to each other your awareness of all the details of exactly how the group formed. What part did you take in forming the group, and how did you feel as it formed? Were you active, or did you wait to be chosen? Who took most responsibility for the formation of the group—by stating his desires and prefer‑ ences, making suggestions, etc.? How did the group decide who had to leave if there were too many people? Take about five minutes to share your awareness of the process of group formation. . . .

I want exactly five (or whatever number of groups you want)

people to volunteer as beginnings for groups. You have no other responsibility except to help begin the process of dividing up into groups. If you're willing to do this, please stand up against the wall somewhere, while everyone else moves toward the center of the room. . . .

As the process of group formation proceeds, I want you to be aware of what happens and what feelings you have about what happens. Now I want each of these five people to choose someone of the opposite sex that you would like to have in the group with you, and ask this person to come and stand with you at the side of the room. . . .

Now I want each of the five people who were *just chosen* to each choose a person of the opposite sex that you would like to have in your group, and ask this person to come and stand with you. . . . (Continue this until everyone is chosen.) Now sit down in a small circle. One at a time, talk to the person you chose and tell him what it is about him that led you to want him in your group. Talk directly to the person you chose, and speak loud enough so that everyone else in the group can hear. After you have all done this, express how you felt during this choosing process—how you felt while waiting to be chosen, how you felt as you were chosen, and how you felt when choosing another person for your group. Take three or four minutes to share your experiences. . . .

(This often brings up strong feelings and feelings of being un-wanted and left out, memories of being chosen last for sports in childhood, etc.)

Pair up with someone of the opposite sex that you don't know well and would like to know better. . . .

(Then do several pair experiments—some *Mirroring*, a couple of *Sentence Completions, You've Got It; I Want It,* etc.)

Now join together with one (or two) other pairs to form groups of four (or six) and sit down. . . . I want each person, in turn, to introduce his partner to the group in the following way: Face your partner and look at him, and tell him everything you were aware of in the interaction you have just had—what you noticed about him, and what he expressed of himself, how you feel toward him, etc. Talk directly to your partner, and talk loudly enough so that the others in your group can hear you easily. Each take at least two or three minutes to do this. Any questions? O.K. Go ahead. . . .

Introductions

An excellent way to introduce the members of a group to each other is to begin with a short simple fantasy journey such as *Rosebush, Mirror, Motorcycle,* or *Statue of Yourself,* and then ask each person to express their experiences in detail in first-person present tense.

I want you first to get to know each other in pairs, and later I'll ask you to introduce your partner to the group. (Choose one or two pair experiments such as *It's Obvious That—It's my Impression That—* or *You've Got It; I Want It.*)

Now I want you each to introduce your partner to the group in terms of what you have actually been aware of during the last few minutes. I want you to look at your partner and talk directly to him, but speak loudly enough so that the whole group can hear you. Tell him what you have observed about him during your interaction and how you feel toward him. I want you each to take at least two minutes to introduce your partner. Any questions? . . . Go ahead. . . .

I want each person to stand up in the center of the circle and to take about three minutes to introduce yourself by expressing your awareness from moment to moment. Talk *to* someone as you do this. As each person does this, I want the rest of the group to be aware of what this person is aware of, and also how he expresses himself non-verbally through his posture, movements, tone of voice, etc. (Demonstrate by standing up in the center as you say this, and then take a few minutes to express your awareness, talking *to* someone as you do this.)

I want you each to introduce yourself by going to each person in the group and communicating with your name only. You may not

use any other words, but you have a wide range of possible inflections, loudness, repetitions, etc. Look into the other person's eyes
and also be aware of how you feel, physically, as you introduce
yourself. As you speak, be aware of what your voice expresses, and
notice how others express themselves as they use their name to
introduce themselves. . . .

(Do the same thing, but use only your name, and the word *yes,
no,* or *maybe* to introduce yourself to each person in the group.)

Close your eyes and get in touch with your physical existence. . . . Become really aware of your body. Get in touch with it,
and your physical sensations. . . . Now I want you to silently repeat
your first name over and over again. Listen to yourself as you do
this, and notice what feelings or images come to you. . . . See if you
can visualize your name as you say it, and see what changes occur in
this image as you repeat your name. . . . Be aware of how you feel as
you repeat your name over and over, and follow whatever feelings or
images emerge into your awareness. Continue to do this for a few
minutes. . . .

Now tell your name and express your experiences to the group
in first-person present tense. . . .

(You can also do this with someone else's name—someone in
the group, or someone important in your life.)

I want us to learn each other's names. I'm going to say my
name, and after a short pause, I want the person on my right to say
his name distinctly, and then slowly name each person who has
already given his name. Then the person on his right will do the
same, and so on. If you can't remember a person's name, ask them,
and then say it and go on. Make sure you are not just memorizing a
list of noises, but are connecting the name with the individual.
Reversing directions occasionally will help you do this. Instead of
naming the people in order from first to last, start with the last
person and move toward the first. . . .

(Names are somewhat superficial cultural tags, but many people
will at least begin to communicate if they know some names. Names
can also reduce ambiguity about who is talking to who.)

Choosing a Leader

Silently look around at the people in your group. *Without talking,* I want each group to choose a leader who will be responsible for seeing that the group follows my instructions. Now take a minute or two to choose a leader non-verbally—*without words.* . . .

Now that each group has chosen a leader, I want you to be aware of *how* this leader was chosen. Take a few minutes to discuss what the actual sequence of events was that resulted in this choice, and to decide which group member actually took the most active part in choosing the leader. . . .

The person who took the most active part is the person who actually led in this situation, so from now on *he* is the official leader of your group.

Giving and Receiving Appreciation

Form groups of 6-8 and sit in a circle, with enough room in the center of the circle for a person to sit comfortably. . . .

In this experiment I want you to experience expressing what you like about the others in your group and to become more aware of how you feel as you give and receive these messages of liking and appreciation. One person at a time will sit in the center, and as long as he is in the center, he must remain silent. I'll give you time for discussion and feedback later. The person to the left of his sitting place in the circle begins, and tells the person in the center 3 or 4 things that he appreciates about him. I'm not asking you to be phony. You can find 3 or 4 things you like—even in your worst enemy. Be as superficial or as deep as you like, but be honest and express things that you really do like. Look at the person in the center, speak directly *to* him and be very *specific* and *detailed.* Don't just say "I like you" or "I like your hair." Say *exactly* what you like about the person or his hair. For instance: "I appreciate the way you really listen to what someone says, and when you are listening, your smile turns up on the left and you tilt your head to the right a little; I feel as if you're really listening to me, and I like that."

After this person has said 3 or 4 things he likes, he says "pass" and then the person to his left says 3 or 4 things he likes about the person in the center—and on around the circle, until everyone has expressed their appreciations to the person in the center. Then the person in the center returns to his place in the circle, and the person to his left moves to the center. Continue in this way until everyone has sat in the center and received appreciation from all the others. When you have finished, sit as closely as is comfortable, and share your experiences with each other. Say anything that you wanted to earlier, but didn't. Many people, especially the last to sit in the center, will not have had a chance to respond to what others have said about them.

I want you to be particularly aware of your physical sensations as you give and receive these messages of liking. Is it easy and enjoyable for you to express your liking, or do you feel a lot of discomfort and tend to avoid communicating directly to the other person? Can you really accept and enjoy what others say to you, or are you uncomfortable and tend to avoid, dismiss, or reject these messages of liking? . . . Any questions? . . . I need a volunteer in each group to be the first to sit in the circle. . . . O.K. Go ahead. . . .

(A lot of good feelings and trust can develop through this experiment if you stay with actual awareness. Don't let it degenerate into vague general statements of praise, compliments, reassurance, etc. These "good intentions" may produce temporary good feelings in people who believe such fantasy statements, but nothing real can happen. If you have time, continue with the *Non-verbal Expression* experiment that follows.)

Non-Verbal Expression

(This is most productive with people who have had at least some significant previous contact with each other. It is especially good when it follows the preceding experiment, *Giving and Receiving Appreciation.*)

Form groups of 6-8 and stand in a circle. One person will begin by moving to the center of the circle, and facing the person who stands to the left of his place in the circle. I want the person in the center to look at the person he is facing, and take a moment or two to get in touch with how he feels towards this person. Then silently express how you feel non-verbally, using some kind of physical contact. Then move to the next person and do the same, and so on, until you return to your place in the circle. Then the person on your left moves to the center and does the same until everyone has done this. When you are finished, sit down in a circle, and share your experiences. Also say anything that you wanted to say earlier but couldn't.

When you are in the center, try to really get in touch with how you feel about each person and let this feeling flow into some kind of non-verbal expression. Don't just go around hugging everyone, or shaking hands with everyone. Differentiate your movements, and be aware of them. You might feel like hugging one person, shoving another away, barely touching another, etc. When you are in the circle, be aware of the specific details of the movements, hesitations, etc. of the person in the center as he interacts with others. Notice not only *what* he does, but *how* he expresses himself non-verbally. Does he move smoothly or jerkily, spontaneously or with deliberation, etc. Any questions? . . . I need a volunteer in each group to step to the center of the circle and begin. . . . O.K. Go ahead. . . .

Three Wishes

Everyone take a minute or two to silently make three wishes that could be satisfied right now, within the group. . . .

Now each person, in turn, tell the group your wishes, and as far as possible carry them out. If satisfying your wish actively involves someone else, respect their feelings if they don't want you to act upon your wish. After you have all expressed and acted upon your wishes, discuss this experience for 5 or 10 minutes. . . . Any questions? . . . Go ahead. . . .

I hope most of you realize now that it is possible to act upon *many* of those impulses and wishes that you usually inhibit and suppress. The range of behavior that is actually possible for you—and also often exciting and nourishing—is *much* wider than what you usually permit yourself. Healthy functioning requires involvement with other people in giving to and receiving from others whatever you *and* they feel like exchanging. Our fear of rejection prevents the expression of many impulses that are very positive and nourishing, as well as many others that are at least harmless.

Now I'd like you to try to expand the range of behavior you permit yourself even more. Each person think of three wishes that you thought of before but censored and did not express for some reason. . . .

Now each person, in turn, tell the group your censored wishes, and see if you can satisfy any of *these* wishes. After you have each expressed and acted upon your wishes, discuss this experience. Go ahead. . . .

Pass a Mask

(Groups of 5-7 or more, sitting in a circle.)

I want you to play a game called "Pass a mask." I want one of you to turn to the person on your right, and make your face into a "mask"—some kind of fixed expression. Hold this mask long enough for the person on your right to copy it. This person has to copy your mask, and when he has copied it he continues to hold it and begins to turn his head quickly to the right. However, sometime before his head faces the person on *his* right, he must *change* his face into a new and different mask. Don't plan what mask you will create, just turn your head and see what happens. (Demonstrate.) Then the person on his right copies this mask, turns his head and passes on a different mask, continuing around the circle. I want you to do this for several minutes. Don't talk while you are doing this, and don't use your hands to alter your facial expression—do it with your facial muscles only. Any questions? . . . Go ahead. . . .

Now I want you to change direction. Pass the mask in the opposite direction for a few minutes. . . .

Now close your eyes, sit quietly, and absorb what you have just experienced. . . . I'd like you to recall the masks you created. What did they express? . . . Were they all different or did many of them express much the same kind of feeling or attitude? . . . Does this have any meaning for you? . . . What do these masks express about yourself? . . .

Now consider the others in your group. What were their masks like, and what do these masks express about them? . . . Open your eyes now and silently look around at the others. . . . Take some time to recall the masks they made and what these masks may express about them. . . .

In a minute I want each of you to put into words your awareness of your own masks and what they express, and then after each person has done this, go on to say what you noticed about the masks that others created. Take five or ten minutes to do this now. . . .

Now close your eyes again, and make a mask that is most characteristic of the masks you made before. . . . keep this mask on your face for awhile, and really get in touch with what this mask is like, and what it expresses about you. . . . Now *become* whatever your face expresses in this mask. If your mask is fierce, become fierce; if your mask is stupid, become stupid. Become whatever your mask expresses and be aware of how you feel as you do this. . . . Now begin to make some small noises that express how you feel now. . . . Notice if your attention wanders to the other noises in the room, or if you want to conform to some of these noises. If this happens be aware of it, and then focus your attention on your own feelings, and your own sound that expresses these feelings. Now let these sounds become somewhat louder. . . . In a moment I'm going to ask you to open your eyes and interact with the others in the group. Continue to keep your mask on and make noises. Stay in touch with your face as you now open your eyes and interact with the others in your group for a few minutes. . . .

Again take a few minutes to share your experience of doing this. . . .

(This is a lively and active experiment that most people enjoy very much. *To the extent that the masks are spontaneously created,* they will express much of the person's more important feelings and attitudes which he may have been unaware of. You can also do much the same kind of experiment and pass something else instead of masks. You can also pass gibberish, animal noises, grunts, screams, laughter, humming, hand gestures, handshakes, other kinds of physical contact, etc.)

Robot-Village Idiot

Everyone stand up and move around a little to loosen up. In a moment I want you to all become robots—machines in human form that move stiffly and mechanically. These robots have no words, but lots of noises from the machinery—grinding, whirring, clicking and clanking, etc. Begin by making some kind of robot noises and mechanical movements, and discover what kind of robot you are. Become a robot now and move around the room. Make some kind of physical contact with the other robots and interact with them for several minutes. Be aware of how you feel as you do this. . . .

O.K. Stop. A robot is completely and rigidly *over*-controlled by a mechanical mind. Next I want you to become the village idiot, a person who is *under*-controlled—whose mind is almost non-existent. I am *not* asking you to make fun of people with mental handicaps. I want you to *experience* how you *feel* when you are under-controlled. Idiots also have no words, but lots of incoherent noises, grunts, etc. Begin by making some noises and slack, shuffling movements, and move into being this idiot. Become a village idiot now for several minutes, and move around the room making physical contact and interacting with the other idiots. Be aware of how you feel as you do this. . . .

Now continue to be a village idiot and find another idiot to pair up with. . . . Spend a couple of minutes in a non-verbal dialogue of sounds, movements and physical contact. As you do this, be aware of how you feel and what goes on between you and your partner. . . .

Now stop. Become a robot again, and continue this non-verbal dialogue with your partner for a couple of minutes. Be aware of how you feel now and how this compares with your experience of being a village idiot. . . .

Now become a village idiot again and continue this interaction with your partner for a minute. . . .

Now sit down together and share your experiences with your partner. How did you feel in each role, how did you express yourself, what did you notice about your partner? etc. Take about five minutes to do this. . . .

Hand Conversation

I want everyone to pair up with someone of the opposite sex (if possible) whom you don't know well, but would like to get to know better. ... Now find another pair that you both would like to get to know better and form a group of four. Get agreement from all four that you're interested and willing to be together for awhile and get to know each other better. ... (If there are leftovers, form groups of six, five or three.) Now stand in a circle so that you are next to the two others in your group that you would most like to know better. ... Now silently sit down comfortably in a small circle in such a way that your hands are free and so that you can touch elbows easily....

Now close your eyes and get in touch with your body. Keep your eyes closed until I ask you to open them. Notice what is going on inside your skin. ... Become aware of your breathing, ... and notice any tension or discomfort. ... See if you can become more comfortable. ... Now bring your hands together as if they were strangers, and let them discover each other. ... How do these hands meet and discover each other? ... What are these hands like, physically? ... And how do they move and interact? ... Now let your hands come to rest together. ... Again get in touch with your body, and what is going on inside you....

In a minute or two I'm going to ask you to reach out to the people on both sides and get to know their hands. Right now, I want you to become aware of what you experience as you leave the present and begin to anticipate the future. ... Be aware of what thoughts, images and fantasies you have, ... and notice how your body feels in response to these images and fantasies about the future. ... Now see how much you can return to the present by focusing exclusively on your physical functioning now—your feelings of excitement or tension, etc....

Now reach out slowly and contact the hands on each side of you. Say hello with your hands, and then gently get to know these hands. ... As you do this, realize how the thoughts and fantasies in your head get between you and your sensations. ... Notice that when you pay attention to the words and images in your head, what you feel in your hands fades or disappears. ... And notice that the reverse is also true: When you focus your attention on your hands and their contact with these other hands, the words and images in your head tend to fade away. . . . So really get to know these hands you are touching. What are they like? . . . How do they feel? . . . How do they move? . . . If these hands were people, how would you describe them? . . .

Now I want you to try expressing different feelings and attitudes through your hands. As you do this, also be aware of how these other hands express the same feelings.

First, express playfulness. . . .

Now be caring and tender. . . .

Now express dominance. . . .

Now be submissive and pleading. . . .

Be alive and active. . . .

Now dead and passive. . . .

Express arrogance. . . .

Now be timid. . . .

Don't be too rough, as you express anger. . . .

Now be loving. . . .

Now express irritation. . . .

Express joy and happiness. . . .

Now be sad and depressed. . . .

Be rejecting. . . .

Now express acceptance. . . .

Now that you have a "vocabulary," have a conversation with these hands. See if you can express to each other how you feel, and what is going on between you. . . . For example, is your interaction mostly caring and communicating, or is it a contest of strength? . . . Is one more active and one more submissive and withdrawing? . . . Would you like the other to be different? See how much you can communicate with your hands. . . .

Now very, very slowly begin to say a silent goodbye to these hands you have been touching. . . . Slowly say goodbye and bring your hands back to yourself. . . . Be aware of your hands, and how you feel now that you are by yourself again. . . . Quietly absorb whatever you have just experienced. . . .

In a minute I'm going to ask you to open your eyes and tell each other what you discovered about yourself and the others through this hand conversation. Talk *to* someone, and do this in the first-person present tense, for example: "I don't feel very active, and I notice the roughness of your skin, and I'm surprised that you are so tender and gentle—" or whatever your experience is. Open your eyes now, and share your experiences for about ten minutes. . . .

I hope you had some experience of how much a person can express himself through his hands. Many of us don't have much physical contact with others, and this separates us and prevents us from relating to others. Except for meaningless rituals like shaking hands, many of us touch others only in anger or love. Some people have so little touching in their lives that when they do feel close to another person they cling to each other physically, and often drown in each other sexually. I'd like you to realize that there are many other ways to relate to another person physically.

We learn to lie and disguise with our words, but when we touch, we usually can't help expressing something of what we really feel. If you can be more aware of how you and others touch each other, you can learn more about what is really going on between you. Your awareness of things that you touch during daily life also becomes more lively.

One objection that some people have to this experiment is that they had difficulty communicating to two different hands at the same time. This is certainly true, but one value of this is to show you how differently two different people express themselves. Now I'd like to give you a chance to communicate with only one person with your hands.

Pair up with someone else in your group, and sit facing your partner with your eyes closed. Sit quietly for a little while and tune in to what is going on within you. . . . Bring your own hands together and let them become acquainted again. . . . Now reach out both your hands to your partner and get to know these hands. . . . What do these hands express? . . . How are the two hands different? How do you feel about these hands? . . . And how do you express how you feel through your hands? . . . Now I'd like you to try alternately "talking" and "listening" with your hands. One of you hold your hands fairly still while the other "talks" with his hands, . . . and then reverse this, as if you were speaking back and forth. . . . Now make some demands on these hands. How would you like them to be different? . . .

Now try playing some games with your hands. Try imagining that one of you is a typewriter that the other is typing on. . . . Now play "tag" or "hide and seek." . . . Now play some games of your own. . . . Be aware of what develops out of the dialogue between you—how you each express yourself, and how you feel doing this. . . .

In a few minutes I'm going to ask you to say goodbye to these hands. Until then, I want you to continue with this silent hand dialogue. Try to express, as clearly as you can, how you feel about these other hands and what they express. . . . Now very, very, slowly bring this conversation to a close, and silently say goodbye to these hands. . . . Bring your hands slowly back to yourself and quietly be aware of what you feel in your hands and in your body now that you are by yourself. . . .

Now open your eyes and take a few minutes to discuss your experiences with your partner. Speak *to* your partner and speak in the first-person present tense. . . .

Now pair up with a new partner. . . . (Repeat this last section.)

Exaggeration or Reversal

I want the group to decide on an exaggeration or reversal for each person in the group. This is some instruction that helps a person to become more aware of himself—an order to announce, exaggerate or reverse what he usually does. For instance, if a person is usually apologizing, either with his words or tone of voice, he could be told to begin everything he says with the words "I'm apologizing—" Or he could be told to exaggerate what he does by pleading on his knees, or told that he must make everything he says into a boast or a brag—the opposite of apologizing. Focus on one person at a time and quickly get several suggestions for an exaggeration or reversal and then get group agreement on one of them. Be sure that what you choose can be imposed in this situation here and now, and be sure that each person realizes clearly what he is to do. . . .

Now that we each have an exaggeration or reversal, spend the next ten minutes with this in effect. During this time, stay as much as you can in the here and now of your experiencing. Be sure that the others comply with what the group has agreed upon, and tell them when they forget. Be aware of how your own instruction affects what you do and how you feel, and notice how the others are affected by theirs. Express as much of your awareness as your instruction will allow. . . .

Now the instructions are removed. Take a few minutes to express anything you could not express earlier about how you experienced the last ten minutes. . . .

Role and Reversal

I want the group to decide on a specific role that fits each individual in the group. Focus on one person at a time and quickly get several suggestions for a role that expresses one way this person impresses you. Realize that there are *many* possibilities for roles. When you have decided on an appropriate role for this person, go on to make this role more specific and detailed. If you have decided on the role of nurse, go on to describe what kind of nurse she is. Is she a tough, strong, no-nonsense nurse, or is she a cheerful young candy-striper? After you have done this, decide on a simple sentence that would be appropriate for this person to say in this role. For my nurse example, an appropriate sentence might be "Cheer up now, this won't hurt a bit and you'll be well in no time." Now decide on these roles and sentences for everyone in the group, and be sure that each person understands exactly what role and sentence he has been given. . . .

Now that we each have our roles and sentences, I want us all to play these roles for the next eight minutes. Really invest yourself in this role, and interact with the others in the group in whatever way is appropriate for this role. As you interact with others, alternate saying this given sentence with saying any other sentence you want to. O.K. Go ahead. . . .

Now stop and absorb your experience of doing this. . . . How did you feel in your role, and what did you notice about yourself and others as you did this? . . . Now take about five minutes to share your experience of playing this role. . . .

Now take a few minutes to realize what the exact opposite of your role and your sentence could be. For instance, the reverse of a young candy-striper nurse whose sentence is "Cheer up now, this won't hurt a bit and you'll be well in no time," is an old patient who groans "Ohhhh, this is going to hurt and I'll be sick for a long time." You might want some help from others in your group to decide on the exact opposite of your role and sentence. . . .

Now that we all have our opposite roles and sentences, I want us all to play these roles for the next eight minutes. Really invest yourself in your role, and interact with others in the group in whatever way is appropriate for this role. As you interact with others, alternate saying this opposite sentence with saying any other sentence you want to. O.K. Go ahead. . . .

Now stop and absorb what you experienced while playing this reverse role. . . . How did you feel in this role, and what did you become aware of as you did this? . . . Which role was easiest for you to play, your original role or the reverse? . . . What did you notice about others as they did this? . . . Now take five or ten minutes to share your experiences and your observations with each other. . . .

Now I want everyone to switch back and forth between your original role and its reverse. As you interact with others, play one role for about twenty seconds, and then switch quickly to the reverse. Do this for about eight minutes. . . .

Again share your experience of doing this. . . .

(This experiment can also be very useful if you ask each individual to choose his own detailed role and short sentence instead of having the group decide.)

Face Touching

Pair up with someone of the opposite sex that you don't know well but would like to get to know better, . . . and then hold hands so that it is clear to the others who you are paired with. . . . If you have to pair up with someone of the same sex, quickly decide which of you will be a "man" or a "woman" so there will be no confusion with the instructions later on. Now find another pair that you would like to be with, and form a group of four. . . . If you are a same-sexed pair, *don't* get in a group with another same-sexed pair. Now find another group of four, and form a group of eight. (Place left-overs in groups of six, or ten; you may have to break up one group of eight in order to do this.) . . . Now sit down in a circle silently facing your partner. . . .

Now I want all the women to close your eyes and keep them closed until I tell you to open them. Now all the men stand up and move around the outside of the circle quietly, . . . and then sit down in front of one of the women, without saying anything or making any noises that would identify who you are. Look at this woman's face carefully and notice all the details of each part of her face. . . . Then reach out very gently and begin to touch and caress her face. . . . Take some time to do this. . . .

Now very slowly and gradually end this caress, bring your hands back to yourself, and sit quietly for a while. . . . Women keep your eyes closed, while the men stand up again, . . . move around the outside of the circle for a while, . . . and then return to sit down facing your *original* partner. . . . Now I want the women to open your eyes and express your experience of having your face touched. Talk to the whole group, and don't try to guess who was with who—you'll have time for that later. Tell how you felt while being touched, and how you experienced the fingers that touched you. Were these hands confident or hesitant, was the touch light or firm, etc.? Take about five minutes to really express all the details of your experience. . . . You have a couple of minutes left now, so finish up. . . .

Now I want the women to close their eyes again, . . . and the men to stand up again and move around the circle quietly, . . . and then sit in front of a different woman than last time. . . . Again really look at this woman's face and notice all the details, . . . and then reach out gently and begin to touch and caress this face for a while. . . .

Now very slowly end this touching, bring your hands back to yourself, and sit quietly for a while. . . . Women keep your eyes closed, while the men stand up again, . . . move around the circle, . . . and then return to sit down facing your *original* partner. . . . Again I want the women to open your eyes and express how you experienced having your face caressed this second time. What differences did you notice between the two experiences? Take five or ten minutes for this.... You have a couple of minutes left now....

(Now repeat all the same instructions above, but asking the *men* to close their eyes while the *women* move quietly around the circle, etc. At the very end, give them a minute or two to discover who touched who, if they wish. It is quite important to maintain this secrecy earlier, because some people will say much less about their experience of being touched if they know who touched them.)

Animal

Find a comfortable position and close your eyes. Now imagine that you are in a dark room and that at the other end of this room there is a dark movie screen. Gradually there will be some light on the screen, and as the light slowly increases, you will begin to see an image of an animal that represents yourself.... As the screen slowly gets lighter, look at the image very carefully.... What kind of animal is this? ... What is it like? ... What is its posture or attitude? ... What is it about to do? ... Is there anything special or unusual about this particular animal? ... Examine it very carefully and notice even more details.... Move closer to it and continue to look and discover even more about it....

Now become this animal. Identify with it. ... What is your existence like as this animal? ... Describe yourself as this animal. Say to yourself silently: "I am—" "I have—" What are you like as this animal? ... How do you feel, physically, as you become this animal? ... Look around—what are your surroundings like? ... And what do you do in these surroundings? ... How do you interact with these surroundings? ...

Keep your eyes closed, and now actually take a physical posture that expresses your being as this animal. If you were this animal, what kind of position would you take? ... How do you feel as this animal? ... What are you about to do as this animal? ... Now stay pretty much in place, but make small movements and actions of the kind that this animal would make. ... Get more in touch with the feel of being this animal. . . . How do you exist as this animal? . . . Now begin to make some small noises that this animal would make. . . . What kind of noises do you make as this animal? . . . Now make these noises louder. . . . Now move around more, and stay with being this animal. . . . Continue to be this animal and make these sounds and movements. In a moment I want you to open your eyes and interact physically with the other animals for several minutes. As you do this, be aware of how you feel, how you move, and how you relate to these other animals. O.K. Open your eyes and interact. . . .

Now sit quietly for a while and consider your existence as this animal. Don't try to analyze it, just stay with your experience and absorb it. . . . What do you recognize in this experience? . . . Do you see any connection between this experience and your everyday life? . . .

Now come together into groups of 5 or 6 people, and each tell your experience of being this animal. Tell about your surroundings, and how you relate to these other animals. Do this in first-person present tense, as if it were happening now. For instance: "I am a black Persian cat with a red collar and I feel very aloof and self-satisfied—"or whatever your experience is. Try to tell all the details of your experience of being this animal. Take the posture of this animal, and become this animal as you tell about yourself. Take about ten minutes for this. . . .

Now close your eyes, . . . and become your animal again. . . . Take a posture that this animal would take, . . . and again start to make whatever movements and noises this animal would make. . . . In a moment I'm going to ask you to open your eyes and interact *only* with the other "animals" in your own group for a few minutes. O.K. Open your eyes and interact with these other animals. . . .

Now discuss *how* you interacted with each other as these animals. . . . Were you active, passive, aggressive, loving, etc.? Which other "animals" did you interact with, which did you avoid, and how did you feel in these interactions? . . .

Now take a little while to sit quietly and absorb more of your experience of your "animalness." . . . Say to yourself silently, "I am a cat. I live in a protected house, and I avoid other big animals—" or whatever your experience is of being this animal and interacting with these other animals. . . .

Now discuss to what extent your fantasy of being this animal expresses the kind of person you are—how you act and how you relate to others. Can you at least see that for the others in your group their fantasy expresses quite a bit about themselves? Take about five minutes for this. . . .

Now close your eyes again, . . . and become your animal again. . . . Find a posture that this animal would take, and again get into the feel of being this animal. . . . What is your body like? . . . How do you feel? . . . What is your life like? . . . Where are you and what are your surroundings like? . . .

Now imagine that you are in some kind of enclosure that restricts your freedom. . . . Examine this enclosure. . . . Discover what this enclosure is like. . . . How are you enclosed, and what is this enclosure made of? . . . Really investigate it in detail. . . . Touch it and test it, until you really know what it is like. . . . Go around and examine all parts of it. . . . Are there any possible ways to get out? . . . How do you feel in this enclosure? . . . What is outside this enclosure? If you can't see outside your enclosure, imagine what is outside. . . . What does this enclosure keep you away from? . . .

Now imagine that you talk to this enclosure, and that the enclosure can talk back to you. . . . What do you say and what does the enclosure answer? . . . Now change roles. Become the enclosure and continue the dialogue with the animal. . . . What are you like as the enclosure? . . . How do you feel? . . . What do you say to the animal? . . . Continue this dialogue for a while. Switch places on your own and play both parts. . . . As you carry on this dialogue, be aware of the character of the interaction between the enclosure and the animal. . . . What is going on between the two? . . .

Now become the animal again, and continue to explore and test the enclosure until you find a way out of it. . . . How do you get out of this enclosure? . . . When you do get out, explore what it is like to be outside this enclosure. . . . How do you feel? . . . What are your surroundings like now? . . . What is your life like, and what do you do? . . . What happens to you? . . . Compare your situation outside the enclosure with your existence when you were inside. . . . Talk to the enclosure again, . . . and see what the enclosure answers you. Keep up this dialogue for a while. . . . Now go back inside the enclosure, just for a look around. . . . How do you experience being back inside the enclosure? . . . Do you prefer being inside or being outside? . . .

Now slowly say goodbye to the enclosure. . . . Keep your eyes closed, and when you are ready, return to this room and your real body, . . . and quietly absorb your experience for a little while. . . . In a minute I will ask you to open your eyes and share your experience of being this animal in the enclosure with the others in your group. Again, tell your experience in first-person present tense, as if it were happening now. . . . O.K. Open your eyes and take about ten minutes to express your experiences in detail. . . .

Again consider to what extent your experience with this fantasy enclosure expresses something important about your life, and how you are restricted. . . . Take a few minutes to tell each other how you see that your fantasy expresses something about your existence— your life situation. . . .

Blind Object Exploration

Sit in a complete circle, without any gaps, and put on blind-folds. Don't talk at all; I want you to be as silent as possible during this experiment. (Dim or turn off lights to discourage peeking.) I'm going to give you each an object to handle and explore with all your senses except vision. We use our eyes so much that we tend to ignore our other senses and we forget how they can be used. We often use vision not to really see, but to dismiss. I glance up and see a tree, categorize it, put it in a pigeonhole, and look away. I don't usually take time to really look at it and contact it—see its special qualities and how it is in some way different from other trees. (Begin to pass out objects: see list of possibilities at end.) I'm going to give you each an object. When I do, try to find out as much as you can about it. Touch it, squeeze it, smell it, listen to it, put it to your cheek, etc. Notice to what degree you want to "know what it is" rather than just discover it with your senses. Even if you recognize it as a familiar object, see what more you can discover about it. Even if you have seen or handled this object many times, see if you can be open to the possibility of discovering something new that you never noticed before. Imagine that you are a small child and that everything is new and interesting. Now you each have an object to explore. I'm going to give you about a minute to discover all you can about this object. . . . Now I want everyone to pass your object to the person on your right, and take about a minute to explore your new object. . . .

(Repeat the instruction to "pass objects to the right" or "pass again" every 45 seconds to a minute. Remember where a prominent object began, so that you will know when the circuit is complete.)

Now place your object behind you and sit quietly and be aware of how you feel physically. . . . Be particularly aware of your hands. . . . How do they feel after exploring all these objects? . . . Now use your left hand to discover your right hand as if it were a new and strange object. . . . Now let your right hand discover your left hand in the same way. . . . How are your two hands different? . . .

In a minute I'm going to ask you to reach out to both sides and discover the hands on either side of you. Right now, I want you to be aware of how you feel about doing this, and what you imagine it will be like to do this. . . . I also want you to realize that this is a guess, a prediction *about* your future experience. You can't *know* what the future will be like, and if you cling to your prediction, this will prevent you from experiencing the situation itself when it does happen. . . .

Now reach out to both sides and discover these hands. . . . What are these hands like? . . . See if you can suspend your thinking and your judgments, and just be aware of the sensations in your hands. . . . Are these other hands active or limp, rough or gentle, heavy or slender? . . . Play games with these hands. . . . Now communicate silently with your hands, and tell these hands you are holding how you feel toward them. . . . Now very slowly say goodbye, . . . bring your hands back to yourself, . . . and again experience your hands, and how you feel physically. . . .

Now I want you to keep your eyes closed, and stand up and hold your hands in front of you. Move around in the circle until you meet someone else. When you meet someone else, bring your hands together and discover what this person's hands are like. I will help pair up people who can't find someone to be with. Take a little time to get to know these hands. . . . Play a game. . . . Have a conversation. . . . Silently communicate how you feel toward these hands. . . . Without words, slowly say goodbye with your hands, . . . and move on until you find someone else to discover. . . .

Pair up again, and this time, get to know this person's hands, . . . and also their forearms. . . . Really discover what these hands and arms are like. . . . Now slowly say goodbye, . . . and move on for awhile. . . .

Pair up again, and get to know this person's hands and forearms, . . . and include their upper arms too. . . . Again discover each other with your hands. . . . Now slowly say goodbye silently, . . . and move on to someone else. . . .

Pair up again, and get to know this person's hands, . . . and arms, . . . and now include the shoulders and the back of the neck. *Don't* touch the front of the neck—some people are very sensitive there. . . . Discover what this person is like. . . . Now slowly say goodbye with your hands, . . . and move on to someone else. . . .

Pair up again, and get to know this person's hands, . . . arms, . . . and shoulders and back of the neck, . . . and then include the hair and head, . . . and now the face. Be very gentle and careful—particularly around the eyes and mouth. . . . What is this person's face like? . . . Join hands again and express to each other how you feel. . . . Now slowly say goodbye with your hands, . . . and move on. . . . *Don't* find a new partner this time: just find a place to stand quietly and get in touch with how you feel now. What is your physical experience now, after this touching and being touched? . . .

Some people object to this kind of experiment, because they are afraid that touching another person in this way will lead directly to sex. My intention is just the opposite: I want you to realize that there are many possibilities between total isolation and total physical union, and if you do this exploring as you would with a child or an animal, you can discover this. Most people do need and want some physical contact. If you can enrich your life with some experiences of sensitive physical contact, you will be much *less* likely to feel a strong need for sex, with all its awkward consequences and complications. . . .

Now take your blindfold off and quickly form groups of 5 or 6 with as balanced sex ratio as possible, and share your experiences. . . .

(*List of sensory objects:* Basically, choose objects that are interesting to *touch, smell, hear,* etc. Don't use something that will drown out everything else. For instance, if you include a cut onion, no one will be able to smell anything else; if you include a large bell, no one will be able to hear the rustle of silk cloth or leaves. Also, of course, don't use something that could be poisonous, dangerous, messy or unpleasant, or something that is so fragile that it will quickly deteriorate. Here are some things I've used: a small bell, a short cedar board, a piece of driftwood, a chamois skin, a piece of velour cloth or silk, an abacus, a small branch of pine, fir, or other evergreen, a sprig of rosemary or some other herbs, a lemon, a rose or other flowers, a stapler, a ceramic pot, a small box with something inside, a piece of fur, a piece of soft rug, an interesting smooth rock, a bleached bone, a bare branch, a yam, an apple, a branch with seeds that rattle, a clean shoe, a pine cone, a piece of bark, a good-sized seashell.)

End of the World

Put on the blindfolds I'm giving you. . . . Now I want you to imagine that you have all been blinded by the flash of an atomic bomb. You are now in an underground shelter, and you know that the ventilation system will stop in about twenty minutes and then you will all die. *There is absolutely no possibility of escape from this room.* You have twenty minutes to live, and you have only this room and the things and people in it. I want you to be aware of how you feel, and how you make use of these last twenty minutes of your life. What do you do in these last twenty minutes? I'll tell you when the time is up. . . .

O.K. The time is up. You are all dead. . . . I want you to take a few minutes to absorb this experience, and recall how you felt and what you did during this time . . Now join together in groups of five or six *without removing your blindfolds.* . . . Now remove your blindfolds and tell each other about your experience in first-person present tense, as if it were happening now. Take about ten minutes for this. . . .

Now I'd like you to contemplate how much of your life you continue to delay and put off to some future time—a time that may never come. Why wait until the end of your life to do these things? Can you afford to wait? Take a few more minutes to discuss this in your group. . . .

(You can also just pass out the blindfolds, tell people to put them on and wear them for twenty minutes—and see what happens. Or you can structure the situation a bit more by forbidding talking, etc.)

Spaciogram

I want everyone to stand up and move around the room silently. . . . As you move around the room, notice what part of the room you feel most comfortable in. Also be aware of how you feel as you move toward and away from different people in the room. . . . Who do you feel more comfortable with, and who would you prefer to stay distant from? . . .

Now gradually choose a place in the room that you would like to occupy, and sit there. As others sit down you may want to change your place so as to be closer to, or farther away from, someone else. . . . Continue to change until you have found the most comfortable place in the room for you. Don't talk, and don't try to get someone else to move. . . .

After everyone has stopped moving, get in touch with how you feel and what it is like to be where you are. Take some time to be aware of your immediate surroundings and what it is that makes you feel comfortable there. . . . How could this place be even more comfortable for you? . . .

Now look around the room to see where everyone is. Who is in the middle of the room, and who is around the outside? . . . What clusterings or groupings do you see? Who is in these groupings, and how do the different clusterings seem different? . . . Who is by themselves? Take a little time to really see what is expressed in this arrangement. . . .

Stay where you are. Now I want each person, in turn, to say how you feel in the place you have chosen, and what it is about your place that makes you feel most comfortable there. Be specific about how you feel, and give details about what it is that you like about this place. . . .

Continue to stay where you are, and share what you experienced as you moved around the room and then found the place you are most comfortable in. . . .

(A simplified version of this is to ask everyone to get up and move around and then stand at one of two—or three or four—walls of the room, and to change location any time you want until you are most satisfied with your location. This can be a useful way of becoming aware of the polarization or fragmentation in a group.)

Home Spot

(This is most useful for a group that has met for some time in the same room.)

Now silently become aware of where you are sitting and how you feel there. . . . What is it about this location that you prefer in comparison to the other possible places in the room? . . . See if you can become aware of what makes this home spot special for you. . . . Now look around the room and decide which place in the room is most *unlike* the place where you are now. . . . What place is most different from your home spot? . . . Now I want everyone to silently move to this different place—or as close to it as possible if someone else decides to sit there too. . . . Now silently get in touch with how you feel in this new place. . . . What is this new place like? . . . What do you dislike about this place and what do you like about it? . . . Compare your experience of this place with your original place. . . . Now can you express more about what you like about your original home spot? . . .

Now I want you to stay where you are and express your experience of being in these two different places. Tell how they are different to you, and how you feel differently in them. . . .

Now return to your original place, and again get in touch with what it is like and how you feel there. . . . See if you can discover even more about what is special about this place for you. . . .

Again I want everyone to express what they are aware of now in their home spot in comparison to the different place. Can you say anything additional now about what is special about this spot to you? . . .

Connection

Everyone stand up and move slowly around the room silently. . . . Don't talk. Be aware of how you feel as you do this. . . . Be aware of who you feel drawn to and who you would prefer to stay distant from. . . . As you continue to move slowly around the room, begin to make whatever physical contact you feel comfortable making with the others. . . .

Now I want you to silently make and maintain some physical contact with *one* other person in the room. . . . Now I want each of these pairs to remain together while each of you makes physical contact with one other person in the room. . . . Now make whatever additional contact you can make and would like to make with anyone else in the room. . . . Now as long as you stay connected with these same people, make any changes of position or other adjustments that you want to make. . . . Now look around the group and become aware of how the group is connected. . . . How many contacts has each person made? . . . Who looks comfortable in their contacts, and who looks awkward and strained? Has anyone tried to make so many contacts that he is all stretched apart and pulled out of shape? . . . Who is in the center, and who is on the outside with only the two required contacts? . . .

Now stay connected, while each of you, in turn, describes your awareness of how you are connected and how you feel in this position. After everyone has done this, reflect on how this arrangement is an expression of how you are connected with people in your everyday life. Go on to share anything else you want to about this experience. . . .

Telegram

For the next five minutes, restrict your sentences to one or two words only. Be aware of how you feel, and the interaction in the group as the flood of words is slowed to a trickle and you have to choose one or two words to carry your message. . . .

Shoulder Massage

I want each person to silently find someone else that they would like to give something to and stand behind that person. . . . Eventually you can make this into a circle with everyone facing clockwise. . . . Now sit down in a close circle and silently massage or rub the back, shoulders and neck of the person in front of you. Close your eyes and don't talk. Communicate with the person in front of you with your hands, and communicate with the person behind you with noises. Experiment with different kinds of massage and listen to the noises from this person to find out what parts he wants massaged, and what kind of massage or stroking he likes best. Make noises to tell the person behind you what kind of massage you prefer. Do this for about five minutes. . . .

Without talking, turn around and face the other direction in the circle and massage the back of the person who was previously massaging you. Again communicate forward with your hands and backward with noises for about five minutes. . . .

Now take a few minutes to talk with the person in front of you and behind you and share your experience of massaging and being massaged. How did your massages differ, and how well could you communicate with each other, etc.? . . .

Underwater Organism

(Groups of about 6-10 best.)

Sit in a circle, close your eyes, and get in touch with what you experience physically. . . . Very slowly reach out your hands and touch the hands on each side of you. Imagine that you are a single cell, moving slowly together with other cells to form a single underwater organism. Without breaking contact, stand up and very slowly make the circle smaller as you gradually increase your contact with the people on either side of you. Contact these people through hands and arms, ... and gradually explore their upper arms and shoulders, ... and now move your arms slowly across their backs and contact the hands coming from the other side of these people. ... Eventually you will be side to side, linked not only with the people next to you, but also with the next people around the circle. ... Now imagine that this underwater organism is standing in a shallow sea, being gently moved by the waves. ... You can feel the gentle waves slowly swaying you back and forth, as the sunlight filters through the shallow water overhead. ... Begin to hum together softly now, and bring your humming together as you have brought your bodies together into this single organism, and continue this for a few minutes. ...

Hand Heart

Stand in a circle, close your eyes, and get in touch with your physical existence. ... Become aware of what is going on inside you. ... Now reach out on both sides and touch the hands and arms on both sides of you. ... Really explore these hands and arms. ... What are they like? ... How are they different, and how are they similar to yours? ... Continue to explore these hands and very gradually move your hands toward the center of the circle. Imagine that all these different hands, with all their different qualities, are going to slowly come together and combine in the center of the circle to form a large heart that beats with a slow rhythm. ... As your hands come together in the center, let the heart begin to contract very slowly, ... and then expand again. ... Imagine that your arms are blood vessels carrying blood to and from this heart that nourishes you and connects all your bodies together. ... Gradually give up control of your hands and let them become a part of this beating heart. ... As you do this, the heart will begin to beat more smoothly and regularly, and gradually take on a life of its own. ... Focus your attention on this beating heart, and notice how the beat changes on its own from time to time. ... Continue to be aware of the feelings in your arms and hands, and *very* gradually open your eyes and look at the beating heart and its arteries, ... and then silently look at the faces of the others in the group for a minute, as you continue to feel the beating and pumping of this heart that connects you and nourishes you. . . .

Group Machine

Form groups of 3-5 people, and *don't talk*. In a moment, I'm going to ask the people in each group to come together and become a machine. As you come together to become this machine, I want each person to make *sounds, movements,* and *physical contact* with at least two other people. Ham it up a little and enjoy yourself. Don't talk, don't plan, and do remember the three essential ingredients: *sounds, movements,* and *physical contact* with at least two other people. Now come together and become a washing machine for about four minutes. . . .

Now stop, close your eyes for a minute and get in touch with your physical existence. . . . What is going on inside you? . . . How do you feel? . . . I want you to become aware of *how* you express yourself and *how* you interact with the others in your group machine. To what extent did you want to plan and organize the machine? To what extent did you feel self-conscious, uncomfortable, and unable to let yourself go? How did the others in your group enter into being the washing machine? Did they participate with a lot of energy and vitality, or were they hesitant and somewhat paralyzed? . . . Who was most energetic and involved, and who participated least? . . . Now open your eyes and share your experiences; tell each other how you felt and what you noticed about yourself and others for five or ten minutes. . . .

Now that you have discussed your experiences and feelings of self-consciousness, I want you to become another machine. Again do this without talking or planning and with sounds, movements, and physical contact. See if you can let go more, and really enter into the activity of this machine. As you do this, be aware of how you feel and how you interact with others. Now become an automobile for about four minutes. . . .

Now stop and close your eyes for a minute, . . . and again get in touch with how you feel physically. . . . How do you feel now? . . . Absorb your experiences of the last few minutes, and become aware of how your express yourself. What part of the car did you become, what kinds of noises and movements did you make, and how did you feel as you did this? . . . How did you interact with the other parts of the car—vigorously or quietly, smoothly or with conflict, etc.? . . . How did you feel about these interactions? Who did you enjoy interacting with most and least? . . . Become aware of all the details of what went on as the group interacted. . . . Now take five or ten minutes to share your own experiences and your awareness of others. . . .

Next I want you all to become any kind of machine you want, as long as you make sounds, movements and physical contact with others. Don't talk or plan; just start moving and making noises. If you get bored with being a part of this machine, change to being a part of a different kind of machine that you enjoy more. As you do this, continue to be aware of how you express yourself through your noises, movements and physical contact, and how you feel and interact with the others. Now be any kind of machine you want for about six minutes. Go ahead. . . .

Now stop, and again close your eyes and absorb this experience. Again reflect on what you experienced, and how you express yourself. . . . Now again take about five minutes to share what more you have discovered about yourself, the others in the group, and how you interact with each other. . . .

(Other good machines to become: printing press, typewriter, airplane, power lawn mower, or any other machine with lots of moving parts and action. You can also do essentially the same kind of experiment by forming a group *animal:* octopus, elephant, dog, horse, monkey or any animal with lots of possibilities for activity and movement.)

Trust Circle

Form groups of exactly seven people (7 is ideal; 8 or 9 is O.K.) and balance sex as much as possible. . . . Stand in a circle and spread the smaller people evenly around the circle. . . . Now one person move to the center and cross your arms in front of your chest. . . . The others in the circle move up to this person and hold him lightly with your hands for a while. (Demonstrate this and what follows with one group.) I want the person in the center to close your eyes and while keeping your body straight, relax your ankles. You will begin to sway to one side, and the person on that side will hold you up. Then gently pass the center person around the circle or across the circle, . . . and very gradually increase the size of the circle. . . . Then continue passing the person for awhile, . . . and then slowly reduce the size of the circle. End by holding the person again for awhile, and all hum softly as you do this holding at the end. (or: end with *Lifting and Rocking*—see the experiment that follows this.) . . . Got the idea? Before you start, I want to mention several very important points:

The basic idea is to give the person in the center an experience of trust—he must trust you not to drop him, and you must be trustworthy enough to provide him with a comfortable, trusting situation.

Don't be rough and *don't* throw the person around. You can be smooth and gentle, even if you gradually make the circle quite large. If you find that the person is getting a rough ride, make the circle a little smaller for a while.

Don't talk or laugh. Try to do the whole thing in complete silence, so that the person in the middle can really get in touch with his experience without distraction.

Everyone in the circle should place one foot forward, and one foot well behind the other. If you do this, you can hold up quite a lot of weight even if you are not strong. If you stand close to the person in the middle, you will have less weight to hold up, so if you are small or if he is big, stand closer and keep the circle smaller. If anyone has a bad back, they should either stand close or not take part in this.

Watch the feet of the person in the center. As you pass him around, his feet may shift to one side of the circle. If this happens, shift the circle so that his feet are again in the center. If you don't stay aware of this, you may suddenly find yourself trying to support more weight than you want to. If you do find yourself with more weight than you can hold, let the person down to the floor as slowly and gently as you can.

The person in the center should relax as much as possible and still keep his body pretty straight. Don't bend your knees or hips. Leave your feet flat on the floor and let your ankles go completely limp. If the person in the center seems quite tense, take it slow and easy, and see if you can encourage him to be more trusting. Any questions? . . .

O.K. Begin now with the gentle holding. . . . Now slowly begin passing the person around, . . . and gradually increase the size of the circle, . . . and pass the person around for awhile. . . . Now reduce the size of the circle again, . . . and now gently hold the person in the center and all hum together. (or: *Lifting and Rocking*—see following experiment.) . . . Now someone else move to the center of the circle and begin again. (Repeat, using just enough instructions to remind the group, or to maintain timing of several different groups.)

Now sit down together and each tell your experience of being in the center, and what you noticed about the others—both when they were in the center, and when they were in the circle. Could you relax in the center? How did the others pass people around—with gentle caring, or as if they were loading boxes on a truck? Take about ten minutes to share experiences. . . .

(If you have fewer people, or want to do this in groups of four, another trust experiment is this: One person stands with his eyes closed while one person stands or crouches directly behind him and one person behind at each side of him. The person with eyes closed gradually tips backwards and falls, and the three behind catch him with their hands and arms under his back and shoulders. Be cautions when you begin, and with anxious people—don't let the person fall very far before catching him. When you become confident, you can let him fall until he is quite close to the floor before catching him with your arms.)

Lifting and Rocking

Form groups of seven people (or 8 or 9) and stand silently in a circle. Be silent; there should be no talking or laughing, etc. during any of this. Someone who wants to be lifted and rocked move into the center of the circle, fold and interlock your arms across your chest, and close your eyes. . . . Now someone fairly small stand directly behind the person in the center, with stronger people on both sides of him in the circle. (Demonstrate all this and what follows with one group.) Move up to the person in the center and place your hands on him and hold him gently for a while.

The person in the center should relax as much as possible and yet still keep his body fairly straight. . . . Then slowly tip the person backwards to a lying position, and shift your hands under him until you are holding him horizontal with your hands and arms under him. The small person behind will cradle the head, and the stronger ones on each side will support the chest and back, while others will hold up the hips and legs. Try to provide complete and comfortable support and keep the whole body fairly straight and level—don't let one part of the body hang down or dangle. Then begin to rock back and forth slowly or around in a small circle without moving your feet, as if you were rocking a baby. Hum together softly as you do this. Continue this for awhile. . . .

Then, if the person being rocked isn't too big for the others, slowly lift him up until he is supported on your hands over your head, and rock him there for a short time, . . . and then *very* slowly lower him to the floor, being sure to keep him level. As you lower him, gradually reduce the distance that you rock him back and forth. Do this so that when you reach the floor, he will be barely moving and he won't scrape along the floor. Also, as you near the floor, move your hands toward the edge of his body so that you can easily pull them out without disturbing him when his body comes to rest on the floor. It is possible to do this so gently that the person doesn't realize when his body is resting on the floor. Then gently remove your hands and be quiet for a little while and let the person stay undisturbed with his experience until he wants to open his eyes. . . .

(This can be a very beautiful experience of being cared for, *if* it is done with care and gentleness. It can be very moving for people who feel alone and distant from others. You can also begin by lifting the person from a lying position on the floor. It's a little more work and it's awkward forcing your hands under the person.)

Group Back Massage
(Groups of 8-10; can also do it with 6 or 7.)

One person lies comfortably, face down with elbows out and hands up near his head. The leader kneels at the head, and three or four people kneel at each side of the person lying down. The whole massage is done without talking, with the person at the head leading and coordinating the others through gestures of his hands and head. *Everyone should try to massage in the same way, and with the same strength, as indicated by the leader.* Massage the entire body, including the head, fingers and feet. Move back and forth over whatever parts of the body are nearest you, and try not to leave any parts out. The massage consists of several episodes of about twenty seconds, with about a ten-second pause after each, so that the receiver can quietly experience his body. Each episode involves only one way of using the hands—rubbing, slapping with palms, etc. Each episode should begin very lightly, then gradually increase, and then decrease and end very lightly, so there is no sudden contact at the beginning and no sudden break of contact at the end. Also, the earlier episodes should be fairly vigorous and stimulating, and the later episodes lighter, ending with very gentle massage, or static application of pressure at only one or two points along the spine. Here's a good sequence: (Demonstrate)

1) *Slapping*: with palms down. . . .

2) *Chopping*: with edge of hands. . . .

3) *Tapping*: with fingertips. . .

4) *Kneading*: place fingertips in a circle, then bring them together and up. . . .

5) *Walking*: use one or two fingers and thumb as if they were legs. . . .

6) *Rubbing*: with palms moving in a circle. . . .

7) *Pressing*: with palm, very gradually increase pressure, hold, and then very slowly reduce pressure. Do this only once. . . .

8) *Stroking*: with fingertips, back and forth lightly. . . .

9) *Pressing*: with fingertips. End by removing one finger at a time, beginning with little finger. . . .

10) Leader (only) places two index fingers somewhere on spine, about a foot apart. Then increase

pressure on one finger, while decreasing pressure on
the other. Alternate once or twice, then very gradually lift low pressure finger completely off, and then
the other. Then wait silently and let the receiver
enjoy his experience as long as he wishes. . . .

You can vary this sequence with many other possibe ways to
massage. You can rub with palms, with fingers, with knuckles or the
heel of your hand. You can also knead with the palms or between
thumb and fingers, stroke with the palms, etc. *It is very important
that everyone do the same thing at the same time, in as much the
same way as possible, and that all begin and end at the same time.* If
you don't do this, the receiver will have a strange and disconcerting
experience instead of a pleasant one. Be aware of what the others are
doing and stay with them. The leader can silently indicate by moving
his hands before each episode, how he wants everyone to massage.
Any questions? . . . O.K. Go ahead. . . .

Secrets

We keep secrets because we imagine that if we were honest and
open, there would be some kind of unpleasant consequence—others
wouldn't like us, would take advantage of us, would be disgusted and
reject us, etc. This experiment gives you a chance to reality-test some
of your catastrophic expectations without suffering any consequences. I want to collect your secrets *anonymously* on these slips of
paper (give out paper), and then you can see how people respond to
your secrets without knowing whose they are. You can also get some
idea of what kinds of things others are keeping secret from you.
Close your eyes now and think of two or three secrets about yourself
that you would *least* want the others in the group to know. What
information about yourself do you think would be most difficult for
you to reveal or be most damaging to your relationship with the
people here? . . .

Now I want you to write your secrets on the pieces of paper I
gave you. Write them clearly, and with enough detail so that anyone
reading them will know exactly what you mean. For instance, don't
just write "I'm afraid of people," say exactly which people you are

afraid of and what you fear from them, such as "I'm afraid of strong men who might injure me physically." *Please don't be phony.* Either write a real secret that is important to you, or just write that you are unwilling to write down any of your secrets. . . . When you have finished writing your secrets, fold the paper twice and place it in a pile in the middle of the floor. As you put your paper on the pile, shuffle the pile a little, and go back to your place. . . .

Now that everyone has put their paper in the pile, I want each person to go to the pile and pick up one, and then sit down again. . . .

In a minute I want one person to read the secret on the piece of paper he picked up *as if it were his own.* Begin by saying "This is my secret: I—" Try to imagine that you really become the person who wrote this secret, and see if you can express something more about how you feel *as this person with the secret.* Even if the secret seems not important to you, it was important to someone, so please respect that. After one person has read "his" secrets, I want the others in the group to say how they feel toward this person who has just revealed "his" secrets. Don't say anything except your *feeling responses:* "I feel disgusted," "I'm surprised," "I don't care that you do that," or whatever your response to each secret is. If any secrets are true of you, and you are willing to admit it, please do so. After everyone in the group has given his response, go on to someone else who reads his paper as if the secrets were his own, while the others give their feeling responses. Any questions? O.K. Go ahead. . . .

Now take about ten minutes to discuss anything you want to share about what you experienced or discovered through this experiment. How did you feel as someone else read your secrets and as the others responded? How did you feel as you heard the others' secrets, etc. . . .

(To get in touch with the catastrophic expectations and the part of you that insists on keeping secrets, ask people to think of several secrets that they wouldn't like other people to know. . . . Then switch roles and become these other people or "society" and talk silently to yourself as if you were these other people. . . . Now continue to be these people responding to your secrets and let your words come out in a whisper or a mumble. . . . Now let your words become louder and louder. . . . Become aware of what you say, and then go on to share experiences, etc.—see the *Secrets* experiment in the *Pairs* section for other possibilities.)

. (In a group that has built up a good deal of trust and warmth, try the following streamlined version of the same experiment. Sit in a close circle, holding hands with eyes closed, and sit quietly for awhile. Then each person, when you are willing, tell a deep secret that you have some fear of revealing. After everyone has done this, open your eyes and give your feeling response to these revealed secrets.)

Imaginary Clay

I have a large piece of imaginary clay in my hands. It can be molded, rolled, drawn, stretched, patted, etc., into absolutely *anything*. (Use hands to pantomime molding the clay into different shapes, etc.) Now I'm going to give a piece of this clay to one person in the group, and I want this person to get the "feel" of this clay with his fingers and then spend a couple of minutes making the clay into some other shape. Be aware of your hands as they move with this imaginary clay, and see what kind of creation emerges from this movement. When you are finished, give what you have created to anyone else in the group that you feel like giving it to. Then it is his turn to create something out of this clay to give to someone else. Continue this until each person has had at least one chance to shape the clay. Do all this without *any* words or talking. Listen and observe. Any questions? . . . O.K. Here is your clay. (Pantomime giving out clay.) Go ahead. . . .

Now silently absorb what you were aware of in yourself, and what you noticed in the other people as you modeled this imaginary clay. How did you feel as you received the clay and as you were modeling the clay? Were you mostly "self-conscious" or could you really get into the feel of the clay and the movements of your hands? Did you think and plan while you were doing it, or could you let go and let something happen of itself? Who did you choose to give your creation to? What did you notice about the others as they shaped the clay? What did each person create and how did you feel about each creation? What was the *process* of creation like with each person—the style or technique that each person used. Did one person carefully draw out the clay, while another just quickly and carelessly tossed something together? As one person gave his creation to another, what was the interaction like, and what went on between the two people? Was it a gift, a discard, a missile? When a person received the clay, did they enjoy what was given to them, or immediately smash it and start to reshape it? Did some people receive several gifts while others got only one? Reflect on all the details of what went on and share your awareness with each other for about ten minutes. . . .

Sculptor

Now pair up with someone and stand facing each other without talking until everyone is paired up. . . . Now I want the taller person in each pair to be a sculptor, and the shorter person to be clay. I want the sculptor to take some time to look at your partner and become really aware of him. Notice how he holds his body, the tilt of his head, etc. . . . *Without planning*, gently begin to change his posture so that you exaggerate what you are aware of. If you are aware of his head tilted back, tilt it back further. Use your hands as if you were molding a clay or wax statue. I want the person who is being molded into a statue to be aware of how you feel during this modeling. . . . Continue to change your statue's position until you are satisfied with the result. When you are through modeling, step back and examine your statue to see what it is like and what it expresses. . . .

Now face your statue and make your body into an exact copy of your statue. I want both of you to get the feel of this statue and what this statue expresses. . . .

Now switch places. Now the shorter person is the sculptor. Take some time to look at your partner and become really aware of him. . . . Then, without planning, gently begin to mold your partner, . . . and continue until you are satisfied with the statue you have created. . . . Then step back and examine your statue to see what it is like and what it expresses. . . . Then make yourself into an exact copy of your statue, and both get the feel of being this statue.

Now take a few minutes to share your experiences with your partner. Tell each other what you became aware of in yourself and in your partner as you did this. . . .

(When each individual statue is finished, you can also bring them all together into interaction with each other in a group sculpture or tableau, if you wish.)

Huddling

(Best in large groups. Ten people is about minimum.)

Close your eyes and stand up. . . . Get in touch with your own experience as you stand alone. . . . How do you feel physically? . . . Notice when you become occupied with thoughts or images, and return to your physical existence. . . . Now leave your arms at your sides and begin to move slowly toward the center of the room. . . . Be aware of what is going on in you as you move toward the others. What fantasies occur to you, and how do you feel? . . . Keep your eyes closed, and when you reach the others in the center of the room, gently contact the others as if you were a covey of quail seeking warmth in the winter. . . . Now gently and slowly weave your way through these other people, and be aware of how you feel as you do this. . . . When you come to the edge of the group, stay there a little while, and be aware of how you feel there, and then turn around and gently burrow your way into the group again. . . . Take a little time to really become aware of how you experience this. . . .

Imitation Circle

(Requires at least ten people.)

Each person in the group find a posture that is comfortable for you. Now each person pick one person who is within the ¼ of the group on your right. It doesn't matter who you choose, and no one has to know who you have chosen. . . . When I say "go," I want each person to imitate this person you have chosen. Copy the posture, facial expression, movements, noises, etc. Imitate everything this other person does, and continue to do this for several minutes. O.K., go. . . .

(No great insight in this one. Many people are surprised at the result. It's fun and it livens people up nicely if they have been sitting still for awhile or if the group energy is low. Try it.)

Nature of Man

I want you to discuss the nature of man for about five minutes. I want you to make statements about the basic nature of man. Don't ask questions, and don't get hung up in deciding who is "right," or what "basic nature" really means. Do share your ideas and beliefs and listen to the feelings and opinions of the others. State your ideas about the basic nature of man in detail, so that the others can know exactly what you mean. It may help if you begin with, "Mankind is basically—" Then finish this sentence with your idea and give some evidence or specific examples to show exactly what you mean. Any questions? . . . O.K. Go ahead. . . .

Now silently absorb the discussion you have just had. . . . And now silently summarize your own beliefs about the nature of man. . . . Look around the group and summarize the statements that each other person made. What is each person's idea of the nature of man? . . .

Now I want you each to say the *same* statements that you made earlier, but instead of saying "Mankind is basically—" say "*I* am basically—" Also identify with all your evidence and examples. If you said "Man is basically warlike. Look at all the war and conflict in history," change this to "*I* am basically warlike. Look at all the wars and conflict in *my* history." As you say these sentences, be aware of how you feel as you say them. Be aware of whether you can really identify with them and feel "Yes, that is true of me," or whether you resist the identification, and feel "No, that is *not* true of me." How do you feel as others say their modified statements? Can you recognize the truth in what they say about themselves? Do this identification now, and after everyone has done this, go on to share what you experienced while doing this. . . .

Art, Movement and Sound

The process of artistic creation in different media has been a means of self-expression for millenia. By deepening awareness of the creative *process,* we can resolve and clarify this expression of ourselves. This resolution and clarification releases energy, and permits us to develop and grow further, and we can realize that every area of our lives can become a medium for growth, creation, and self-expression.

Left-Right Drawing

(Materials: one very large set of oil pastels for each 8-10 people, and several large pieces of good heavy white paper about 2' x 3' per person. You can also use other media, of course. Oil pastels are quite cheap, they are much nicer than crayons, and are much less messy than paints. The very large sets have a rich variety of beautiful colors that provide a wide range of possibilities for self-expression.)

Without talking, go to the box of oil pastels and let your right hand choose a color that fits your right hand, and let your left hand choose a color that fits your left hand. Make a small mark on paper with the colors you have found, to be sure that these are the colors you want. When you have chosen your colors, take one of the large pieces of paper and find a place to sit down where you can be by yourself quietly. Be sure that there is some space around you, so that you will not be distracted by the people near you. Don't draw anything on your paper until I tell you to. . . .

Now hold one color in each hand in front of you where you can see them easily, and look at these colors for a while. . . . Now close your eyes and take these colors with you as images, and just watch what these two colors do. If you can't easily take your colors with you when you close your eyes, open your eyes, look at your colors for a while, and then again close your eyes and take the colors into your private world of images and see what these colors do. . . . These colors might move around, might form abstract images, or grow into images of recognizable things. Just let go, and take a little time to observe what these colors do. . . .

In a minute I'll ask you to open your eyes and silently draw with both these colors on your paper. You can draw some of the forms or images that came to you when your eyes were closed, or draw whatever emerges. Use both hands alternately, or at the same time if you wish. As you draw, focus your awareness on the *process* of drawing and creating. Notice how the pastel feels in each hand, how the colors appear on the paper, how each of your hands moves, and how the two colors interact on the paper. Notice any "shoulds" that restrict what you are doing, and let them go. As much as you can, let go of goals and just be aware of what is happening as you draw—what do the colors want to do, and how do your hands feel like moving? Let the materials and the process of drawing lead you and direct you as you draw. O.K. Open your eyes now and draw quietly without talking for about ten or fifteen minutes. . . .

Now I want you each to take several minutes to express your experience of doing this to the others in the group. Hold your drawing so that the others can see it. Tell which color belongs to each hand, and describe your awareness of the process of creating your drawing—how your hands moved, how the colors interacted and how you felt as the colors created forms and images on the space. (Demonstrate doing this with your own drawing. For example: "Red is my right-hand color and purple is my left-hand color. I realized immediately that I didn't want to draw simultaneously with both hands, so I let them alternate. Initially the red was much more active, sort of swooping and taking over most of the paper, and the purple was feeling a little defensive, like "stay out of my territory." I also quickly found out that the purple could easily overmark the red but it was harder for the red to overmark the purple. I made a bunch of squiggles with the purple, and then I went in with the red and filled in the space between the purple. I came over here with red where there was already purple, and then the purple made it solid so that the red couldn't get in. Toward the end I began blending the colors more, and I liked that." Now go ahead and describe your awareness of your process of making this drawing. . . .

Now that you have each described your experience of drawing, I want you to silently reflect on this. . . . To what extent do your two hands and their two colors express two sides of your personality and how these two sides interact? . . . Do the two colors keep separate on the paper, or do they interact? Do they cooperate, or are they in conflict? . . . What do the colors themselves express? . . . To what extent can you see that the process of creating this drawing expresses something about your own functioning? . . . What do you notice about the others' drawings—what the two colors seem to express, how they interact and what each person said about his process of creation? . . . What differences or similarities do you see as you look around at all the drawings? . . . Realize that each person knows most about his own process. Others' comments and observations are useful only if they are offered freely and easily, without demanding that they be accepted as correct, etc. Now take about five or ten minutes to share your observations and discuss them. . . .

Self-Drawing

Without talking, go to the box of oil pastels and pick out several colors that you would like to draw with. If you can, pause and quietly let the colors choose you. Make a small mark on paper with the colors you find, to be sure these are the colors you want. After you have chosen your colors, take one of the large pieces of paper and find a place to sit down where you can be by yourself quietly. Be sure that there is some space around you so that you will not be distracted by the people near you. Don't draw anything until I tell you to. . . . Now close your eyes, and get in touch with your body and the actual sensations that you can feel. . . . Become aware of how you feel inside. . . . Now let some visual images come to you that somehow express your inner self and how you feel about your life. . . . These images might be abstract forms or they might be something that you can recognize, but they somehow represent yourself as you really are. . . . Take a little while to let these images develop. . . .

In a minute I'm going to ask you to open your eyes and to create a drawing that represents yourself with these colors you have chosen. If you decide that you need different colors, quietly go to the box and choose whatever colors you need. As you draw, focus your awareness on the process of drawing and how you feel as you create. Let go of specific goals, and just be aware of how your hands move and how the color appears on the paper. Let these materials and the process of drawing take over, so that the colors and your hands decide where and how to draw next. Let a line go as far as it wants to, stop when it wants to, change direction when it wants to, etc. Open your eyes now and take about ten or fifteen minutes to make a drawing that represents yourself. . . .

Now hold your drawing so that the others can see it. I want you each to take three or four minutes to describe your drawing of yourself. Do this in *first-person present tense as if you were describing yourself.* For instance, "I have a lot of criss-crossing lines, I am mostly confused and muddy-looking. On my right side I have harsh jagged angry red lines cutting into my peaceful blue and green," etc. Also express your awareness of the process of creating yourself and how you felt about what was happening. For instance, "At first I had only these harsh red lines, and a lot of space which I didn't like. Then as I tried to fill up the space, I became all confused and cluttered, so then I made this patch of peaceful blue and green," etc. Also be aware of how you feel and what you notice as you describe yourself. Now each take a few minutes to describe your drawing in first-person present tense. . . .

Now that each person has described his drawing, I want you to silently reflect on this experience. . . . What did you discover about yourself and others as you expressed yourselves through these drawings? . . . What similarities and differences did you notice in the drawings? . . . Now take another five or ten minutes to share your observations and discuss them. . . .

(A variation of this self-drawing asks each person to begin by choosing three colors that he likes most and three colors that he dislikes most and insist that he use all of these colors in his drawing. Or you can ask each person to first make a self-drawing with colors that he likes, and then make a self-drawing with colors that he dislikes. Then describe these two drawings and the process of creating them, and compare the two. Drawing with the disliked colors is usually more frustrating, and it can also be quite expressive and revealing.)

(You can also draw a part of yourself that you do or don't like, or a feeling that causes you difficulty. You can also draw some important person in your life—spouse, parent, child, boss, lover, etc.—or some force that affects your life—worry, disease, devil, god, old age, authority, etc. A drawing of your whole family can express a great deal about how you feel toward them and how you relate to them.)

Drawing Dialogue

I want you each to go to the box of oil pastels and quietly choose a color that expresses some important aspect of yourself. . . . Now silently pair up with someone who has a different color than you do. Each pair take one of the large pieces of paper and find a place to sit down. Put the paper between you, and sit at opposite sides of the paper. . . . Hold your color in the hand that you *don't* write with. In a minute, I want you to begin to silently draw together on this piece of paper. Don't divide the paper and make separate drawings, and don't plan, discuss, or decide what you will draw together. Just begin to draw slowly and focus your awareness on the process of drawing and how you feel as you interact with your partner. Let your awareness and your feelings flow into the process of drawing. You might alternate drawing, or draw at the same time, or even gently move your partner's hand for a short time and draw with his color if he is agreeable to this. Begin to do this now, and take ten or fifteen minutes to interact with your partner as this drawing develops between you. . . .

Now tell each other what you experienced as you worked on this drawing together. Express what you were aware of as you interacted and how you felt during this silent dialogue. How does this drawing and the process of making it express the kind of relationship you have with your partner? Take about five minutes to do this. . . .

(You can also do this with three or more people, or with a family. This kind of experiment can express a great deal about the patterns of relationship and interaction that exist within a family.)

Experimenting

(Need lots of good-sized sheets of cheap paper for the following experiments.)

Go to the box of oil pastels and choose several colors that please you. Then take ten or fifteen sheets of paper and sit down somewhere. . . . I want you to experiment with different ways of putting colors onto the paper. I also want you to be aware of how you feel as you experiment with these different ways of drawing. Notice which ways are pleasing to you and which ways are less satisfactory to you. Now imagine that the color in your hand is a flying bird. Move your hand as if it were a bird swooping down to make some marks on the paper. . . . Now change to another color and imagine that the pastel is an ant, and see what kind of marks it makes as an ant. Use the same paper until it gets too crowded; then put it aside and start on a clean sheet. Change colors each time you change ways of drawing. . . . Now imagine that the pastel is a whip. . . . Now it is a bulldozer or scraper. . . . Now it is a massaging hand. . . . Now it is a motorcycle. . . . Now it is a horse. . . . Now it is a rattlesnake. . . . Now it is a knife. . . . Now it is a cat's tongue. . . .
Now continue further on your own for the next five minutes. Think of something that moves, and then let the pastel become that and see how it puts the color on the paper. . . .

Now take a clean sheet of paper and use several of the ways of drawing that you like *best* for the next couple of minutes, and be aware of how you feel as you do this. . . .

Now take another clean sheet of paper and use several of the ways of drawing that you liked *least* for the next couple of minutes, and be aware of how you feel as you do this. . . .

Now sit quietly for a minute or two and contemplate these last two sheets of paper. Be aware of what it is that you like and dislike about these different ways of applying color. . . . How did your hand move differently on each of these two sheets? . . . How did you feel as you drew on these two sheets, and how does the color look on the paper? . . . Are there any ways in which the liked and disliked ways of drawing express opposing qualities, such as slow-fast, big-small, etc.?

Now place your sheets where the others in the group can see them. Take turns expressing your awareness of the process of drawing, and what you like and dislike about these different ways of drawing. After each of you have done this, take another five or ten minutes to compare the differences and similarities in the ways that each person drew as each thing—bird, horse, etc. Then discuss anything else you became aware of in this experiment, or in each others' drawings. . . .

Emergence

Go to the box of oil pastels and quietly choose three colors that you like, and that are pleasing to you when they are together. Make heavy marks with these three colors side by side on paper, to be sure that you like them together. When you have found three colors that you like, take several pieces of paper and sit down by yourself somewhere you won't be distracted by the people around you. Don't draw on the paper until I tell you to. . . .

I want you to choose any simple line-form—a rectangle, a circle, a part of a circle, an angle, two lines crossing, etc. (Show examples.)

□ ○ ∟ ⊂ ⊃ ⊂ ℓ ∧ = ∪ ⟨

I want you to use only this one line-form, and draw this one form on your paper in different ways. You can draw it in different colors, different sizes, different orientations, overlapping or separate, etc. (Show an example.)

Do this easily and experimentally, without any goal except to be aware of the whole process of doing this—the feel of the chalk in your hand, the colors, the emerging patterns, and how you feel as you do this. After you have done this for a while, some pattern or object will begin to emerge in your drawing. Instead of just being a bunch of line-forms in different colors and sizes, you will be able to see something definite emerging—some object, perhaps several things, a person or a face, etc. When something specific begins to emerge from your drawing, notice how you feel toward it and see if you can continue to develop it while still using the same line-form for a while. Then stop using this line-form and develop the emerging thing still more, drawing, connecting, or shading in any way you want while still using the same three colors. Any questions? . . . Begin doing this now without talking, and take about ten minutes to do this. . . .

Now take a couple of minutes to silently look at your drawing and review the process of creating it and what went on in you as you did this. . . .

Now hold your drawing where the others in the group can see it and describe your awareness of the process of creating it—the different stages of development, how you felt, what you did, etc. Then take a few more minutes to discuss your awareness of each other's drawings—the colors and line-forms each person chose, what emerged from each person's drawing, and what this might express about each person. . . .

Now take another sheet of paper. I want you to repeat this same drawing experiment, but this time do it in the reverse of the way that you just did it. For instance, if you previously used a hard angular line-form, this time choose a soft, curving line-form. If you previously began with a cluster of forms in the center of your paper with the same color, begin this time with scattered forms in different colors. If you previously used heavy strokes to make dark lines, this time use lighter strokes to make fainter lines. As much as possible recall how you did this experiment the first time and reverse your way of doing it. Again start by making these line-forms while focusing on the process. See what emerges and then develop whatever emerges, first with the same form and then drawing any way that you want to. Again take about ten minutes to do this. . . .

Now silently look at the drawing you have just made, and focus your awareness on whatever emerged and developed in it. . . . Really become aware of it in detail. What are all its qualities and characteristics? . . . Now identify with whatever emerged. . . . Become it and describe yourself. . . . What are you like, . . . and how do you feel as this thing? . . . What is your life like, and what do you do? . . . Really get into the details of your experience of being whatever emerged from your drawing. . . .

Now I want you to hold your drawing so that the others in the group can see it. I want you to continue to identify with whatever emerged in your drawing and take a few minutes to describe yourself in first-person present tense. Really express all the details of being this thing. After you have each done this, take another five or ten minutes to share anything else you noticed about others' drawings and your own, discuss the process of making them, etc. . . .

Name-Writing

Go to the box of oil pastels and choose a color that pleases you and expresses something about you. Also take about ten sheets of paper from the stack, and sit down quietly somewhere you won't be distracted by the others near you. . . . In all of these experiments I want you to hold your pastel in the hand that you *don't* write with.

Now I want you to slowly write your name backwards, as if your name were reflected in a mirror. Use the top half of the sheet of paper to do this, and be aware of how you feel as you write your name backwards with your unaccustomed hand. . . .

Now use the bottom half of the paper to do the same thing as before—writing your name backwards with your unaccustomed hand—but now do it with the *least possible effort*. Be aware of what you experience as you do this. : . .

Take another sheet of paper and write your name forwards in such a way that you fill the whole sheet of paper. . . .

Now on the same piece of paper, write your name as small as you possibly can. . . .

Now put all these signatures where the others can see them, and tell each other about your experience of doing these different kinds of name-writing. . . .

Take another piece of paper and write your name very slowly with your unaccustomed hand. Use this signature to draw a time-line map of your life up to the present time. The finished signature will somehow represent the different periods of your life and what you experienced at these times. . . .

Take another piece of paper and on one half of the sheet, use your name to draw a sketch of yourself as you really are. . . .

Now on the other half of the same sheet, use your name to draw a sketch of yourself as one of your parents sees you. . . .

Take another sheet of paper and on half of it use your name to draw a part of yourself that you like. . . .

On the other half of the same sheet, use your name to draw a part of yourself that you don't like. . . .

Now place your signatures where everyone can see them and take turns telling about them and how you felt as you did them. Describe your time-line signature and your sketches of yourself in detail, and express your awareness of the process of doing them. After everyone has done this, take some time to discuss what you notice about each others' signatures and what they express. . . .

Self-Sculpture
(Materials: For each person, have about 5-10 pounds of modeling clay and a piece of cardboard or plywood about two feet square for modeling on. You can use cheap paper painter's "drop cloths" to keep clay off a good floor or rug.)

I want you each to take a good full double-handful of clay. Also get a board to put the clay on and find a comfortable place to sit, with some space around you. ... Now take a few minutes to get acquainted with the clay. ... Feel its texture and weight. ... Feel the way it changes shape as you explore it with your fingers. ... Try different ways of shaping it—squeezing, patting, rolling, pulling, pushing, stroking, punching, etc. ... Discover what this clay is like and what it is capable of. ...

Now that you have explored your clay, shape it all together into a fairly round ball and set it gently on your board in front of you. Close your eyes, sit in a comfortable position, and focus your awareness on your hands and fingers that have just been exploring this clay. ... Notice how your fingers and hands feel. ... Now turn inward even more and let your attention flow into the different areas of your body. ... Become aware of what you feel in each different part of your body. ...

Now visualize an image of your round ball of clay, and imagine that it will slowly change and shape itself into an image of yourself. This image might be a fairly realistic representation, or it might be quite abstract. Don't try to change this imaginary ball of clay; let it change itself slowly into some representation of yourself. ... It might go through quite a few changes, or perhaps form two or more images of yourself. ... Whatever it does, just watch it closely as it develops, without interference from you. ...

Now keep your eyes closed and reach out to the real ball of clay in front of you, and hold it gently in your hands for a little while. ... Focus your attention on your hands and fingers, and let them begin to move and get acquainted with the clay again. ... Now I want you to begin to create an image of yourself out of this clay with your eyes closed. As you do this, focus on all the details of the *process* of shaping the clay—how the clay feels, how your fingers move, the images that come to you as the clay changes shape, etc. ... As much as you can, let the clay and your fingers lead you in this shaping, and see what develops out of this process of shaping yourself out of clay. ... You will have about fifteen minutes to do this. ...

(Give a little warning near the end of the time period.)

Now slowly open your eyes and look at what you have made out of the clay. . . . Continue to work on it a little if you wish, but don't make any major changes in it. . . . Look at it carefully and be aware of what it is like—all its properties and characteristics. . . . How do you feel toward this image of yourself? . . . Now identify with this sculpture. Become it, and describe yourself. . . . What are you like? . . . How do you feel as this sculpture? . . . What is your existence like? . . . Explore all the details of being this sculpture. . . .

Now I want each person, in turn, to take a few minutes to describe your self-sculpture. Identify with your self-sculpture and tell about yourself in detail—what you are like, how you feel, what your existence is like, etc. . . . Do this all in first-person present tense. After each person has done this, take another five or ten minutes to share your awareness of each other's self-sculptures, any similarities or differences you notice, what they express to you, etc. . . .

Body Movement

Ideally, have a very large area to move in, such as a gym with a wood or cork floor. Any large room with a clean smooth floor will do. A large expanse of lawn is fine on a nice day that is neither too cold nor too hot. Wear loose or flexible clothes that don't hinder your movements. Remove shoes and socks, and as much of your clothing as you feel comfortable without.

Basically, the aim is to focus attention on your body and let go, so that your body can do whatever it wants to do without planning or direction. As you focus attention on your body, you will become aware of parts of your body that want to move. Let these parts move in any way they want to—choppy, graceful, awkward, flowing, or whatever feels right for the parts that are moving. The parts of your body that move may bring other parts of your body into movement too. Some movements may change and develop into other kinds of movement before they stop. As some movements stop, others may emerge, or your body may want to rest or pause for a while. Continue to focus your attention on your body and let it do whatever it wants to do. Move in whatever ways you want to, for as long as you want to. As you do this, your body may want to make sounds, and images may come to you. Let these sounds and images also become part of your movement, and continue to see what emerges and develops from these expressions.

Most of the experiments that follow are more structured than what I have just described. I have also suggested music to be used with some of them, which structures the situation further. This structure makes it easier for most people to get moving in certain ways, and at the same time prevents certain other ways of self-expression that would emerge with a different kind of music or without music. African drumming is excellent for stimulating people and getting them to move and loosen up, and also makes it very difficult to move slowly or flowingly.

Although music is useful to break people out of habits and inhibitions, it is also important to explore how you limit and inhibit yourself, and what parts of your body are tense and held in. Be sure that any music you use is stimulating and expressive, and as little structured as possible and appropriate to the experiment. Don't use music with words, because this will impose additional structure. *No* music is far preferable to bad or inappropriate music. With a new group, or a group that is tight and self-conscious, a lot of music and structure is useful to get them going. After this loosening up, do other experiments with less structure and without music to allow more self-expression and self-awareness to develop. Experiments with eyes closed are particularly important for a group that is new or self-conscious. This helps to prevent people from judging their own movements and comparing them with others. Since no one else can see, either, it also reduces fantasies of others' observations and judgments. Keeping eyes closed also helps focus attention on the body and what it feels and expresses.

I have made some specific suggestions for music to use with some of the experiments below. As you try some of these experiments, you may find that some other selection feels as good or better to you, or to the people you are working with. Try using different selections with the same experiment to see what effects they have, and choose what is most useful. I have made no suggestions for music with some experiments because they are much more useful without music. Once people are loosened up somewhat, all these experiments are best without music. The lack of external structure provides the greatest freedom for self-expression and self-discovery.

Breathing into Your Body

Find a place with plenty of space around you and lie down. Close your eyes and find a comfortable position. . . . Take some time to become aware of your body. . . . Now focus your attention on your breathing. . . . Notice all the details of your breathing, as the air flows effortlessly into your body and then out again. . . . Feel the air as it moves into your nose or mouth and down your throat, and feel your chest and belly expand to receive this life-giving air. . . .

Now imagine that you breathe into other parts of your body. Imagine that some of the air that you breathe in flows down into your pelvis, on down your legs, and into your toes. Imagine that your legs expand a little as you breathe in this air, and contract a little as you breathe out. . . . Do this for a couple of minutes.

Now try breathing into your arms and fingers for awhile, . . . and notice how you feel as you do this. . . .

Now breathe into your head and neck. . . .

Centering

Now tune into your lower stomach or the small of your back. Somewhere in this area is a center from which all your movements go outward. Now move slowly toward this center in any way you want, . . . and now move slowly outward from this center. . . . Continue this alternation between moving toward your center, and then away from your center. Be aware of how you move, and how you feel as you do this for the next few minutes.

Compression-Expression

(Piano music of Erik Satie, Vol. 1. Angel S-36482.)

Keep your eyes closed. I want you to exaggerate this alternation between slowly withdrawing toward your center, and then moving outward toward the world. Continue to do what you have been doing, but exaggerate it and see what else you can become aware of

in your feelings and movements as you do this. . . . Now exaggerate it
still further, so that you alternate between compressing yourself into
a very tight ball, and then expressing yourself toward the world. . . .

   Now continue this alternation between compression and expression, but open your eyes as you move outward. As you move
outward, direct your movements silently toward another person.
Open up to this person into some position that feels good and hold
this position for several seconds. Then slowly withdraw to compression and close your eyes. Then move outward again and express
yourself toward someone else, and hold this position for awhile. Be
aware of what goes on in these silent interactions: how you feel, how
you and others move, and what these movements seem to express. . . .

Grounding

   Stand up with your eyes closed and become aware of how you
are standing. . . . Explore any tension you feel, and see if you can
release it. . . . Now focus your attention on your feet and legs, . . .
and the contact of your feet with the ground. . . . Without moving
your feet, be aware of how your weight is distributed between them.
. . . Is most of your weight on the heel, or on the ball of your foot?
. . . Is there more weight on the inside edge of your foot or the
outside edge? . . . Notice any differences you feel between your feet.
. . . Be aware of how your feet contact the ground. Do your feet
receive the ground, grip it, draw back from it, etc.? . . . Now be
aware of how your legs feel, and notice any differences between
them. . . . How do they support your upper body and connect you to
your feet? . . .

   Now begin to move your feet and legs a little, and continue to
explore your contact with the ground as you move. Notice how your
legs and feet feel as your weight shifts. . . . Now open your eyes and
continue to experience your feet and legs as you walk slowly. . . .
Notice how your feet contact the floor and how you stride. . . . Do
you strike the floor, or stamp, grab, caress, slide, etc.? . . . Now walk
at your usual speed, and continue to be aware of your feet and legs.
. . . Now walk quickly. . . . Now run slowly. . . . Now be aware of
how your contact changes as you slow to a fast walk, . . . and then to

your usual walking speed, ... to a slow walk, ... and finally stand still again with your eyes closed. ... Stay with your experience for a little while. ...

Toward-Away

Keep your eyes closed and imagine something specific that attracts you very much—something that you would like to move toward. ... Visualize it clearly, and be aware of how you feel toward it. Be particularly aware of what you feel in your face. ... Now let your feelings flow into slow movement toward it, and be aware of how your body moves and feels. ... Move toward this thing that attracts you, and then take some time to touch it and contact it in whatever way you want to. ...

Now move slowly away from this thing, and let your movements express how you are still drawn back to it, even though you are moving away. ...

Now stay where you are and imagine that very close to you is something specific that repels you strongly—something that you would like to move far away from. Visualize it clearly, and be aware of how you feel toward it. Be particularly aware of what you feel in your face. ... Now let your feelings flow into slow movement away from this thing, and be aware of how your body moves and feels as you move away. ...

Now I want you to move back toward this thing that repels you and experience your feelings toward it more clearly. Begin to move back toward this thing and be aware of how you feel and how you move. ... Approach this thing closely. When you reach it, take some time to examine it and discover what it is like. ... Discover more about what it is that repels you, ... and go on to discover what other qualities and characteristics this thing has. ... Can you discover something about this thing that you can appreciate—something that actually attracts you toward it? ... Go on to discover more about it. ... Now again move slowly away from this thing, and be aware of how you feel and move as you do this. ...

Tensing

Find a place with plenty of space around you and lie down.

Close your eyes, and find a comfortable position. Focus your attention on your body and be aware of where your body feels comfortable and at ease, and where it feels tense or uncomfortable. . . . Now tense your body as hard as you can for a few seconds—really hard, . . . and then let go completely. . . . Do this several more times, and stay aware of how your body feels as you do this. . . .

Cocoon

(Debussy: Reverie, on Laurindo Almeida: Reverie for Spanish Guitars. Capitol p 8571. Start music as breaking out of cocoon begins.)

Find a comfortable closed-up position on the floor in which you feel safe from the world. . . . Close your eyes and keep them closed until I ask you to open them. Imagine that you are in a cocoon, surrounded by a soft strong shell that protects you. . . . Take some time to explore your existence inside this cocoon. . . . Discover what this cocoon is like, and how you feel there. . . . Discover how much space you have in your cocoon, and how much you can move around inside it. . . .

Now slowly break out of your cocoon. . . . Find your way out of this protective shell, and be aware of how you feel as you emerge into the world. . . . When you emerge, begin to stretch in any way that feels comfortable. . . . Each time you stretch, let your stretching flow into some kind of noise. . . . Now become this noise and let it flow back into your stretching. . . . Explore all the possible ways of stretching your body. . . .

Gravity

(Tchaikovsky: Dance of the Sugar Plum Fairy, on Laurindo Almeida: Reverie for Spanish Guitars. Capitol p 8571. Start music when gravity is reduced.)

Continue to stretch and move any way you want to with your eyes closed, and focus your attention on your experience of gravity. . . . Feel how the force of gravity pulls you, and how this force is transmitted through your body to whatever parts are supporting you. . . . Feel how your whole body responds to the pull of gravity as you move and change position. . . .

Now imagine that the pull of gravity is doubled or tripled, so that you are very heavy, and every move you make takes tremendous effort. . . . Be aware of how you move in this heavy gravity, and how you feel. . . . Now slowly pull yourself to a standing position against this tremendous force, . . . and then sink down again to rest on the ground. . . .

Now imagine that the pull of gravity is reduced to about half normal, so that you are very light, and moving your body is easy and effortless. . . . Be aware of how you move and how you feel in this light gravity. . . . Now open your eyes and continue to move around any way you like in this light gravity. . . . Notice whether you feel like continuing to move by yourself, or whether you want to interact with the movements of others. . . .

Exploring Possibilities

(Olantanji: Drums of Passion, Columbia CL1412, or other African drumming.)

Stand comfortably with space around you, and close your eyes. I want you to explore the possibilities of movement in the different parts of your body. Start with your fingers and hands, and see how many different ways they can move. . . . Now also bring your lower arms into this movement. . . . Now let movement flow up into your upper arms as well. . . . Now let movement flow into your shoulders and neck and head. Continue to move your arms and hands. . . . Gradually, movement will flow into your whole body. . . . Now let movement flow into your chest and torso, as you discover all the possibilities of movement there. . . . Now let movement flow into your hips, . . . and on into your thighs and knees, . . . and finally into your lower legs, and your ankles and feet. Discover all the ways that your feet and legs can move. . . . Now continue to let your whole body move in whatever ways feel most comfortable for you. . . .

Continue to let your whole body move. Open your eyes now, and explore different kinds of movement. First, explore bending. Bend all the different parts of your body in as many ways as you can. . . . Now explore swaying. . . . Now writhing. . . . Now twisting. . . . Now jerking. . . . Now undulating. . . . Now rocking. . . . Now rotating. . . . Now flowing. . . . Now continue moving for a while in whatever ways feel most comfortable to you. . . .

Now explore moving with different noises and sounds. I'm going to make a sound and I want you to continue repeating this sound on your own and let this sound flow into your movement. Now explore how you move to this sound: Buzzzzzzz. . . . Now move to Grrrrhhhh. . . . Now Chnnhhh. . . . Now Shhhhhhh. . . . Now Zap. . . . Now Owooooo. . . . (Make up any other sounds you like.) Now make whatever noise you feel like making right now and let this noise flow into your movement. . . .

Now pair up with someone else for a little while and have a dialogue of sound and movement. Be aware of how the other person moves, and let your response to him flow into movement and occasional noises. . . . Now find a new partner and interact with him through movement. . . . Be aware of how your movements are different with this new partner. . . . Now again find a new partner for a new dialogue. . . . In what ways are your movements similar, no matter who your partner is? . . . Go on to other new partners, and explore how you interact with them through movement. . . .

Dancer

(Borodin: "In the Steppes of Central Asia." Or "Both Sides Now" on Gabor Szabo 1969. Skye SK-9.)

Find a comfortable sitting position with space around you. . . . Close your eyes, and get in touch with your physical existence. . . . Notice what is going on in your body. . . . I want you to imagine that you are alone at the edge of a large sunny grassy meadow with lots of space to move and dance. Look around at this place and be aware of it and how you feel there. . . . A person who loves to move and dance will come into this meadow without noticing you, and begin to move and dance freely. When this person comes, just watch the grace and beauty of the movements and dancing for a while. . . . Soon this dancer will notice you, and come over to see you happily. Then the dancer will offer to show you how to move and dance, and insist that you dance together in the meadow. Begin by just moving in place with the dancer, and then begin moving around the room with your dancer. You will have to open your eyes to avoid bumping into other people, but keep your attention on your dancer and dance together.

Growing

(Aldo Ciccolini: Piano music of Erik Satie, Vol. 1, Side 1 Band 1. Angel S-36482. Or some light Chopin piano music, such as Ballade No. 2 in F major Op.38.)

Lie down on your back with space around you, and get in touch with how your body feels. . . . Now imagine that your left hand is a small flower bud that very slowly grows and moves up toward the sunlight, . . . slowly opens its petals to the breezes and the rain, . . . then begins to wither as its energy goes into forming seeds, . . . and gradually sinks down toward the ground again with its seeds. . . .

Now bring your body into a closed position and become a seed. . . . What kind of a seed are you? . . . It is springtime now, and you begin to sprout and move, sending a small root down into the soil and a small shoot up toward the sunlight. . . . Continue to grow and move, and be aware of how your body feels as you slowly unfold from this seed and grow into some kind of plant or tree. . . .

Evolution

(Gabor Szabo: Spellbinder, Side 1, Bands 1 and 2. Impulse AS 9123.)

Lie down with space around you, and close your eyes. Imagine that you are inert matter on the bottom of a prehistoric sea. There is water all around you—sometimes gentle currents, and sometimes raging crushing waves of water. Feel the water flowing over your inert surface. . . .

Now as life develops, you become some kind of seaweed or underwater plant. Listen to the drumming, and let the sounds flow into your movements as the currents of the water move you. . . .

Now become a simple animal that crawls along the bottom of the sea. Let the drumming flow through your body and into your movements as this underwater animal. . . .

Now move slowly toward land, . . . and when you reach land, grow four legs and begin crawling around on the land.

Explore your existence, and how you move as this land animal. . . .

Now gradually become upright on two legs, and explore how you move and exist as a two-legged animal. . . .

Now continue your moving, and open your eyes and interact with the others through these movements. . . .

Separation and Connection

(Aaron Copland: Clarinet Concerto. Columbia MS 6497.)

Find a place with space around you. . . . Close your eyes and get in touch with your body. . . . Explore your physical sensations, and what is going on inside you. . . . Now begin to reach out with your hands and feet, and explore the space close around you. . . . Be aware of how you feel, by yourself in this space. Do you feel like staying here alone in this space, or do you feel drawn to move and be in touch with others? . . . If you want to, begin to move around more now. When you contact someone else, squeeze his hand if you want to stay in touch with him. If he wants to stay in touch, he will squeeze back. From then on, maintain contact and continue to move together as if you were both part of one organism. You can change the way you touch this person as long as you stay connected somehow. You can also absorb others into this organism if you want to and if they are willing. Continue to move for another five minutes and either interact or stay separate, as you wish. . . .

Now slowly withdraw from whoever you are touching, until you are alone again. Take a little time to experience being by yourself again. . . .

Incomplete

I'm going to divide the group in half, and I want this half to sit down. . . . Now I want the half that is standing to move around the room as if you were something incomplete. Don't talk; just move, and make noises if you wish. Become something incomplete and moving, now, and continue to do this. . . .

Now I want the people sitting down to get up and complete one of these incomplete things with your movements and actions, and continue to interact for awhile.

Unusual Angles

Now I want you to look at each other from unusual angles and head positions without talking. Bend over and look at one person sideways for a little while. . . . Then move on to someone else and look at them with your head upside down between your legs, . . . and go on to explore all the possibilities of meeting others from unusual angles and positions for a few minutes. . . .

Movement Dialogues

Now pair up with someone and begin to interact without talking, in a dialogue of movement. . . . Be aware of how you feel, and what goes on between you in this interaction. . . .

Now silently say goodbye to your partner through movement, and move on to a new partner for another movement dialogue. This time I want you to imagine that one of you is a sorcerer and the other is his subject who is completely in the power of the sorcerer's magic. Continue this dialogue of movement for a couple of minutes, and be aware of how you each express yourselves. . . .

Now switch places, so that the sorcerer now becomes the subject in a new dialogue. Again be aware of how you feel and move. . . .

Now say goodbye through movement and move on to a new partner for another movement dialogue. This time I want you to imagine that one of you is joy, and the other is sadness. Have a movement dialogue between sadness and joy and be aware of how you each express yourselves. . . .

Now switch places, so that joy becomes sadness in a new dialogue. . . .

(There are many other possibilities of opposite roles, feelings, and qualities: teacher-student, parent-child, policeman-criminal, male-female, rehearser-spontaneous person, boredom-excitement, acceptance-rejection, love-hate, calm-upset, emotional-unemotional, strength-weakness, tender-rough, active-passive, patient-impatient, etc.)

Flame

Now find a comfortable resting position lying on the floor. Close your eyes, and quietly get in touch with your body.

Now imagine that you are a fire just beginning to slowly flicker into life. Let these flames become movements. . . . Where in your body do these small flames start, and how do these flames grow as they move upward and outward, growing into the air above? . . . Be aware of what kind of fire you are as you move and grow. . . . Do your flames burn steadily, or do they leap upward, alternately flaring and then retreating? . . . How do you feel as fire? . . . Continue to be this fire as it burns brightly, and explore the space around you. . . . Continue to be these flames, as you open your eyes and move around interacting with these other flames. . . . Pair up with another flame and have a dialogue of movement for a little while, . . . and then move on to another partner for another dialogue. . . . Now move on and find a place where you have space around you. Stay in this place and close your eyes. Your flames are beginning to die down now, and soon your fuel will be all gone. Be aware of how you feel and how you move as your flames gradually decrease, . . . then flicker and fade, . . . until the last flickering flame disappears, and only glowing embers are left. . . . Stay with your experience and absorb it for a little while. . . .

Chanting

Sit down in a circle, close your eyes, and get in touch with your body. Sit upright, and imagine that a flexible string at the top of your head gently pulls you up so that your spine straightens and your belly and chest open up a little. Don't strain and tighten your body, and do let your body move or sway a little to be sure you are not holding yourself rigidly. . . .

Now focus your attention on your breathing, . . . and the movements of your chest and belly as you breathe. . . . As you do this, keep the word "smoothness" in mind. . . . Let your breathing and your body become smooth—without kinks or knots. . . . Notice the smoothness of your breathing, as the air flows smoothly into your lungs without effort. . . . Feel your whole body become more calm and smooth. . . . Now let this smoothness of your body and your breathing expand to include the air around you. . . .

Now let your mouth open a little, and when you feel ready, let a sound form as you exhale. Make whatever sound emerges with the least possible effort as you continue to focus your attention on the smoothness of your breathing and your body. Don't try to make this sound—just let this sound flow out of you easily. As you let this sound flow, your smoothness will expand to include the others in the room, and their smoothness will include you. Gradually all of you will come together into one smooth sound or chant. Pause for breath, and pause whenever you begin to tense and lose some of your smoothness. The chant may change from time to time—rise and fall in volume, change in pitch, etc. Let it flow, and let your own sound flow easily with the chant. Continue the chant for several minutes. When you feel ready to let your own smooth sound emerge, begin this blending of smooth, easy sounds that will form the chant. . . .

Sound Dialogue

Stand up with space around you, and with your partner facing you about four feet away. . . . Close your eyes and let your body go as much as you can while standing. . . . Be aware of your shoulders, your belly, and your chest, and let go of any tensing that you find. . . . Be aware of your throat and neck, and let them go. . . . Let your jaw go, so that it drops a little and your mouth opens slightly. . . .

Stay in touch with your breathing, and with all these parts of your body that participate in making sounds. When you feel ready, let a sound grow inside you and emerge without trying to make any particular sound. Let this sound emerge without effort. When it does emerge, be aware of what it is like without trying to change it. Just be aware of it, and notice how it grows or changes. Take turns doing this, and be aware of the qualities of your sound as you make it. Do you let it die out slowly as you come to the end of your exhalation, or do you stop abruptly, or squeeze the last possible bit of air out even though you begin to tense and the sound wavers? Pause after making your sound and get in touch with your own breathing and be aware of your body while your partner makes his sound. Then make your sound again. Do this for a few minutes.

Now that you have become familiar with your comfortable sound, increase the volume without changing pitch, and then experiment with changing the volume from loud to soft. . . .

Now be aware of your mouth, lips, and tongue as you make your sound, and slowly explore how they can modulate your sound. Play with the five vowels a e i o u while making the same sound. ... Continue to be aware of your mouth, lips, and tongue, and experiment with how they modulate your sound. ...

Now keep your eyes closed and have a sound conversation with your partner. Continue to use this one sound that is most comfortable for you, using different volume and modulation to express yourself. Focus your attention on your feelings toward your partner, and on your partner's sounds and your response to these sounds. Let this awareness flow into the sound you are making as you carry on this dialogue with your partner. Continue this dialogue for a couple of minutes. ...

Now pause for a little while to silently absorb your experience. ...

Now open your eyes and share your experience with your partner for a couple of minutes. What were your sounds like in this dialogue? What did they express, and what did you feel, physically, as you did this? ...

(This experiment can also be done in a small group of no more than eight or ten people. Begin with everyone finding their sound at the same time, then get each person's sound by itself, by touching each person on the shoulder in turn. Then move people silently into pairs for dialogues without their knowing who they are paired up with. Do dialogues with one pair at a time so that everyone can be aware of the others' dialogues as well as their own, and so that a pair in dialogue is not distracted by the others' sounds.)

Awareness Poetry

Find a place where you can be alone, and get in touch with the flow of your awareness. Pay attention to what you are aware of from moment to moment. Then let your awareness flow into words *as if* it were free-verse poetry. Don't try to make it into a poem—just let your awareness flow into words. Do this silently in your mind at first, and then speak these words out loud as they come to you. ...

Now do the same thing, and let your attention flow back and

forth between your awareness of inner feelings and responses and outer things and events. Let this awareness flow into words for a few minutes. . . .

Awareness Singing

Now I want you to add sounds to this expression of your awareness in poetry. Begin by getting in touch with your inner experiencing and let this flow into some kind of sounds, as in the *Humming* experiment. When you are flowing easily with these sounds you are making, let your awareness flow into words as well as sounds, *as if* it were a song. Don't work to shape or structure these expressions into a song, just let sounds and words flow for a few minutes. . . .

(You can also go on to add other ways of self-expression: let your awareness also flow into movements, or into painting, etc.)

Afterword

The process of writing this book has been mostly very satisfying, and in spite of being tired of it right now, I'm pleased with how it has turned out. A lot has emerged in me through watching it change and grow in my hands, and many things have become much clearer to me as I try to express them to you. As I have rewritten some sections and responded to criticism, I have often realized that portions of what I had written were not grounded in my awareness, but were left-over bits of fantasy junk that I was still clinging to. I'm sure that there are still other portions that I haven't yet recognized as junk. Now that I've written a book, I'm in danger of becoming a guru to whom you may listen in preference to your own awareness.

Awareness is basic, and you can only discover this through your own experiencing. If you stay with your own awareness, you will find that my words are sometimes useful as ways to lead you into new territory, and none of my mistakes can lead you far astray. If you take my words as more real than your experience, there is no limit to the damage you can do to yourself and others. You will only be in contact with fantasy: images, ideas, thinking, and beliefs that will take you further from your awareness of your own experiencing.

In the past, I spent some time searching for gurus. At first I was unsuccessful, because no one could meet my expectations of someone who could answer all my questions and solve all my problems. Later, when my expectations were more reasonable, I found a few outstanding human beings and I learned from them how to do for myself what I wanted them to do for me. More recently, I find myself learning most from parts of the world that I had previously rejected as being very un-guru-like. Perhaps if I continue to flow with my awareness, I will become open enough to let everything in my world be my guru, teaching me through my ongoing experiencing.

I hope you will take this book simply as a report of some of my tools and explorations as of this moment. I feel a bit like an explorer who has paused during the winter to make crude maps and notes describing my travels. As soon as I have written these words, my life and my awareness goes on moving and changing—sometimes with love, joy or pleasure, and sometimes with turbulence, anger, or unhappiness. The events of my life are sometimes like waves that will crush me on the rocks if I resist them. But I am learning to go with the waves like a surfer: I can use their power to carry me joyously instead of destroying me; I can enjoy the movement and beauty of the rushing water instead of being blinded and paralyzed by my fears.

There are immense destructive powers loose in the world. These powers are mostly created, maintained, and guided by fantasies: fears, ideologies, ideals, images, beliefs, assumptions, thinking, planning, tradition, custom, etc. Many of those who cling to these fantasies—and quite a few innocent bystanders too—are being destroyed by these powers. A growing number of us are waking up from our dreams and nightmares and getting in touch with the reality of our own experiencing. As we do this, we become personally free of these fantasies and we withdraw our participation in the destructive power that these fantasies generate. This is the revolution of awareness over fantasy, and of the living over the dead. Most revolutions ask you to give up your life for a cause. The revolution of awareness is happening because more and more of us are insisting on living our own lives, and refusing to give up our lives for fantasies.

You can only join us by living your own life fully, with awareness. By being ourselves, rather than images, we can respond to each other directly and come together in honest response-ability.